# UNINFORMED CHOICE

*Copublished with the Eagleton Institute of Politics,*
*Rutgers University*

# UNINFORMED CHOICE

## The Failure of the
## New Presidential
## Nominating System

# Scott Keeter
# and
# Cliff Zukin

**American Political Parties
and Elections**

**general editor:
Gerald M. Pomper**

**PRAEGER SPECIAL STUDIES • PRAEGER SCIENTIFIC**

New York • Philadelphia • Eastbourne, UK
Toronto • Hong Kong • Tokyo • Sydney

**Library of Congress Cataloging in Publication Data**

Keeter, Scott.
  Uninformed choice.

  (American political parties and elections)
  Bibliography: p.
  Includes index.
  1. Presidents—United States—Nomination. 2. Pri-
maries—United States. 3. Political participation—
United States. I. Zukin, Cliff. II. Title. III. Series.
JK522.K43 1983        324.5'0973        83-19237
ISBN 0-03-061588-7

Published in 1983 by Praeger Publishers
CBS Educational and Professional Publishing
a Division of CBS Inc.
521 Fifth Avenue, New York, New York 10175, USA

3456789 052 987654321

Printed in the United States of America
on acid-free paper

This book is dedicated to our parents.

# PREFACE

This is a book about how our nation chooses presidential leadership. It is not, however, a book about "voting behavior." When citizens cast their votes for the Democratic or Republican candidate they are simply engaging in the final act of a long and somewhat mysterious decision-making process. Long before people enter the voting booths in November they have made decisions—or had decisions made for them—that winnow a once-crowded field to a choice between two finalists. As the long season of presidential primaries unfolds, voters come to recognize candidates' names, learn something about many, form impressions about some, and strengthen or change their opinions of a few. It is this larger process upon which we have focused our attention.

How citizens are introduced to, and form evaluations of, potential leaders is of course an important question to a democratic society. It is also a question that has taken on added significance in the last decade. The political system has undergone a fundamental change with regard to how candidates for the presidency are selected. It is the citizenry as a whole, rather than a cadre of party activists, who now have the power to determine which candidates will contest the general election. Since 1968, the real action has moved to the primaries, and the real actor has become the public.

As much as social scientists might like to think their job is description rather than prescription, social inquiry is always value-laden. The choice of a topic for study says that the researcher thought it was important. We think that self-government is important and began the research program that led to this book with the hope that what we found might help improve the democratic process. As our title indicates, we found the quality of public participation in nomination politics to be unhealthily low, and incompatible with standards commonly associated with informed decision making.

The new system of presidential nomination makes for uninformed choice both by the individual and for society as a collectivity. A precarious democratic process must lead to precarious results. Indeed, we toyed for a while with the title of "random selection," feeling that it captured the increased role of fortune and idiosyncracy in the new system. However, we feel it is important to state at the outset that the quality of citizen input is not completely, or even mostly, a function of the capacity of the public to participate. Rather, the nature of citizen input is a function of the structure and environment in which it is made. We find that the contemporary system of presidential nomination presents a most inhospitable climate for rational and informed participation. The public is presented with a series of difficult choices in an information-starved atmosphere. Under such circumstances blaming the voter is akin to blaming the victim.

Certainly, citizens could be more interested in presidential nominations, but this lack of concern may be saying the same thing many party leaders and seasoned Washington observers are saying: this is no way to pick a president. Moreover, while we lament an impoverished information environment, the media, much like the general citizenry, are behaving about as well as one might expect given their values, incentives, structure, and resources. We do suggest it would be profitable for journalists to engage in some introspection as to their working definitions of "newsworthiness." Currently there is quite a wide gap between "reporting the news" and "informing the public."

Our work has benefited from the help of many people—friends and colleagues—who gave us support, encouragement, and good advice along the way. They may rightfully share some of the credit for what appears here, but should not be held responsible for the occasions on which we have failed to respect their good judgment. Several graduate students at Rutgers University should be thanked for their research assistance: George Barna, J. Robert Carter, Jr., Barbara Christensen, Mabel Hsueh, Robin Snyder, and Jim Woolford. The Center for Computer and Information Services at Rutgers provided technical assistance and gave freely of space and time on their machines to help us with the enormous tasks of data analysis; in particular we are grateful to Gert Lewis and Don Robertson. Three different organizations contributed their respondents: The Center for Political Studies at the University of Michigan, CBS News and the *New York Times*, and the Eagleton Poll of Rutgers University.

Our colleagues Christine Harrington, Carol Nackenoff, and Charles Noble listened skeptically and asked good questions about why all of this matters. Herbert Asher, C. Anthony Broh, John Glascock, Doris Graber, C. Richard Hofstetter, and Harry Wray read earlier versions of the research presented here and helped us with their comments and suggestions; the help of Michael Delli Carpini is especially acknowledged. Gerald Pomper saw the potential for a manuscript in this research at an early stage and helped to keep us on the right track. His help and encouragement are gratefully noted.

Alan Rosenthal and the Eagleton Institute of Politics provided generous research support, without which this project could not have been done. The Department of Political Science and the Research Council of Rutgers University also provided assistance. Our biggest debt is to Fran Waldman and particularly Judy Luckus, who typed the manuscript and kept the project organized. We also thank them for their constant encouragement and dedication.

Finally, we want to acknowledge each other. This book has truly been a collaborative effort; we have listed authorship by the vagaries of the alphabet. We share with pride whatever contribution this book makes as well as the responsibility for any errors of analysis or interpretation.

# CONTENTS

# LIST OF TABLES

# LIST OF FIGURES

FIGURE

# UNINFORMED CHOICE

# 1
# NEW SYSTEM, NEW QUESTIONS

Presidential elections in the United States must be a source of puzzlement to foreign observers.

In 1976, a peanut farmer who had served for one term as governor of a small southern state rose from obscurity to capture the nomination of the nation's largest political party. In the wake of political scandal in Washington the farmer ran as an outsider, smiling, saying "Trust me. I'll never lie to you." Despite having no party base and engendering only lukewarm support from the leaders of his party he carried the Democratic Party's banner into the general election.

The peanut farmer ran against a sitting president who had never been elected to national—or even statewide—office. In fact, the non-elected president had come within a whisker of losing his party's nomination to a famous Hollywood actor-turned-politician. In a close election, the peanut farmer won.

Four years later the public decided the farmer had not measured up to the job and elected the actor president.

To some this will seem an abstractly perverse view of U.S. presidential elections; yet these are essentially the facts of the 1976 and 1980 elections. The "meaning" of these facts is of course open to debate and interpretation. The political optimist marvels at the openness of the system. *"It is living proof of the American dream that any boy can grow up to be president—farmers and actors, men of advanced learning and those of 'simple common sense,' cold and warm men, industrious and indolent men, boring and inspiring men, pragmatists and ideologues. Power has flowed from the party bosses to the citizen. We have a much wider selection of potential leaders to choose from than ever before."*

*"True enough,"* responds the political cynic. *"But it may not be quite as open as you have described. After all, it is still only 'boys' who grow up to be president, and it appears to be quite helpful if one is an unemployed millionaire. More to the point, I am less concerned with the* process *than the* outcome. *The public did not view Carter as an able leader, which is the primary reason Reagan won. By the middle of his term, Reagan's job performance rating was similar to Carter's. Even members of his own party in Congress and his own staff had questioned how in touch the president was with basic political, social, and economic realities. I worry about how much people actually know about these potential leaders when they make their choices. I have yet to be convinced that your open system produces the best leaders."*

This is a book about how the public chooses leadership under the new system of presidential nomination. The opening of the nomination process to the rank-and-file is one of the most significant "reforms" in recent political history. Former Democratic Party Chairman Lawrence O'Brien called it "the greatest goddamn change since the two-party system." These reforms have consequences that are of the most fundamental nature for the selection of leadership. Both optimist and cynic would quickly agree that Jimmy Carter would not have been nominated by Democratic Party leaders in 1976. Moreover, as we shall see, the base of the Reagan candidacy in 1980 was built on his challenge to Gerald Ford in 1976—a challenge that Republican Party leaders tried to snuff early in the nomination season and surely would have derailed had they retained the power to do so.

The question of who exercises power over presidential nominations is a primordial one. No more critical a decision confronts a republic than the selection of leadership. And, it may be argued, the selection of candidates who will contest the general election is even more important than the choice made in the general election. If the two candidates are talented and principled men, the public cannot lose; if both men are fools, the public cannot win. What has been cloaked as reform and change in a process may be unfrocked in naked political terms: *the people* now have the power to decide who will run for president.

Indeed, the change in the role of the mass public in selecting presidential candidates has been so great since 1968 that we may talk of the *old system* and *new system* of presidential nominations. The principal actors under the old system were groups of party regulars. State caucuses and national conventions were attended by elected officials and party professionals—people who were interested in politics on a daily basis and who paid attention to public affairs. The style of decision making could be called discursive; party leaders discussed, bargained, compromised, and selected. Candidates usually rose through party ranks in a system that was admittedly not always democratic, but the party professionals tended to produce candidates accustomed to working with diverse groups and to forging a consensus among the competing factions within the party.[1] Popular participation was largely illusory under the old system; party leaders were able to control the nomination. As late as 1968 Hubert Humphrey received the Democratic nomination without contesting a single primary.

Party reforms adopted in the wake of the tumultous 1968 Democratic Convention radically changed the configuration of presidential nominations in the United States. Taking a cue from Al Smith's maxim "the cure for the ills of Democracy is more Democracy," and stating "in the American two-party system no decision is more important . . . than the choice of the party's presidential nominee,"[2] party reformers ceded the power to nominate to the people. Between 1968 and 1980 the number of people participating directly in delegate selection increased from 12 to 32 million. Over the same period the proportion of delegates elected in primaries has risen from 36 to 75 percent. Under the new system, as Gerald Pomper has noted, "Nominations are no longer seen as the decision of distinct and legitimate factions whose interests must be compromised, or vindicated, or vanquished but at least acknowledged."[3] Rather, they are now viewed as the rightful decisions of "the people." Clearly, under the new system the people are in charge, even if no one is in control.

The right to vote is a hallmark of democracy—defining it, becoming its symbol, and being held dear by the populace. It is next to impossible politically to oppose this right, for it is a preeminent value by its very definition. This helps to explain why opening the nominating system to more meaningful public participation was greeted largely without criticism—or even a great deal of thought about possible consequences. As the McGovern-Frazier Commission noted, "We are less concerned with the outcome than the process."[4] Some important consequences of the new system have been documented elsewhere: increased influence of the mass media,[5] decreased influence of party leaders,[6] changes in candidates' strategies and the conduct of campaigns,[7] and changes in campaign financing,[8] among others. *Our focus is on the citizen.* Our concern is with the responsibility that accompanies the right to vote in a democratic system—the responsibility to make informed judgments.

Despite the increased role played by the parties' rank-and-file, relatively little attention has been given to the nature of public participation. With the experience of three elections conducted under the new system we now have evidence for examining the factors that influence citizens as they exercise their new power and make critical decisions about their country's leadership. We seek to explain the process by which citizens come to know and accept—or reject—candidates for president before the nominations are formally decided. We explore the nominating contests of 1976 and 1980, examining how citizens learn about and form opinions of candidates through the series of caucuses and primary elections. Our focus on the citizen within the current structure of presidential nomination politics leads to a number of basic questions:

—How interested in, and attentive to, presidential nominations is the public?
—How much, and what, does the public learn during the nomination season about the people who wish to lead them?
—How does the public form opinions about the candidates? How do opinions change in response to events of the campaign?
—How much do voters know about the candidates when they are called upon to cast their ballots in primary elections?
—How *representative* is the decision-making process under the new system? What are the effects of the early campaign tests in Iowa and New Hampshire—do the "winnowing" states accurately reflect or distort the preferences of the nation as a whole?

The answers to these questions transcend their scope. They go beyond concerns about the growth of candidate knowledge and opinion formation, leading to an evaluation of the criteria employed by the public in selecting leadership. The question of how adequately the public plays its assigned role in the new system begs a larger question: Is this a "good" system of nominating presidential candidates? The answer to this question in part rests on the selection of a standard against which the empirical realities of citizen behavior in presidential nominations may be juxtaposed—a set of expectations to act as foil and context for the findings. The standard we shall utilize most often is the one responsible for bringing about the transference of power from party leaders to the partisan electorate—a variant of democratic theory. A number of values are embodied in this concept. First is the value of citizen participation, both to the system as a whole and to the individual citizen. Second is faith in the collective wisdom of "the people." By focusing their attention on process, reformers have generally adopted the position that "the essence of democracy is to take chances on the free choice and wrong decisions of the people."[9] Third, democratic theory values an informed electorate. Citizens are presumed to be interested, attentive, and sufficiently knowledgeable about basic choices to make informed decisions.

Much of course goes under the rubric of democratic theory. Both the new and old systems can be called democratic. The new system obviously finds a haven in mass participation and the divinity of direct democracy. The watchword is government-by-the-people. The old system of nomination politics rested on a consent-of-the-governed philosophy and comfortably argued that intraparty democracy is not necessary—and may even be dysfunctional—for interparty democracy.[10] We deal at greater length with the question of standards in the following chapter on representation, and again in the concluding chapter of the book.

Apart from the normative concern of democratic theory, we are interested in public reaction to politicians from a scientific perspective. We know very little about how people form evaluations of public leaders, especially newcomers such as John Anderson and George Bush. Even in politics, first impressions matter. And the public gets introduced to the various candidates not simply as individuals, but as representatives of a system of government and as potential presidents. We suspect that over time even basic attitudes about political parties and the political system and its leadership could be affected by experiences with the new system of nomination politics. While fewer citizens participate in the nomination phase than in the general election, it is one of the few times when a substantial portion of the public is engaged in politics. Tracking changes in public opinion through the nominations of different candidates by different parties in different elections allows us to discern regularities and identify differences in new system nominations, shedding light on the dynamics of general public opinion and on public response to presidential aspirants.

## PLAN OF THE BOOK

The remainder of this chapter provides background for what is to come. The next section describes the sources of data used in our analysis. The making of the new system of nomination politics is then traced, followed by a brief history of the Democratic and Republican nominating contests in 1976 and 1980. As noted, the focus of Chapter 2 is on representation and the new system in the context of democratic theory.

The second part of the book, Chapters 3 through 7, presents data on what and how citizens learned during the nomination campaigns. Chapter 3 provides a basic context, presenting information on citizen interest, involvement, and media use. The pattern of growth in awareness of candidates for the presidency is the subject of Chapter 4, while Chapter 5 looks at citizen learning of candidates' issue positions, ideological stances, and character traits over the course of the campaign. Chapters 6 and 7 investigate how opinions about candidates form and change in response to events of the campaign. In the final chapter we return to the issue of standards and to questions about the nature of representation, offering our general conclusions as to the adequacy and desirability of the new system of presidential nomination.

## SOURCES OF DATA

We are relying on three sources to inform our discussion of citizen learning in the 1980 election. First, through the Eagleton Poll of Rutgers University, we interviewed some 15,000 New Jerseyans between October 1979 and October of 1980. While the data collected in these cross-sectional studies come from a single state—and one holding its primary at the tail end of the nomination season—and may not be representative of the nation as a whole, the large number of interviews conducted immediately before and after most of the significant events of the campaign allows us to observe the dynamics of public opinion in nomination politics from a better vantage point than ever before.

The second source of data is a set of monthly surveys conducted during the nominating period in 1976 and 1980 by the *New York Times* and CBS News. These data are not tied as closely to the formal events of the nominating campaign as are the New Jersey data; however, they have the advantage of being based on national samples. Moreover, the 1980 surveys allow us to validate the representativeness of the Eagleton samplings by showing the close parallel between public opinion in New Jersey and the nation as a whole.

Finally, we have used data collected in the National Election Study (NES), by the Center for Political Studies (CPS) at the University of Michigan. This source of information is less useful in describing the dynamics of nomination politics, because of the lengthy time interval between waves of interviewing (and other reasons discussed in Appendix A). Surveys were conducted in February, April, and June of the nominating season. However, the NES incorporated a *panel* design, where the same respondents were interviewed on more than one occasion. This allows us to analyze individual-level change, while the Eagleton and *Times*/CBS data allow us to look only at aggregate change in the population.

Each of the three data sources has unique advantages and disadvantages; each is most appropriate for some analytic tasks and inappropriate for others. We frequently move from one to the next depending on the specific questions being addressed, and have tried to give readers a basic justification of our choices without being overly technical or ponderous. Interested readers should consult Appendix A, which gives sampling information, ties survey waves into specific events of the campaign, and discusses the strengths and weaknesses of each data source.

## THE MAKING OF THE NEW SYSTEM

For more than a century, presidential candidates have been nominated by the parties' national conventions. Throughout this period, the delegates to the conventions were selected in the states, according to rules and procedures that varied from state to state.[11] Until very recently, the conventions were composed of delegates representing the views and preferences of party organizations in their states. Because rules for delegate selection were not uniform, and because there was no centralized control over the process, the way conventions were constituted could hardly be called a "nominating system." Much of the delegate selection was isolated from the activities of politicians seeking the nomination, and for most of the nineteenth century active campaigning for the nomination was viewed as unseemly. The conventions' decisions were a result of bargaining among party leaders from around the country.

Turn-of-the-century Progressives who attempted to eliminate corruption and open the government to broader public participation succeeded in persuading a majority of states to institute primary elections as a means of nominating candidates for office, and many states adopted primaries to select delegates to the parties' national conventions as well. However, with the passing of Progressive fervor, most states returned to more closed, party-based methods of delegate selection. Nevertheless, enough states retained primaries that "mixed system" was an appropriate label for the presidential nominating process for much of this century. Most of the delegates were selected through caucuses or conventions, but some were selected in primaries. A candidate could win the nomination without running in the primaries, though some aspirants used them to demonstrate electoral appeal.

Radical changes in the party rules and state laws governing delegation selection were made in the early 1970s, transforming a decentralized, patchwork-quilt process into a true system. The Democratic Party provided the impetus for the changes, and the Republican Party, while not seeking to alter its procedures, was swept along since many of the changes were mandated by state law and thus applied to both parties. The changes were reinforced by federal legislation on campaign financing in 1974, which established government subsidies paid directly to candidates for nomination. By 1976, presidential nominating procedures in the United States bore little resemblance to any method ever used before.

The election of 1968 was the catalyst for change. In retrospect, the circumstances of 1968 which led Democrats to reform their delegate selection procedures appear to have been idiosyncratic and unique. Yet many broader forces beyond a beleaguered incumbent, a divisive war, and a contentious convention impelled changes. The public was becoming more mobile, while innovations such as network television meant that Americans saw much the same news and increasingly shared a common culture regardless of where they lived. Television and other improved means of communication enabled candidates to reach the public directly, without relying on intermediary institutions such as the political party. In response, the public was relying less upon partisanship as a guide to the selection of leaders, and parochial concerns and traditional ways of viewing the world became less important. This "nationalization" of politics led logically to changes in how the most national of political offices—the presidency—would be filled. Party leaders in the cities and states had once spoken for their constituents' particular interests in determining presidential nominations, and in turn had been able to influence the thinking of those constituents and to deliver their votes. Now, the leaders found themselves increasingly out of touch with a more heterogeneous citizenry, and simultaneously less able to control the information received by those citizens or to influence their behavior. The practical consequence of these changes was to increase the power and discretion of individual candidates relative to the power of the national party, while increasing the power of the national party relative to the state organizations.

Despite the evident dissatisfaction of much of the Democratic rank-and-file with the Johnson administration's Vietnam War policies, the 1968 convention nominated Vice-President Hubert H. Humphrey for president. Candidates opposed to the war had done well in the primaries that year, while Humphrey had not entered any of the contests. The one candidate who might have translated the primary verdicts into convention success, Robert Kennedy, was assassinated the night of his victory in the California primary. The convention that nominated Humphrey was held in Chicago, whose mayor—Richard Daley—was an old power-broker who symbolized the oligarchic, conservative control of the party that thwarted the efforts of younger, more liberal elements. Daley's police were seen by national television audiences clubbing anti-war protesters outside the convention, and this spectacle, along with the revulsion of many of those inside the convention, showed Americans a divided party and served to devalue Humphrey's nomination. The general election was a contest among Humphrey, Republican Richard Nixon, and George Wallace, who ran as a third-party candidate. Despite trailing Nixon badly in the post-convention polls, Humphrey caught up but narrowly lost the election.

Though unable to stop the nomination of Humphrey, the efforts of reformist elements in the party led to the creation of a commission to examine the ways of opening the party to greater participation by rank-and-file Democrats. This commission, headed first by South Dakota Senator George McGovern and later by Minnesota Congressman Donald Fraser, recommended several changes in procedures for selecting convention delegates. Many of these suggestions were accepted and applied to the 1972 convention in which McGovern himself was nominated. Among the changes were: the establishment of quotas for each state's delegation in order to increase the representation of blacks, women, and young people; the requirement that delegate selection rules in each state had to be written and publicized, and caucus meeting dates within a state had to be uniform; a rule that no delegates could be appointed *ex officio* by the state party leadership, and that no delegates could be selected, regardless of method, before the year of the presidential election.[12]

The McGovern-Fraser Commission did not suggest, or even expect, that primaries be used to comply with the requirements, but in fact several states switched from caucus or convention methods to a primary in order to ensure compliance. At the time, most primaries did not bind delegates to particular presidential candidates. Indeed, in many states, the candidate preferences of delegates running in the primary were not indicated on the ballots. Nevertheless, the primaries became more important. The Democratic nomination in 1972 saw the early front-runner, Maine Senator Edmund Muskie (the vice-presidential candidate in 1968) eliminated from competition quite early when he failed to run as well as expected in the first primaries. McGovern took advantage of the new rules by organizing cadres of enthusiastic volunteers and packing the early caucuses, while also using volunteers for door-to-door campaigning in the early primary states. His strategy paid off with a fast start that discouraged competition, and a late challenge by Humphrey was not sufficient to deny him the nomination.

Despite the intention of reformers to make the convention more representative of Democratic Party members, the delegates in 1972 were decidedly unrepresentative of the views of a majority of Democrats.[13] The nominee was, in the opinion of most observers, outside the mainstream of the party. McGovern was beaten badly by Nixon, and after the elections, the Democrats once again established a reform commission. Headed by Baltimore Councilwoman Barbara Mikulski, it suggested rules, subsequently adopted by the party, that mandated allocation of convention delegates in proportion to the strength of the presidential candidates and which bound delegates to those candidates for at least one convention ballot, both in caucus and in primary states.[14] Fearing the influence of highly committed ideologues such as those who helped nominate McGovern, many party leaders pressed for greater use of primaries, rather than caucuses, for the selection of delegates. In 1976, 29 states held primaries to select delegates, and did so in ways that provided for a more accurate translation of a candidate's performance into delegate strength. After 1976, the Democrats tightened this linkage even further by requiring that delegates list their candidate preference on the ballot, and run as a part of a slate, rather than as individuals. Candidates receiving more than a specified percentage of the vote (which varied from 15 to 25 percent in 1980) were allocated at least some of the delegates on their slate. Many states automatically listed all declared candidates on their ballots, forcing a candidate to withdraw his name if he wished not to run in the state.

Ironically, supporters of the new rules believed that they would produce a more representative and deliberative convention, even as the binding rule took discretion away from the individual delegates.

Proportional allocation of delegates within the states was expected to produce a situation in which no candidate could obtain a first-ballot nomination, while at the same time guaranteeing that ideological minorities would not be overrepresented at the convention.

The Republican Party, less concerned about issues of representation than the Democrats, undertook no comparable reforms. Yet since delegate selection procedures are subject to state laws, the number of Republican primaries increased along with Democratic ones. In many cases, proportional allocation of delegates and the binding of delegates to specific candidates was also mandated by state law. The Republican Party has adopted few national rules for delegate selection, and on many of the issues over which the Democrats wrestled mightily, the Republican rules explicitly defer to the state party organization or to the applicable state laws.

The nominating environment was also affected by national legislation on the financing of campaigns, passed in 1974. The 1972 burglary of the Democratic headquarters at the Watergate Hotel in Washington, D.C. was financed by money contributed to President Nixon's campaign organization, the Committee to Re-elect the President. Subsequent investigation revealed widespread abuses, as huge sums of money were used for a variety of illegal and unethical campaign practices. Spurred by these revelations, and the rapid increases in the costs of presidential campaigns, Congress passed a comprehensive package of campaign finance laws, which applied to nominations as well as the general election. The laws limited the amount of money any individual or group could contribute to a candidate, and required that amounts over $200 be publicly disclosed. Most importantly, the legislation established public funding of nomination campaigns, with the money given directly to the candidates. The rules required that, in order to be eligible for public funds, a candidate raise a minimum of $100,000, with at least $5,000 in each of twenty states, in contributions no larger than $250 each. Contributions of $200 or less would be matched by the government, and funding would continue through the primaries as long as the candidate received at least 10 percent of the vote in consecutive primaries. An overall spending limit was set, and ceilings were set for expenditures in each state as well.[15]

This legislation interacted with the new delegate selection rules to have a considerable impact on the nominating system. The provision of public funds directly to candidates further shifted initiative and control in the system to the candidates and away from the parties. It made running for president more affordable and thus

**TABLE 1.1**

**The Growth of Presidential Primaries**

|  | 1968 | 1972 | 1976 | 1980 |
|---|---|---|---|---|
| *Democratic Party* | | | | |
| Number of states using a primary to select or bind convention delegates | 17 | 23 | 29 | 29 |
| Percentage of all votes cast by delegates chosen or bound in primaries | 37.5 | 60.5 | 72.6 | 71.4 |
| *Republican Party* | | | | |
| Number of states using a primary to select or bind convention delegates | 16 | 22 | 28 | 33 |
| Percentage of all votes cast by delegates chosen or bound in primaries | 34.3 | 52.7 | 67.9 | 76.0 |

*Source:* James Ceaser, *Reforming the Reforms* (Cambridge, Mass.: Ballinger, 1982), p. 33.

contributed to the large field of aspirants to the Democratic nomination in 1976 and the Republican nomination in 1980. The spending ceilings affected strategies; some candidates doubtless could have raised and spent more than they were permitted in certain key states. One candidate in 1980 (John Connally, a Republican) declined to accept public funds so that he could raise and spend as he pleased. Despite an $11 million budget, he obtained only one delegate, demonstrating that money may be necessary but it is not sufficient to obtain the nomination. Yet for most candidates, the rules require a relatively large effort to raise money in the appropriate amounts, and mean an early trip home when failure in two primaries closes the public fund pipeline.

Thus by 1976, the nominating system was based almost entirely upon elections, with most of the convention delegates selected in primaries and bound by those results. The candidates vie for the delegates in public contests, supported by funds raised independently of the parties. The convention delegates gather to ratify the result determined during the delegate selection contests, and the winner then wears the party label.

The magnitude of the change can be seen in Table 1.1, which shows for each party the number of states using primaries and the percentage of convention votes cast by delegates selected in primaries during the period from 1968 to 1980. In 1968, just over one third of the delegates were chosen in primaries; by 1976, nearly three fourths were. And, as described above, primaries not only proliferated but also changed in ways that ensured a more faithful correspondence between a candidate's popular vote and the number of delegates won.

By 1980, the Democratic Party's rule making succeeded in bringing virtual uniformity to its nominating procedures. Only two primary states—Illinois and West Virginia—held primaries that were not strictly proportional contests in which voters selected a candidate or a slate pledged to a candidate. The Republican rules have remained more diverse. Sixteen states held strictly proportional elections, eight used some variation of winner-take-all at the district and state-wide level, while two (plus Puerto Rico) used state-wide winner-take-all. Three states held primaries in which no candidate names were listed, and five (plus the District of Columbia) selected individual delegates who listed their candidate preference.[16] The remainder used the caucus/convention system.

## THE NEW SYSTEM IN ACTION: THE NOMINATIONS OF 1976 AND 1980

Although we have only four nominations in the new system with which to judge the effects of the changes, certain patterns are evident in the contests of 1976 and 1980. In both years, incumbent presidents faced serious challenges within their parties, challenges of the sort seldom seen in nominating politics under the old system. And in the party out of power, a large field of contenders fought in the early contests. The races were characterized by fast shrinkage of the field, and a relatively early determination of the winner.

The new party rules, along with changes in campaign finance laws, point logically to the kinds of contests seen in 1976 and 1980. In the past, incumbent presidents held effective control of the party machinery and could engineer their renomination without having to fight public battles with rivals. The proliferation of primaries eliminates the use of an "inside strategy," and permits an opponent to force the incumbent to stand before the public in a series of elections. Laws limiting expenditures may hurt incumbents more than challengers, since incumbents usually can raise money easily. The limitations hurt challengers who need to spend to become known, but this is perhaps balanced by the fact that a president has less time to campaign than does a challenger—especially a challenger who may, like Reagan in 1976, be unemployed. Thus, a strong candidate (especially one from the wing of the party not represented by the presient) may look at the rules, weigh the costs, and say "why not?"

In the party out of power, the rules, the finance laws, and the tendency of journalists to seek new and exciting characters, combine to encourage a large number of hopefuls to ante up for the initial rounds. The early contests are held in smaller states, permitting fledgling candidates to focus their efforts in hopes of striking a responsive chord with the public and attracting a share of the extensive press coverage accorded the first tests. In the Democratic Party especially, the allocation of delegates in proportion to the candidates' caucus or primary performance is an added incentive, particularly for the less well known. Public financing provides a source of funds previously unavailable to candidates seeking nomination, and spending limitations help to equalize the disparity between the better-known and the lesser-known.

Much of this book's discussion of the process of public learning about the candidates and the formation and change of attitudes about them is tied to the events of the contests in 1976 and 1980. Here is a brief review of the four nominations in those years.[17]

### 1976: The Republicans

Sitting presidents ordinarily had not worried much about challenges from within their own party. But Gerald Ford was not an ordinary incumbent, and he barely prevailed over challenger Ronald Reagan in a very close convention vote. A number of circumstances contributed to Ford's vulnerability. First was the fact that he held the presidency by virtue of two resignations. He was appointed to the vice-presidency in 1973 when Spiro Agnew resigned after pleading no contest to charges of income tax evasion. When Richard Nixon resigned in 1974, facing certain impeachment and conviction, Ford became president. Ford thus lacked the legitimacy—and the experience—of having won a presidential election. Second, he had alienated many people by granting Nixon an unconditional pardon for any crimes committed during his presidency. And third, resting upon a shallow base of public support, he was forced by the new nominating rules to run in primary elections against a challenger who brought several important assets to the contest. Reagan was an effective speaker and campaigner, and was well known both for his acting career and his work as a corporate spokesman for General Electric. Strongly conservative, he represented a highly organized, fervent, and well-funded segment of the Republican Party. His support was strongest in the southern and western states, which now had a greater voice in the nomination due to reapportionment of delegates by the Republicans. Unemployed at the time, he was able to devote his full attention to defeating Ford.

Although he ran far behind Reagan in preelection polls in New Hampshire, Ford managed to finish first in that state's primary, 49 percent to 48 percent. Because of the polls, and Reagan's earlier prediction of a victory, Ford's one-point margin was considered a success by journalists. The following week on March 2, Ford received almost two thirds of the vote in Massachusetts. The next contest was one week later in Florida, a "sun belt" state considered to be a potential loss for Ford. Reagan's campaign managers had forecast a big victory there before the primaries began, but Ford once again finished first with 53 percent to Reagan's 47 percent. The following week, Reagan managed only 40 percent to Ford's 59 percent in Illinois, and many analysts, supported by allies of Ford, said that Reagan's cause was lost.

Reagan was able to keep the wolves—in the form of party leaders pressuring him to withdraw—off his door with a first-place finish in North Carolina on March 23 (52 percent to 47 percent) but did not have another success until May 1, when he won all 96 Texas delegates. On May 4, he barely edged Ford by 2 percent in Indiana, a state in which the polls had shown him trailing. He won 45 delegates to Ford's 9, while also finishing first in Alabama and Georgia. Amazingly, at this point in the campaign Reagan led in total delegates accumulated, 366 to 292 for Ford.

During the final month of primaries, each candidate had notable successes. Ford prevailed in Michigan (his home state), and in West Virginia, Tennessee, Kentucky, Oregon, and Rhode Island. Reagan finished first in Nebraska, Nevada, Idaho, South Dakota, and Montana. On the final day, Reagan won all of the large California delegation, besting Ford 66 percent to 34 percent in the popular vote.

But he finished behind Ford 57 percent to 43 percent in Ohio, and was not on the ballot in New Jersey.

Overall, Reagan received a slightly higher percentage of the vote in contested primaries than did Ford, but Ford held a slight lead in committed delegates. The search for uncommitted or vacillating delegates continued until the nominating vote was held at the Republican National Convention. Ford prevailed, getting 1,187 votes to 1,070 for Reagan.

### 1976: The Democrats

The multitude of declared candidates for the Democratic nomination was perhaps more noteworthy for who it did not include than for who it did. Only George Wallace among the contenders was favored by more than 10 percent of Democrats in an early-January Gallup poll. Massachusetts Senator Edward Kennedy chose not to run, and Hubert Humphrey, who wanted to run, decided to wait for the call that might arise if the primaries did not determine a winner. Indeed, the size of the field led to predictions that no candidate would be able to obtain enough delegates to win the nomination on the first ballot. After the first ballot, delegates would no longer be bound to the candidate for whom they were chosen, and a deliberative or "brokered" convention could result.

In fact, no candidate *was* able to obtain enough delegates directly to win a first-ballot victory, but Jimmy Carter's lead over all the other candidates was so large that he won a first-ballot nomination anyway when slates of uncommitted delegates were ceded to him. Carter built his lead by starting fast, thus eliminating almost all of the early field. He held his lead against strong late entrants by taking advantage of the proportional allocation of delegates, while maintaining his image as a winner by finishing first in at least one primary on each election day.

Of all the candidates, Carter had the best understanding of the new rules. His long-time adviser, Hamilton Jordan, had devised a strategy that emphasized a strong early effort to obtain favorable (and free) attention from journalists, while building for a contest in every primary state. Carter was a talented "retail" politician who left a good impression in the small-scale, personal appearances characteristic of campaigning in the two important early states, Iowa and New Hampshire. The first official event of the nominations was the Iowa precinct caucuses, held on January 19. Iowa Democrats met in schools, churches, and homes to select delegates to county conventions, to be held in March. The county conventions would select delegates to district conventions, who in turn would pick delegates to the state convention (in May) which would select Iowa's delegates to the Democratic National Convention. The new party rules required all caucus participants to declare their presidential preference. At the precinct caucuses, 39 percent of those in attendance said they were uncommitted. Twenty-nine percent said they favored Jimmy Carter. Birch Bayh, next in popularity, was favored by 11 percent. Carter's first-round success eventually translated into 20 of Iowa's 47 national convention delegates, or a little more than 1 percent of the 1,505 needed for the nomination. But journalists were impressed; here was a little known former governor who not only came across well to Iowa Democrats, but was a crafty politician as well.

Boosted by the favorable publicity from the Iowa caucuses, Carter finished first in the New Hampshire primary on February 24. Although he got only 28 percent of the vote, he received copious national publicity. The following week, he finished fourth in the Massachusetts primary with 14 percent. Washington Senator Henry Jackson was first with 22 percent, Arizona Congressman Morris Udall second with 18 percent, and George Wallace third with 17 percent. Yet Carter maintained his "momentum" by finishing first in Vermont, leading Sargent Shriver 42 percent to 28 percent. The grim winnower, feeding on candidates as they ran out of money, took Birch Bayh two days later.

The Florida primary on March 9 was viewed as an important test of Carter's ability to gain southern votes against George Wallace. Jackson also campaigned in Florida, hoping for support among retired citizens, defense employees, and Jewish voters. Carter received 35 percent of the vote, while Wallace got 31 percent and Jackson 24 percent. Former Pennsylvania Governor Milton Schapp, who got under 3 percent in Florida, was claimed by the winnower four days later. In the following two weeks, Carter finished first in Illinois and North Carolina. Shriver, Harris, and Wallace, all acknowledging the futility of their continued campaigning, dropped out.

The contests on April 6 demonstrated clearly that a candidate's actual performance in gaining delegates was less important than the journalistic interpretation of what happened. On that day in New York, Jackson won 104 delegates while Carter got only 35 in a complicated primary in which the ballot did not list the names of the presidential candidates. In Wisconsin's primary, Carter received 37 percent of the vote to 36 percent for Udall. Although the delegates were allocated to each candidate in proportion to the vote, the news coverage was not; journalists made much of Udall's failure once again to win, this time in a progressive state expected to be fertile ground for him. Meanwhile, Jackson's success in New York received much less attention than the number of delegates he gained would suggest, perhaps because the rules of the contest made it difficult to report and analyze.

Jackson's last stand was in Pennsylvania, where he hoped a northeastern, industrial constituency would find him more appealing than Carter. But he finished second, with only 25 percent of the vote to Carter's 37 percent, and withdrew four days later.

As the campaign entered the final month, Carter had nearly 40 percent of the pledged delegates, far more than any other contender. He faced two new challengers in May and June, and though he finished second in several primaries, he continued to accumulate delegates and maintain his lead. Idaho Senator Frank Church finished first in Nebraska on May 11, Oregon and Idaho on May 25, and Montana on June 1. California Governor Jerry Brown finished first in Maryland on May 18, Nevada on May 25, and California on June 8. But Carter was able to finish first in at least one election on each primary day, and as the primaries concluded on June 8, he received endorsements and uncommitted delegates from several important party leaders. The nomination was his.

### 1980: The Democrats

Unlike Gerald Ford, Jimmy Carter was an elected president and might reasonably have not worried about a strong challenge from within his party. But as the end of 1979 neared, Carter too was vulnerable. Persistent inflation coupled with slow economic growth had led to a decline in public confidence in his ability to manage public affairs. The most popular Democrat in the polls was not the president, but rather Edward Kennedy. Though urged to run for president in the previous two elections, Kennedy had chosen not to do so. But a combination of circumstances led him to challenge Carter for the nomination. First, he represented the liberal wing of the Democrats, and he regarded many of Carter's actions and policies as contrary to the traditions and ideals of the party. Second, based on the polls and the recommendations of his supporters, he felt that Carter could be beaten. And third, the rules for nomination facilitated a challenge, just as they had helped Reagan against Ford.

One other Democrat also opposed the president. Jerry Brown, remembering his string of first-place finishes in 1976, hoped that he might recapture that magic, or at least be the compromise choice for the party if neither Carter nor Kennedy could obtain a clear victory.

Kennedy did not officially declare his candidacy until November 7, 1979, but "authoritative rumors" that he would run had begun in early September. Yet even before he could declare, two fateful events on November 4th seriously damaged his candidacy. One was an hour-long interview on CBS Television conducted by Roger Mudd, in which Kennedy did not appear sharp, and gave a rambling, partially incoherent answer to Mudd's question of "Why do you want to be president?" Though the interview was seen by a relatively small audience (another network showed the popular film "Jaws," prompting Senator Robert Dole to quip later that most of the audience couldn't tell the difference between Mudd and the fabled shark) its impact reverberated through the political community.

The second, and ultimately more consequential event, was the seizure of the United States embassy in Iran by Islamic militants, who took the embassy staff hostage. Promoting the event as a crisis, President Carter pledged to devote his full attention to securing the release of the hostages. In many previous incidents in which American interests were challenged abroad, the public has responded by strongly supporting the president, and this was to be no exception. Polls conducted during the following weeks found that over two thirds of the public approved of Carter's handling of the situation in Iran. In polls of Democrats taken at the same time, Carter led Kennedy for the nomination. Kennedy compounded his misfortune by criticizing the president's decision to allow the deposed Shah of Iran into the United States for medical treatment, the event that precipitated the seizure of the hostages. And just before the new year, one final international event served to emphasize further the political advantages of incumbency in a time of international turmoil. The Soviet Union sent an invasionary force into Afghanistan to install a regime more friendly to its interests. Carter then backed out of a scheduled debate with Kennedy and Brown in Iowa, and said he would not actively campaign until the crises were resolved.

Thus a complete reversal in the standing of the two candidates had occurred. Carter, benefiting from patriotic "rallying around the flag," was preferred by 59 percent of Democrats attending the precinct-level Iowa caucuses, while Kennedy was preferred by only 31 percent. Though he considered quitting the race, Kennedy persisted, delivering several well-publicized speeches critical of the president. Carter responded, saying that Kennedy's remarks were "very damaging to our country . . . and to the achievement of our goals to keep the peace and get our hostages released." Kennedy replied to the president: "We will rally around the flag. But we need not, we must not rally round the failures of a president that threaten the real interests of the nation. . . ." And so a long and divisive battle for the Democratic nomination had begun.

Though his new-found popularity was to wane later in the campaign, Carter did well in the first month of primaries. He received 47 percent of the vote in New Hampshire, while Kennedy got 37 percent and Brown got only 10 percent. The following week, Kennedy finished first in his home state, but Carter finished first in Vermont. Carter overwhelmed Kennedy in three southern primaries on March 11, and then got a surprising 65 percent of the vote one week later in Illinois, where Kennedy had received the early endorsement of Chicago Mayor Jane Byrne and had hoped to do well. Carter finished behind Kennedy in Connecticut and New York on March 25, damaged by a vote at the United Nations in which the United States joined the rest of the Security Council in condemning Israeli settlements in Arab territory.

But Carter's lead in delegates mounted steadily. He disposed of Brown in Wisconsin, getting 56 percent of the vote, while Kennedy received 30 percent and Brown got only 11 percent. A three week lull allowed Kennedy to focus his attention on Pennsylvania, where he finished first by two tenths of 1 percent. In the remaining five weeks of the campaign, Kennedy did as well as the president, finishing first in California, New Jersey, and several smaller states. But Carter's lead was never substantially reduced, as he recorded some first-place finishes and continued to accumulate delegates even in contests where he trailed Kennedy.

Refusing to concede defeat, Kennedy proposed a debate with Carter, after which each candidate would release his delegates to vote their consciences. Carter refused, and Kennedy's supporters attempted to secure the release of the delegates through a convention vote on the binding rule. This effort failed, Carter was renominated, and Kennedy unenthusiastically endorsed the president.

### 1980: The Republicans

Once again, the party out of power had a plethora of candidates from which to choose. Foremost among them was Reagan, now the leader in polls of Republicans. Two other conservatives had declared their candidacies: Philip Crane, a young and articulate Congressman from Illinois, and John Connally, former Governor of Texas who had been Secretary of the Treasury in the Nixon administration. Connally was a forceful personality well-liked in the corporate world of the "sun belt." With relatively easy access to contributions, and fearing the effects of federal spending limitations on his ability to wage a campaign against Reagan, Connally was the only candidate who chose not to accept federal matching funds.

The other candidates were moderate or centrist Republicans: Tennessee Senator Howard Baker, fairly well known nationally for his polite but persistent questioning during the 1973 Senate Watergate hearings; Illinois Congressman John Anderson, on some issues more liberal than the other candidates; George Bush, a man with a long resume, including stints as CIA Director, Congressman, party chairman, and Ambassador to China; and Kansas Senator Robert Dole, President Ford's running mate in 1976.

Bush campaigned diligently in Iowa, while Reagan, believing his organization's reports that he was already strong enough there, did not campaign personally and chose not to participate in a nationally televised candidate forum. With an amazing turnout estimated to have been nearly 20 percent of Republicans statewide, Bush had more supporters at the caucuses than did Reagan, though the margin was small. Stunned, Reagan's organization regrouped and waged a vigorous campaign in New Hampshire while Bush basked in the rays of press coverage. Aided by substantial "independent" expenditures by conservative groups, and the strong support of arch-conservative publisher William Loeb, Reagan reversed the polls that had shown him trailing Bush shortly after the Iowa caucuses. Just a few days before the primary, Bush made an embarrassing and perhaps fatal mistake. Reagan and Bush had agreed to a two-man debate in Nashua, sponsored by a local newspaper. The other candidates were infuriated by this, and threatened to "crash the debate." Reagan's strategists considered the implications of this, and quietly invited the candidates to come. On the evening of the debate four of the excluded candidates showed up, and Reagan met with them. But Bush refused to acknowledge their presence, and in a memorable scene captured by the national networks' news cameras, sat passively as the four candidates— all distinguished members of the U.S. Congress—were sent off into the snow. The vote on the following Tuesday, with Reagan receiving 50 percent to Bush's 23 percent, was almost anticlimactic.

So few voters had spoken, but so much had been said. Reagan was once again on top, serious doubts about Bush were raised, Anderson (10 percent) and Baker (13 percent) were said to be in trouble. Dole was gone. The following week, Anderson revived, finishing a very close second in Massachusetts and Vermont. Reagan was first in Vermont, and Bush had a much-needed first in Massachusetts. Journalists, intrigued with the didactic Anderson, now had cause to examine him closely, and he received the majority of attention during the week after the Vermont and Massachusetts elections. Meanwhile, a disappointed Baker withdrew from the race.

Connally hoped to ambush Reagan in South Carolina on March 8, and spent heavily there. But his candidacy was ended when he finished with less than 30 percent of the vote to Reagan's 55 percent. Reagan then dominated three southern primaries on March 11. Anderson's best hope came one week later in Illinois, his home state. But even with the help of some Democrats who crossed over to vote for him, he could not prevail, trailing Reagan by over 10 percent. In the following two weeks Anderson finished third in Connecticut and Wisconsin, and decided to run for the presidency as an independent candidate. By this time it was apparent that only a miracle could stop Reagan. Saying that he didn't hear enough prayers, former President Ford declined to try to offer that miracle; at that point Crane, who had hoped to be the beneficiary of the conservative vote if Reagan were stopped, withdrew also.

Bush continued to campaign, focusing his efforts in northeastern and industrial states, and in his home state of Texas. Although he ran a close second in Texas and finished first in Connecticut, Pennsylvania, and Michigan, it was not enough to offset Reagan's sweep of the rest of the country, a sweep accentuated by the Republican apportionment formula. Bush withdrew May 26, and though more than 4.2 million Republican primary voters—one third of the total for 1980—had yet to go to the polls, the campaign was over.

## NOTES

1. Cyrus Vance, "Reforming the Electoral Reforms," *New York Times Magazine* (February 22, 1981), p. 62.

2. Commission on Party Structure and Delegate Selection, *Mandate for Reform* (Washington, D.C.: Democratic National Committee, 1970), p. 10.

3. Gerald Pomper, "New Rules and New Games in Presidential Nominations," *Journal of Politics* 41 (August 1979), p. 789.

4. Commission on Party Structure and Delegate Selection, *Mandate for Reform* (Washington, D.C.: Democratic National Committee, 1970), p. 49.

5. Thomas Patterson, *The Mass Media Election* (New York: Praeger, 1980).

6. Thomas Marshall, *Presidential Nominations in a Reform Age* (New York: Praeger, 1981).

7. The literature is voluminous. For a sampling see: F. Christopher Arterton, "Campaign Organizations Confront the Media-Political Environment," and "The Media Politics of Presidential Campaigns," in *Race for the Presidency*, ed. James David Barber (Englewood Cliffs, N.J.: Prentice-Hall, 1978), pp. 3–54; Ernest May and Janet Fraser, *Campaign '72: The Managers Speak* (Cambridge, Mass.: Harvard University Press, 1973); Jonathan Moore and Janet Fraser, eds., *Campaign for President: The Managers Look at '76* (Cambridge, Mass.: Ballinger, 1977); Jonathan Moore, ed., *The Campaign for President: 1980 in Retrospect* (Cambridge, Mass.: Ballinger, 1981); Sidney Blumenthal, *The Permanent Campaign* (Boston: Beacon Press, 1980); Larry Sabato, *The Rise of Political Consultants* (New York: Basic Books, 1981).

8. F. Christopher Arterton, "Political Money and Party Strength," in *The Future of American Political Parties: The Challenge of Governance*, ed. Joel Fleishman (Englewood Cliffs, N.J.: Prentice-Hall, 1982), pp. 101–39; William Crotty, *Political Reform and the American Experiment* (New York: Harper and Row, 1977), pp. 103–91.

9. American Enterprise Institute Forum, *Regulation of Political Campaigns—How Successful?* (Washington, D.C.: American Enterprise Institute, 1977), p. 17.

10. E. E. Schattschneider, *Two Hundred Million Americans in Search of a Government* (New York: Holt, Rinehart and Winston, 1969).

11. Several good overviews of the evolution of presidential nominating procedures have been written. See especially: James Ceaser, *Reforming the Reforms* (Cambridge, Mass.: Ballinger, 1982), Chapter 2; Thomas Marshall, *Presidential Nominations in a Reform Age* (New York: Praeger, 1981), Chapter 2; and William R. Keech and Donald R. Matthews, *The Party's Choice* (Washington, D.C.: The Brookings Institution, 1977).

12. See the report of the Commission on Party Structure (note 2, this chapter). One member of the commission described the intentions of the reformers: Austin Ranney, *Curing the Mischiefs of Faction* (Berkeley: University of California Press, 1975).

13. Jeane J. Kirkpatrick, "Representation in American National Conventions: The Case of 1972," *British Journal of Political Science* 5 (Fall, 1975), pp. 265–322. In addition to data comparing convention delegates and party identifiers, Professor Kirkpatrick's article includes an extensive treatment of the theory of representation.

14. *A Report of the Commission on Delegate Selection and Party Structure*, Barbara Mikulski, Chairman (Washington, D.C.: Democratic National Committee, 1973).

15. The best available description of the new laws is: Herbert Alexander, *Financing Politics* (Washington, D.C.: Congressional Quarterly, 1976).

16. This effort to describe the nominating system necessarily omits much detail about the procedures in each state, and in particular how the Democrats and Republicans differ. The most thorough treatment of the rules is by James W. Davis, *Presidential Primaries: Road to the White House* (Westport, Conn.:

Greenwood Press, 1980), Chapter 3. James Ceaser provides a readable overview of the post-1968 rules changes in *Reforming the Reforms* (Cambridge, Mass.: Ballinger, 1982), Chapter 3. Other useful accounts include Thomas Marshall, *Presidential Nominations in a Reform Age* (New York: Praeger, 1981), pp. 32–59; and John H. Aldrich, *Before the Convention: Strategies and Choices in Presidential Nomination Campaigns* (Chicago: University of Chicago Press, 1980), Chapter 3.

In 1984, the Democrats will once again permit states to conduct district-level winner-take-all primaries. This change was made partly to induce larger states not to move their primaries closer to the start of the nominating season, so-called "front loading." Other rules changes are discussed in Chapter 8. For a description of the changes see the *Report of the Commission on Presidential Nomination*, James B. Hunt, Jr., Chairman (Washington, D.C.: Democratic National Committee, 1982).

17. Several good accounts of the nominations of 1976 and 1980 are available. Among the best journalistic treatments are Jules Witcover, *Marathon: The Pursuit of the Presidency, 1972–1976* (New York: Viking Press, 1977), written about the 1976 contests, and for 1980, Jack W. Germond and Jules Witcover, *Blue Smoke and Mirrors* (New York: The Viking Press, 1981). See also Gerald M. Pomper, "The Nominating Contests and Conventions," in Pomper et al., *The Election of 1976: Reports and Interpretations* (New York: David McKay, 1977), pp. 1–34; Pomper, "The Nominating Contest," in Pomper et al., *The Election of 1980* (Chatham, N.J.: Chatham House, 1981), pp. 1-37; and Thomas R. Marshall, "A Guide to Recent Presidential Nominations," in his *Presidential Nominations in a Reform Age* (New York: Praeger, 1981), pp. 173–94.

# 2

# REPRESENTATION IN
# PRESIDENTIAL NOMINATIONS

The chief rationale of reformers who oversaw the changes in nominating rules was to strengthen the linkage between the preferences of the party's rank-and-file and the outcome of the nominations. They sought, in short, to make the nominating conventions more *representative* of those who identified with the party. In this chapter, we will first review some of the elements of democratic theory that guided the reformers, and discuss the choices they made. Second, we will note some of the ways in which the structure of the new nominating system distorts representation. And finally, we will examine evidence about the representativeness of the nominating process.

Debate about the perceived failings of the nominating system, during both the Progressive era and in the period following the 1968 election, reflected the enduring tension between proponents of direct democracy and those advocating the use of mediating or representative institutions. The Progressives stood very clearly at one end of the continuum; they believed that whenever possible, the public should speak directly through elections. As a means of eliminating the influence of corrupt party leaders, they urged the use of primary elections for party nominations. The McGovern-Fraser Commission was not as sanguine toward primaries as the Progressives had been. They opposed a national primary, fearing that such an instrument would render parties meaningless and thus destroy them. And they did not argue for more extensive use of state primaries. Their approach to improving representation was multifaceted. One set of recommendations was aimed at eliminating practices that had insulated the convention from rank-and-file opinion, while another set was intended to engineer greater participation by particular groups that had been demographically underrepresented at the conventions.

Acting on the recommendations of subsequent reform commissions, the Democrats (and to some extent, state legislatures) made rules that further strengthened the link between the opinions and preferences of the party members (or more correctly, the members who participate in caucuses and primaries) and the actions of the convention while moving away from rules requiring the convention to "look like" the party membership. With proportional representation and legal binding, the Democrats succeeded in 1980 in producing a convention composed of delegates who had almost no discretion at all in their most important function. They were representative of their states only in the same narrow sense that members of the electoral college represent theirs: they faithfully ratified an outcome that had already been determined.

## NOTIONS OF REPRESENTATION

The U.S. system of government was founded by a middle class elite fearful both of despotism and anarchy. They wanted a government responsive to the wishes and interests of the public—at least, of a public like themselves—but one not too much linked to the ephemeral passions of the masses. Direct democracies, said James Madison, lived short lives and died violent deaths. The solution was a republican government in which the public's opinions would be "refined and enlarged" by being passed through the medium of a representative body.[1] Although citizens have obtained more power with the passage of time—among other things suffrage is nearly universal, referenda are widely used, senators are directly elected, and presidents nearly so—public control of the government remains indirect. Joseph Schumpeter's description of U.S. democracy remains most apt: ". . . the democratic method is that institutional arrangement for arriving at political decisions in which individuals acquire the power to decide by means of a competitive struggle for the people's vote."[2]

The "competitive struggle for the people's vote" has for most of our history occurred under the auspices of the political parties, though many of the framers opposed the idea of parties. In the first party system, presidential nominations were made by caucuses of congressmen. By the middle of the nineteenth century, this method had evolved into the more familiar convention system, in which party leaders from across the nation would gather and negotiate their way to agreement on a candidate. Except for a few elections during the Progressive era, this system provided for little input from ordinary citizens who identified with the parties. Jeane Kirkpatrick describes representation in the brokered convention system:

> Insofar as conventions were conceived as representative bodies, it was party organizations—their leaders and "regulars"—that were supposed to be represented.... The test of a convention was believed to be its ability to pick a winner. Its responsiveness to the rank-and-file was secured—or was believed to be secured—by the party's need to attract and mobilize local party activists in order, in turn, to attract voters and win elections.[3]

Operating under these norms but in the highly charged atmosphere of 1968, the Democratic National Convention (and its decision to nominate Hubert Humphrey) was viewed as illegitimate by many. The Democrats' choices of what to do about this ranged from doing nothing—retaining a representative system in which the representatives were supposed to act for their constituents but were in no way checked by them—to adopting a national primary to select the nominee, the extreme of direct democracy. Though polls showed that the public supported (and still supports) the idea of a national primary, the Democrats were reluctant to reform themselves out of existence. The convention would be kept, but the question was how to constitute it. The delegates must be representative of the party membership, but how was this to be achieved?

The meaning of representation has long been debated. One theorist, Hannah Pitkin, distinguishes between representation as "standing for" and representation as "acting for."[4] In the former, the representative represents the constituents by being like them in some relevant way. This notion of representation was reflected in the actions of the McGovern-Fraser Commission which sought to increase the representation of blacks, women, and young people by mandating that each state's delegation to the 1972 convention include an appropriate proportion of individuals from these three groups. The party later moved away from quotas, although it retained the requirement that half of the delegates be female. The idea of "demographic representation" embodied in the quotas was seen as flawed by many Democrats. It required that someone arbitrarily determine which of a myriad of politically important social characteristics was relevant and should be the basis for mandatory representation. Such an approach was particularly troublesome for a party as heterogeneous as the Democrats. Any number of groups—old people, poor people, Hispanics, white ethnics, and so forth—could rightfully claim to be an important underrepresented constituency. But another, more persuasive reason for turning away from demographic representation was that it did not guarantee and appeared even to conflict with the idea of "preferential representation." The 1972 convention, while *looking* a lot like the Democratic party membership, in other important ways did not *think* or *act* like the party membership.

And so the Democrats moved toward a notion of representation as "acting for" the represented. The delegates to the convention would be selected in such a way that their actions more faithfully reflected what the party membership itself would do if it could attend the convention. But even using this conception of representation, a difficult question remained. To what extent should the delegates act according to what they perceived to be the wishes of the constituents or according to their perceptions of what was in the best interest of the constituents? Many practical as well as normative problems obscure an answer to this. How can a representative always know what the constituents want? Our representatives to Congress should certainly not vote consistently in ways opposite to how we ourselves would vote. But representatives are there in part because we are limited in time, ability, or other resources; consequently we expect them to use their judgment. The question is how independent they should be. At one pole of the continuum is the conception of representatives as statesmen or trustees, basing their decisions on their considered judgments of what is best for the constituency (so-called "independence theories") and at the other pole is the notion of representatives as instructed delegates, acting solely on orders from the constituency (so-called "mandate theories").[5]

The Democrats in the 1970s clearly embraced a "mandate theory" of representation and so made rules to apportion delegates according to the candidates' performance in caucuses and primaries, and to bind delegates to the candidate under whose name they were elected. The concept of delegate as statesman was eliminated altogether for 1980 with the adoption of the rule prohibiting delegates from running as individuals. The party debated this issue at the 1980 convention when forces loyal to Kennedy argued futilely that many Democrats who had voted for Carter in the primaries probably no longer supported him, due to changed circumstances. Accordingly, they pleaded that the delegates should be unbound and free to represent a "changed" constituency.

Ironically perhaps, the reforms undertaken by the Democrats served not to make the conventions more representative of the party membership, but rather as Kirkpatrick points out, more representative of those who have a strong presidential preference and who seek to influence the nomination.[6] Contemporary advocates of "re-reform" argue that party leaders will give more weight to the wishes of the "typical" party member (who may not participate) than will zealots for a particular ideology.[7] This debate points up a difficulty of democracy: self-government is not a passive activity. While our system undoubtedly minimizes the amount of citizen input necessary to sustain it, citizens who wish to be represented must ultimately *do* something besides answer opinion polls. Primaries were perceived as the easiest form of participation available to the party rank-and-file, and thus the one in which representation could occur with the least distortion. The mass media, faithful to the idea of direct democracy, and always suspicious of party bosses, encouraged this perception, and primaries proliferated.

## DISTORTIONS OF REPRESENTATION

The past dozen years or so have witnessed an unprecedented amount of activity by the two parties at the national level. The Democrats have labored with the problems of nomination reform, while the Republicans have built a highly effective, businesslike organization for recruiting political talent and assisting its candidates for office. Yet despite this activity the parties remain relatively decentralized, reflecting the underlying structure of the U.S. federal system of government. Though the rules by which nominations are made have become more uniform, the diversity of the states is not completely downplayed in the presidential nominating contests. Each state is not presumed to be a microcosm of the whole nation, and each is expected to speak with its own voice in contributing to the eventual determination of a nominee. At the same time, states are not equal; some are larger than others, and this fact is reflected in the size of the delegations from each state (though for a variety of reasons perfect proportionality is not preserved). Some states speak earlier than others; in recent elections, speaking earlier meant speaking louder. Some states take on added importance because the people who live there may be strategically important to a candidate. John Kennedy's need to demonstrate his appeal to conservative Protestant voters made the West Virginia primary far more important in 1960 than the state's size would suggest; similar interactions of circumstance and strategy occur in every election year, changing the salience of individual primaries.

The heterogeneity of the primaries and their settings serve to distort representation because the influence of primary voters varies so widely. Ironically perhaps, this heterogeneity springs from efforts to tailor the setting of each primary more snugly to its locale, and to preserve the independent influence of each state. A national primary would be more uniform, but this uniformity would be purchased at a cost—only those candidates who were already well known would have a realistic chance to win. With a national primary, the citizens of New Hampshire would be unlikely to answer the knocks on their doors and find a presidential candidate standing on their front porch. This quaint aspect of our present system, it could be argued, greatly enhances the quality of decision making in the New Hampshire primary because the public comes to know the candidates well.

The rules for delegate selection vary among the states in a number of ways. First is the actual method of selecting and allocating delegates. By 1980, the Democrats conducted almost all of their primaries as statewide elections of candidate slates with proportional allocation of delegates. In 1984, however, states will again have the option to use winner-take-all rules at the level of the congressional district, and many of the larger states are likely to adopt that method in hopes of increasing their clout. Meanwhile, as noted in Chapter 1, the Republicans have continued to use several different systems.

Second, states differ in the rules governing candidates' access to the primary ballot. Despite efforts by the Democratic party to avoid early closure of the ballots (a situation which effectively limits the chances of late entrants to the contest), filing deadlines are not uniform nor necessarily in the same order as the primaries in the respective states. Further, the question of who will appear on the ballot is resolved differently in different states. Many require that the candidate file a petition to appear, but in others officials of the state determine who will be listed. Voters in different states rarely are presented with the same slate of candidates.

A third kind of variation in rules is eligibility to vote in the primary. Despite both parties' efforts to restrict voting to bona fide supporters, state laws make enforcement difficult. Some states allow citizens who are registered with a party to vote only in that party's primary; other states do not require a declaration of party affiliation, and thus allow voters to choose which primary they vote in; still others allow independents to choose which primary they wish to vote in. Crossover voting, as it is called, is not rare, and occasionally has affected the outcome of the primary. Because some primaries are magnified by virtue of the timing, episodic instances of crossover voting can be consequential. If a political party is to be a relatively enduring institution with a mostly loyal membership, participation by members of the opposition party in its most fundamental decisions must be minimal.

Perhaps the most distorting feature of the nominating system is its sequential nature. Because primaries are strung—in no particular order—across three months, what happens in one affects what happens in another. Voters in different states have different kinds of information upon which to base their judgments. Voters in New Hampshire react to the candidates mostly on the basis of the campaign in their state, plus what they may already have known of the candidates (and what they learned from the press during the Iowa caucuses). Voters in Massachusetts one week later have the results of the New Hampshire primary as well as history and the campaign. As we will demonstrate in later chapters, the results of primaries in other places can profoundly affect the way citizens view the candidates.

At the same time that public opinion is being affected (or formed) by the march of the primaries, significant changes occur in the candidates' organizations as a result of those contests. Morale is boosted or deflated, volunteers join up or leave discouraged, and most importantly, money flows in faster or it begins to dry up. The underachieving candidates quickly find themselves unable to sustain their campaigns and are gone.

As candidates drop out, and as voters face each new primary with a different field and a different base of information, so too must the meaning of each primary's outcome be different. Primary results are often interpreted in terms of the struggle of ideological factions within a party, but the changing field makes such analysis difficult and may mean that no candidate from the largest faction wins.[8] For example, in a primary with two liberals and a moderate, the two liberals compete for the vote of like-minded citizens; if they are roughly equally attractive to liberal voters, neither may be able to best a single moderate of similar attractiveness. Once one of the liberals drops out, the other liberal may begin to do much better against the moderate, but by then it may be too late to prevent him from winning the nomination, even if liberals were more numerous than moderates among the party membership.

Thus, the great variety of rules and circumstances under which primaries are conducted means that an individual citizen's choice of whether to vote, and for whom to vote, is a product of a unique mix of factors in each state. Many citizens will be aware that their vote is more or less important than the vote of a citizen in another state. The choice of a candidate is simpler in some states than in others. Voting itself is easier in some places than others. Under such conditions, the meaning of individual primary elections is often ambiguous, and rarely will they be equivalent in importance, either in absolute terms or relative to the size of the party's constituency in that state. A democratic process implicitly guarantees that each participant will have roughly equal power over the outcome. The Supreme Court affirmed this notion in its reapportionment decisions supporting the idea of "one man—one vote." But participants in primaries and caucuses vary widely in their influence on the nomination. Consequently, a most important requirement of representation is not fulfilled and the main goal of reform has not been achieved.[9]

## ASSESSING REPRESENTATION

Evaluating who or what is represented in the confused and changing environment of the nominating contests is not a straightforward task. A number of approaches are possible. One focuses on the outcome: Did the convention nominate the candidate with the most support in polls of the party identifiers? In the postreform contests since 1968, the nominees *were* the leaders in the polls, but in some cases they became the leaders only after it was apparent that they could not be denied the nomination. A similar question could ask: Did the convention nominate the candidate who received the greatest support in the primaries? As measured by delegates won in primaries, postreform conventions have done so; but when primary *voters* are the unit of analysis, one exception stands out: Ford won the nomination in 1976 despite being the choice of fewer primary voters than Reagan.

Moving away from the level of the conventions' ultimate choices, we could ask how representative the convention delegates were of the party membership. We have already reported Kirkpatrick's finding that the 1972 Democratic delegates, while demographically representative, were quite unlike rank-and-file Democrats ideologically. A more recent study found less disjuncture between convention delegates and their constituents. Farah compared poll data with the results of interviews with samples of delegates to all of the postreform conventions. The delegates were decidedly unlike their constituents demographically (with the exception of the Democrats in 1972). Ideologically, the gap between the delegates and the constituents varied across conventions. While the Democratic delegates were "too" liberal in 1972, the Republican delegates were "too" conservative in 1980, though as Farah points out the effect of this incongruity on the party's electoral success was quite different in 1980 than in 1972.[10]

The delegates in the Farah study were asked who or what they thought they represented at the conventions, and were allowed to choose among the party, a particular candidate, the primary voter, or an interest group. Among all sets of delegates except those to the 1972 Republican convention, most said they represented their candidate. This was somewhat more true of delegates selected in primaries than in caucuses, and was especially true of delegates supporting "insurgent" candidates rather than incumbent presidents. Less than 10 percent of the delegates said they represented the voters.[11]

A study of delegates to the 1976 Democratic convention also asked about role obligations, but in a somewhat different way and with strikingly different results. Paris and Shingles asked a sample of delegates what they perceived as "the primary job of a delegate." A plurality (42 percent) responded "to follow one's own judgment as to who would make the best president." The second most numerous response (31 percent) was "to represent the preferences of a majority of constituents." Ten percent said "to choose the candidate who has the best chance of winning for the Democrats."[12] Thus over half of those attending the 1976 Democratic convention viewed their role as more of a trustee or statesman than as an instructed delegate.

A final level on which representation can be judged is that of the participants in the contests themselves, in particular, the primary voters. Here, a number of comparisons are possible. Since primaries are conducted on a state-by-state basis, one comparison is the primary electorate of a state with the party rank-and-file in that state. Another comparison recognizes the role early primaries play in winnowing the field and establishing particular candidates as serious contenders. How representative of the national party membership are the primary electorates of the early states? And finally, ignoring the federal nature of the system, is the party's entire primary electorate representative of all those who identify with the party? We will review research on the first of these comparisons, and then present data of our own addressing the other two.

**Primary Electorates and Party Identifiers in the States**

Very few studies have compared state primary electorates with the populations from which they are drawn. A variety of methodological hazards threaten the validity of such research, particularly with respect to the candidate preferences of participants and nonparticipants. Surveys conducted after the primary are subject to severe "bandwagon effects," in which more citizens report voting for the winner than actually did so. Surveys done before elections may miss important opinion shifts at the end of the campaign (a phenomenon frequently seen in primary elections where citizens know little about many candidates) and, of course, identifying likely voters in preelection surveys is difficult.

Facing such obstacles, Ranney attempted to describe the representativeness of New Hampshire and Wisconsin primary electorates in 1968.[13] Employing a series of corrections and adjustments to identify likely voters he found that the voters were older, richer, and more active in organizations than were nonvoters. On most issues, the voters were not much different from the nonvoters. However, on the most important issue, the Vietnam War, the primary electorates in both parties in New Hampshire were quite a bit more supportive of the war than were nonparticipants. Ranney urged caution, however, since the actual vote for Johnson was lower than his survey of intended voters predicted. Johnson was also better liked among Wisconsin voters than among nonvoters, while for Robert Kennedy the opposite was true.

Better data were available for the 1972 Democratic nomination, and James Lengle performed a careful comparison of the California Democratic primary electorate with the statewide population of Democrats.[14] Even though turnout in that primary was an amazing 64 percent of registered voters, Lengle found that upper-status Democrats were considerably overrepresented in the primary, and that support for the two candidates, McGovern and Humphrey, was strongly related to social status. By weighting the primary results so as to produce a demographically representative electorate, Lengle argued that with universal or proportionally representative turnout, Humphrey and not McGovern would have won the state. Such an outcome could have given Humphrey the nomination, made the general election of 1972 much closer than it was, and in so doing, perhaps altered some of the post-1972 history of the United States.

The upper-status bias produced similar distortions in support for McGovern in Wisconsin, Florida, Michigan, and Pennsylvania. In general, Lengle argues that social status is related to Democratic voters' preferences among three major factions of the Democratic Party: the New Deal, the Southern, and the "New Politics" factions. The status bias inherent in the primary system helps the "New Politics" faction and to a lesser extent, the Southern faction against the New Deal faction, and in so doing, renders the process less representative.

Careful analyses of representation in individual primaries in 1976 and 1980 are not available, but it is likely that the status bias was not as critical in either party's nomination in those years. For example, Reagan enjoyed greater support than did Ford among higher-status Republicans in 1976, but in 1980 was less favored than Bush among those Republicans.

## How Representative are the Early Primaries?

The state of New Hampshire has enjoyed many fruits of being the first primary in each presidential election year. The large field of candidates and the attending legions of volunteers and journalists provide a substantial boost to the Granite State's tourist industry. The state is in the eye of the nation's newswatching public longer than any other. And perhaps most significantly, its citizens usually have more impact upon presidential nominations than those who live in the rest of the nation, though by 1980 they had to share some of that power with the residents of Iowa.

In the postreform period, the power exercised by such a small state has been considered a virtue of the system by some observers. New Hampshire (and a few of the other small, early states) offers new, less well-funded candidates an opportunity to demonstrate popular appeal in a setting of a relative intimacy with the populace. Where a national primary would put a premium on having a large organization and substantial resources for advertising, the New Hampshire primary gives fledgling talent a chance to be noticed. Viewed from this perspective, voters in New Hampshire are exercising a "proxy" for those who live in other states. But New Hampshire is a small state in New England, with hardly any urban population. It is as American as any other state, but its population is certainly not a cross section of the American public nor are its problems necessarily typical of those experienced by the rest of the United States.

Given the atypical character of New Hampshire, what sort of bias is introduced into the nomination process when this state exercises

## TABLE 2.1

### Comparison of New Hampshire Republican Primary Voters and Republicans Nationally

#### 1976

|  | New Hampshire | February National |
|---|---|---|
| Preference | (vote) | (243) |
| Ford | 49 | 60 |
| Reagan | 48 | 35 |
| Don't try to be friends with Russia | (649) | (351) |
| Agree | 56 | 62 |
| Approve abortion | (537) | (381) |
| Agree | 72 | 81 |
| Relax pollution laws | (530) | (365) |
| Agree | 51 | 51 |
| Integrate schools even with busing | (541) | (381) |
| Agree | 15 | 23 |

#### 1980

|  | New Hampshire | February National |
|---|---|---|
| Preference | (vote) | (392) |
| Anderson | 10 | 3 |
| Baker | 13 | 13 |
| Bush | 23 | 32 |
| Reagan | 50 | 40 |
| Wage and price controls | (791) | (448) |
| Favor | 45 | 49 |
| Equal Rights Amendment | (827) | (440) |
| Favor | 51 | 58 |
| Send troops to protect oil supplies | (789) | (434) |
| Favor | 60 | 69 |
| Military spending | (858) | (465) |
| Favors decrease | 6 | 5 |
| Keep same level | 19 | 21 |
| Favors increase | 75 | 74 |

| | Col 1 | Col 2 | Col 3 | Col 4 |
|---|---|---|---|---|
| Attention to presidential campaign | | | (871) | (489) |
| A great deal | | | 55 | 18 |
| Some | | | 40 | 41 |
| Not much | | | 4 | 41 |
| Age | (544) | (407) | (881) | (488) |
| 18–29 | 17 | 27 | 18 | 27 |
| 30–44 | 35 | 26 | 34 | 27 |
| 45–64 | 34 | 27 | 29 | 28 |
| 65 and older | 14 | 20 | 19 | 19 |
| Education | (560) | (407) | (868) | (489) |
| Less than H.S. | 10 | 32 | 7 | 27 |
| H.S. graduate | 31 | 35 | 25 | 39 |
| Some college | 24 | 15 | 24 | 17 |
| College graduate | 35 | 18 | 44 | 18 |
| Income | | | (827) | (473) |
| Less than $10,000 | | | 13 | 16 |
| $10,000–$14,999 | | | 19 | 20 |
| $15,000–$24,999 | | | 36 | 31 |
| $25,000 and above | | | 33 | 33 |
| Respondent ideology | (464) | (381) | (915) | (468) |
| Liberal | 15 | 16 | 10 | 15 |
| Moderate | 26 | 37 | 45 | 43 |
| Conservative | 60 | 48 | 44 | 42 |

disproportionate influence? One way to answer this question is to compare the Republican and Democratic New Hampshire primary electorates with national samples of Republicans and Democrats interviewed at the time of the primary. In terms of demographics and attitudes on most political issues, this comparison should be a valid way of assessing the representativeness of the New Hampshire electorate. Yet we should note that, unlike citizens in the rest of the nation, residents of New Hampshire have experienced campaigns directed toward them. These campaigns serve to inform them about the candidates' personal qualities and opinions on important issues.* Campaigns change the salience of the individual candidates and the importance of the contest. We have no way of knowing what the rest of the nation's public might think, know, or do if they experienced the same communications environment as the residents of New Hampshire. The differences between New Hampshire voters and the national samples could be a result both of the uniqueness of New Hampshire and the campaigns that have occurred there. The comparisons presented here are between primary voters interviewed outside the polling places and national samples of people identifying with the parties, interviewed by telephone.† Selected data for Republicans are shown in Table 2.1, and for Democrats in Table 2.2.

New Hampshire Republican primary voters gave Ronald Reagan more support than did the national samples of Republicans in both election years. In 1976, Ford led Reagan 60 percent to 35 percent in the national poll, but barely edged him 49 to 48 percent on election day. In 1980, Reagan led Bush 40 percent to 32 percent in the national poll but received 50 percent of the New Hampshire vote, to Bush's 23 percent. The campaigns in each year undoubtedly account

---

*The extent of the campaigning is suggested by the fact that as early as December 1982, at least six potential candidates for the 1984 Democratic nomination had each visited New Hampshire several times.

†These comparisons utilize data gathered by CBS News and the *New York Times* in 1976 and 1980. Data were collected in New Hampshire on election day with paper-and-pencil questionnaires given to a sample of voters leaving polling places. Results from these surveys will be compared with the February national surveys of CBS News and the *New York Times*, conducted a few days before the New Hampshire primary in both election years. The national survey was conducted by telephone. Question wording on issue items was identical on the national survey and the exit poll. Note that comparisons in this section are between a party's voters and a nationwide sample of partisans that includes those who will vote in primaries and those who won't.

for much of this disparity, but in 1976 some of the disparity may have resulted from the fact that New Hampshire Republican voters were more conservative than their national counterparts. Sixty percent of primary voters called themselves "conservative" while slightly under half of the national sample of Republicans did so. On various issues, the New Hampshire electorate was a bit more conservative than the national sample: they were 9 percent less supportive of abortion, and 8 percent less supportive of busing to achieve racial balance in schools. In 1980, the New Hampshire Republican electorate looked more like the national sample, with no difference in self-identified ideology and only minimal difference in issue attitudes.

Demographically, the primary voters were much better educated than the national sample of party identifiers; over two thirds of the New Hampshire Republican electorate had at least some college education, compared with just over one third of the national sample. On income, however, the voters were only slightly better heeled than the national sample.

As we might expect, the primary voters reported paying much greater attention to the campaign than did the national sample. Over half of the New Hampshire Republican voters reported paying "a great deal" of attention to the campaign, compared with 18 percent of the February national sample.

Where New Hampshire Republicans were more conservative than Republicans nationally, New Hampshire Democrats were more liberal than their counterparts across the country. This is seen both in the survey item tapping the respondent's ideological self-identification and in the support of liberal candidates. Carter did as well in New Hampshire in 1976 as he was doing in the national poll. But Udall did much better; he had 6 percent nationally, but received 24 percent of the New Hampshire Democratic vote. In 1980, Carter led Kennedy 66 percent to 26 percent nationally in mid-February, but his margin in New Hampshire was much smaller, 47 percent to 37 percent.

Half of New Hampshire Democratic voters in 1976 said they were liberal, compared with just one third of the national sample. In 1980, only one third of the New Hampshire Democrats admitted being liberal, but this was still more than the national sample of Democrats, of which only 24 percent confessed to being liberal. Differences on some issues underscore this point; for example, in 1980, 65 percent of New Hampshire Democrats favored wage and price controls, compared with 56 percent of Democrats nationally. In 1976, half of the national sample favored relaxing environmental controls to help create jobs, but only 36 percent of New Hampshire Democratic voters agreed.

## TABLE 2.2

### Comparison of New Hampshire Democratic Primary Voters and Democrats Nationally

**1976**

| | New Hampshire | February National |
|---|---|---|
| Preference | (vote) | (311) |
| Udall | 23 | 6 |
| Shriver | 8 | 38 |
| Bayh | 15 | 13 |
| Carter | 28 | 29 |
| Harris | 11 | 9 |
| Don't try to be friends with Russia | (436) | (649) |
| Agree | 50 | 60 |
| Approve abortion | (465) | (728) |
| Agree | 72 | 69 |
| Relax pollution laws | (454) | (649) |
| Agree | 36 | 51 |
| Integrate schools even with busing | (454) | (718) |
| Agree | 28 | 26 |

**1980**

| | New Hampshire | February National |
|---|---|---|
| Preference | (vote) | (727) |
| Brown | 10 | 8 |
| Carter | 47 | 66 |
| Kennedy | 37 | 26 |
| Attention to presidential campaign | (619) | (821) |
| A great deal | 49 | 13 |
| Some | 45 | 42 |
| Not much | 6 | 45 |
| Wage and price controls | (560) | (731) |
| Favor | 65 | 56 |
| Equal Rights Amendment | (592) | (758) |
| Favor | 73 | 62 |
| Send troops to protect oil supplies | (581) | (746) |
| Favor | 48 | 75 |

**Left group**

| | (450) | (764) |
|---|---|---|
| Age | | |
| 18–29 | 37 | 29 |
| 30–44 | 32 | 25 |
| 45–64 | 25 | 32 |
| 65 and older | 6 | 14 |

| | (469) | (762) |
|---|---|---|
| Education | | |
| Less than H.S. | 11 | 38 |
| H.S. graduate | 30 | 37 |
| Some college | 21 | 15 |
| College graduate | 38 | 10 |

| | (405) | (696) |
|---|---|---|
| Respondent ideology | | |
| Liberal | 50 | 32 |
| Moderate | 25 | 45 |
| Conservative | 25 | 23 |

**Right group**

| | (616) | (769) |
|---|---|---|
| Military spending | | |
| Favors decrease | 17 | 9 |

| | (610) | (742) |
|---|---|---|
| Spending on domestic programs | | |
| Favors increase | 46 | 33 |
| Keep same level | 25 | 44 |
| Favors decrease | 29 | 23 |

| | (621) | (819) |
|---|---|---|
| Age | | |
| 18–29 | 32 | 34 |
| 30–44 | 38 | 25 |
| 45–64 | 20 | 29 |
| 65 and older | 10 | 13 |

| | (609) | (823) |
|---|---|---|
| Education | | |
| Less than H.S. | 8 | 31 |
| H.S. graduate | 28 | 42 |
| Some college | 20 | 16 |
| College graduate | 44 | 11 |

| | (600) | (799) |
|---|---|---|
| Income | | |
| Less than $10,000 | 13 | 23 |
| $10,000–$14,999 | 23 | 23 |
| $15,000–$24,999 | 38 | 35 |
| $25,000 and above | 25 | 20 |

| | (640) | (767) |
|---|---|---|
| Respondent ideology | | |
| Liberal | 32 | 24 |
| Moderate | 52 | 47 |
| Conservative | 16 | 29 |

Demographically, the disparities seen between Republican voters and the national sample held for the Democrats as well. Nearly two thirds of the Democratic voters had some college education, compared with only 27 percent of the national sample in 1980. Primary voters in New Hampshire had higher family incomes than their national counterparts; 63 percent reported incomes over $15,000 compared with 55 percent nationally. Interestingly, however, 40 percent of the voters said their family finances were worse than they had been one year earlier, while 30 percent of the national sample of Democrats said this.

As was true with the Republicans, Democratic primary voters reported paying more attention to the campaign than did Democrats nationally. Fifty percent of the voters said they had paid "a great deal" of attention, while only 13 percent of the national sample said so.

In 1980, both Democrats and Republicans in New Hampshire expressed much greater dissatisfaction with Carter's handling of the presidency than did the national samples of Democrats and Republicans. One might point to the campaigns waged in the state as the source of much of this discontent; with the exception of Carter himself, candidates of both parties had been traveling around the state attacking his performance in office.

Overall, while we see a tendency for New Hampshire Democrats to be more liberal than Democrats nationally, and New Hampshire Republicans to be more conservative than Republicans nationally, the demographic differences are unexceptional. On the other hand, differences in candidate preference were substantial. On ideological self-placement, the differences narrow from 1976 to 1980; on specific issues, we see differences of around 10 percent on some issues, but no differences on others. The differences in support for liberal and conservative candidates in the primaries was partly the result of underlying ideological disposition of New Hampshire partisans, but almost certainly depended upon campaign-specific factors as well. Some polls suggested that Bush might have done as well in New Hampshire as he was doing in the national polls had it not been for the Nashua debate debacle. And the disproportionate strength of Catholic voters—who were not necessarily more liberal than other Democrats—contributed to Kennedy's stronger showing in New Hampshire than in the national polls.

Similar conclusions may be drawn from an analysis of other important early contests. We compared national samples of partisans with exit polls from primaries in Wisconsin in 1976, and Massachusetts and Illinois in 1980. Demographically, these primary electorates are quite similar to those in New Hampshire; compared with the national samples, they are much better educated, have slightly higher incomes, and are a little older. Politically, no single statement can be made. The 1980 Republican primary electorate in Massachusetts was 8 percent *less* conservative than the national sample, and on some issues the gap was twice that. Massachusetts Democrats were slightly more liberal than Democrats nationally on some issues, but the differences were small. Illinois Republican primary voters in 1980 were, like those in Massachusetts, also somewhat less conservative than the national sample, though on several issues (government aid to minorities, domestic spending, and the Equal Rights Amendment) they were a little more conservative. Illinois Democrats were about 10 percent more liberal than Democrats nationally, both on ideology and on some issues. Wisconsin primary voters in 1976 in both parties were very similar ideologically to the national sample of partisans.

Comparing the candidate preferences of party identifiers nationwide with voters in these early primaries is even riskier than in New Hampshire. We know that the results of the New Hampshire primary affect the public's opinions of the candidates, yet we have no national sample of the public taken between the New Hampshire and Massachusetts primaries with which to establish a comparison. Reagan did a little worse in Massachusetts than he did in the mid-February national poll of Republicans, while Bush did about the same and Anderson did much better. Ted Kennedy got 65 percent of the vote in his home state, despite the fact that Carter was getting 66 percent in the national poll. Of course, candidates are expected to do well in their home states, and journalists will adjust their interpretations of the outcome accordingly.

In Illinois, Carter and Kennedy ran about the same as they had run in the mid-March national poll. By this time, Reagan had become the choice of two thirds of Republicans, but he got about half of the vote in Illinois. John Anderson did much better in Illinois, his home state, than he was doing in the polls. But journalistic expectations—as well as his own—were higher and his performance was viewed as a serious loss.

Wisconsin was an important primary in 1976, especially for Morris Udall. At the time, Udall was favored by only about 10 percent of Democrats nationally, but ran a very close second to Carter in Wisconsin with 36 percent of the vote. On the Republican side, Reagan did a little better in Wisconsin than he was doing in the polls.

## Primary Voters and Nonvoters

A final way of assessing the respresentativeness of primary electorates is to compare primary voters nationwide with the citizens
they are supposed to represent. The 1980 National Election Study
conducted by the University of Michigan's Survey Research Center
(SRC) allows us to identify primary voters with certainty, since the
actual record of turnout for each respondent was verified. We will
compare these voters with primary nonvoters and with general election voters. Since the central question here is how similar primary
voters are to members of their party, we have also divided the respondents according to partisanship.*

While the turnout in presidential primaries is much lower than
that in the general election, the demographic composition of the
primary electorate looks much like that of the general electorate.
Table 2.3 shows the demographic characteristics of our comparison
groups. Here is a brief summary of the relationship between social
characteristics and primary turnout:

—Age is even more strongly related to voting in primaries than it is in
   general elections. Only 10 percent of respondents aged 18 to 29
   voted in a primary, compared with 28 percent of those aged 50
   or older.
—College graduates voted in primaries at the rate of 28 percent, while
   the turnout of citizens with less education varied between 17 and
   20 percent.
—The effect of income on primary voting is seen chiefly at the highest and lowest levels. Over one fourth of respondents with a family
   income over $35,000 voted, compared with only 14 percent of
   those making $11,000 or less. The groups between these extremes
   varied little.
—Men and women voted at the same rate.

---

*About 20 percent of the SRC national sample can be certified as having
voted in a primary, but since the sample in the 1980 study was large (N = 3,587),
we have over 700 primary voters with which to generalize.

The determination of partisanship was made using the standard seven-point
party identification scale. Leaners are included with the party they said they
leaned toward. Note that many of the comparisons made here involve voters
with nonvoters, rather than voters with all citizens.

—Protestants and Catholics voted at about the same rate (20 percent), but 41 percent of the 104 Jewish respondents voted in a primary.
—Twenty percent of whites voted, compared with 15 percent of blacks.

The demographic unrepresentativeness of primary electorates is therefore similar to that of general electorates: older, richer, and better educated individuals are more likely to turn out, and thus exert somewhat more influence over outcomes than they would if everyone voted. Older voters have relatively more power in primary elections than they do in general elections. The richest and best-educated voters make up about 7 percent more of the primary electorate than the group of stay-at-homes. Whether this 7 percent constitutes a politically significant force depends upon the circumstances; for example, if this 7 percent were monolithic in opposition to a candidate favored by those with less education and less income, they would certainly make a difference in many primaries. But given the variety of candidate slates presented in primaries, and the lack of clear, class-based cleavages within the parties, no simple conclusion about the income and education bias can be made. We should note once again, however, that at least in 1980, the upper-income bias was most clearly manifested in the Democratic party. As James Lengle has pointed out, such a bias in the party of lower-status Americans may have important consequences for the stability of the party.[15] We will return to this issue in Chapter 8, after examining other aspects of the representativeness of primary electorates.

Primary voters and general election voters are rated about the same in their knowledge of politics. Interviewers for the SRC were asked after each interview to rate the respondent's level of political information; 48 percent of primary voters and 46 percent of general election voters were rated above average ("fairly high" or "very high") by the interviewers. By contrast, only 33 percent of primary nonvoters, and 24 percent of general election nonvoters were so rated. Republican primary voters were the most highly rated of any of the groups: 54 percent were rated above average, while 42 percent of the Democratic voters were.

Almost no differences exist between primary voters and general election voters on the series of political trust and efficacy items included in the 1980 election study. There are a few differences between primary voters and nonvoters on some of the items, but the differences are generally quite small. Voters are a little less cynical

## TABLE 2.3

### Demographic Characteristics of Primary Voters and Other Groups, 1980

| | Percent of group that turned out | Primary voters | Primary nonvoters | Democratic voters | Democratic nonvoters | Republican voters | Republican nonvoters | General election voters |
|---|---|---|---|---|---|---|---|---|
| Education | | (704) | (2870) | (314) | (1532) | (178) | (1012) | (1828) |
| Grade school | 19 | 11% | 12% | 13% | 13% | 10% | 9% | 10% |
| Some high school | 17 | 14 | 17 | 19 | 19 | 8 | 13 | 12 |
| High school graduate | 18 | 33 | 37 | 33 | 36 | 32 | 35 | 35 |
| Some college | 20 | 20 | 20 | 18 | 20 | 25 | 23 | 22 |
| At least college graduate | 28 | 22 | 14 | 17 | 13 | 26 | 20 | 21 |
| Family income | | (470) | (1870) | (187) | (991) | (127) | (697) | (1267) |
| $11,000 or less | 14 | 14 | 22 | 16 | 26 | 8 | 15 | 16 |
| $11,000–$17,000 | 20 | 15 | 16 | 20 | 16 | 9 | 14 | 15 |
| $17,000–$25,000 | 21 | 26 | 25 | 24 | 25 | 34 | 23 | 26 |
| $25,000–$35,000 | 21 | 23 | 22 | 19 | 20 | 25 | 26 | 25 |
| $35,000 or more | 27 | 22 | 15 | 20 | 13 | 24 | 23 | 19 |
| Race | | (703) | (2872) | (314) | (1532) | (178) | (1012) | (1825) |
| White | 20 | 92 | 87 | 84 | 81 | 99 | 97 | 91 |
| Black | 15 | 8 | 12 | 14 | 18 | 0 | 3 | 9 |
| Sex | | (705) | (2882) | (315) | (1538) | (178) | (1014) | (1832) |
| Male | 19 | 42 | 44 | 41 | 41 | 39 | 48 | 44 |
| Female | 20 | 58 | 56 | 59 | 59 | 61 | 52 | 56 |

| | | (703) | (2873) | (313) | (1533) | (178) | (1012) | (1829) |
|---|---|---|---|---|---|---|---|---|
| Age | | | | | | | | |
| 18–29 | 10 | 13 | 30 | 11 | 26 | 13 | 27 | 18 |
| 30–39 | 16 | 17 | 22 | 16 | 23 | 17 | 20 | 21 |
| 40–49 | 23 | 15 | 13 | 15 | 14 | 14 | 13 | 16 |
| 50–64 | 28 | 30 | 19 | 32 | 20 | 29 | 20 | 25 |
| 65+ | 28 | 25 | 16 | 26 | 17 | 26 | 18 | 20 |
| | | (705) | (2882) | (315) | (1538) | (178) | (1014) | (1832) |
| Religion | | | | | | | | |
| Protestant | 20 | 60 | 60 | 55 | 59 | 74 | 67 | 61 |
| Catholic | 20 | 23 | 23 | 26 | 25 | 15 | 19 | 23 |
| Jewish | 41 | 6 | 2 | 10 | 3 | 2 | 1 | 4 |
| Nontraditional Christian | 12 | 2 | 3 | 2 | 2 | 1 | 4 | 4 |
| Other, none | 16 | 9 | 11 | 7 | 10 | 7 | 9 | 9 |

*Note*: Entries in the first column are the percentage of the demographic group in that row (for example, respondents with a grade school education) that voted in a primary election. Entries in other columns are the percentage of the respondents in that column (for example, all primary voters) who fall into a particular demographic subcategory. Entries in parentheses are the number of cases in each column for each demographic variable.

*Source*: 1980 National Election Study for the Center for Political Studies, University of Michigan. Data made available through the Inter University Consortium for Political and Social Research.

## TABLE 2.4

### Issue Attitudes of Primary Voters and Other Groups, 1980

| | Primary voters | Primary nonvoters | Democratic primary voters | Democratic primary nonvoters | Republican primary voters | Republican primary nonvoters | General election voters | General election nonvoters |
|---|---|---|---|---|---|---|---|---|
| Inflation vs. unemployment | (450) | (1851) | (185) | (1027) | (118) | (680) | (1223) | (1024) |
| Reduce inflation | 37% | 34% | 25% | 29% | 48% | 46% | 35% | 35% |
| Neutral | 36 | 34 | 40 | 34 | 33 | 30 | 36 | 33 |
| Reduce unemployment | 27 | 32 | 35 | 36 | 20 | 24 | 29 | 33 |
| Government services and spending | (595) | (2336) | (263) | (1272) | (154) | (855) | (1564) | (1297) |
| Reduce spending | 36 | 31 | 20 | 22 | 55 | 48 | 36 | 27 |
| Neutral | 21 | 19 | 22 | 17 | 21 | 18 | 20 | 18 |
| Continue services | 43 | 51 | 58 | 61 | 23 | 34 | 44 | 55 |
| Defense spending | (638) | (2385) | (276) | (1294) | (166) | (889) | (1626) | (1321) |
| Decrease | 9 | 11 | 13 | 15 | 3 | 5 | 9 | 12 |
| Neutral | 17 | 17 | 20 | 19 | 16 | 13 | 16 | 19 |
| Increase | 74 | 72 | 67 | 66 | 81 | 83 | 74 | 70 |
| Government guarantee of jobs | (547) | (2104) | (240) | (1139) | (139) | (786) | (1454) | (1132) |
| Should guarantee | 24 | 27 | 35 | 34 | 10 | 16 | 24 | 31 |
| Neutral | 20 | 19 | 24 | 20 | 15 | 15 | 19 | 18 |
| Should not guarantee | 56 | 54 | 41 | 46 | 75 | 69 | 57 | 51 |
| Getting along with Russia | (607) | (2314) | (253) | (1230) | (163) | (876) | (1567) | (1285) |
| Important to get along | 37 | 38 | 45 | 39 | 35 | 32 | 38 | 36 |
| Neutral | 19 | 22 | 18 | 22 | 20 | 22 | 20 | 23 |
| Mistake to try | 44 | 40 | 37 | 39 | 45 | 46 | 42 | 41 |

*Note*: Entries are percentage of respondents in each column with the corresponding opinion on the given issue. Entries in parentheses are the number of cases in the column for each issue.

*Source*: 1980 National Election Study

and feel a little more efficacious than nonvoters. Slightly more primary voters than nonvoters (70 percent to 62 percent) think that there are important differences between the political parties.

Primary voters and general election voters look the same ideologically. The primary electorate, like the general electorate, is slightly more conservative than the group of nonvoters; when the sample is divided by party, this difference is seen only among Republicans.

We examined respondent attitudes on five issues, three dealing with the government and the economy, and the other two with defense spending and relations with Russia.* These data are presented in Table 2.4. On all five issues, the primary and general electorates were indistinguishable. On the domestic issues, the Democratic primary voters were a whiff more liberal than Democratic nonvoters, but the differences in the sample could have occurred by chance. Republican primary voters were more distinct from their nonvoting fellow partisans, and as expected, the difference was in the direction of greater conservatism. But even here, the differences were not dramatic; the largest is seen on the item which asked the respondent's opinion about cutting government services and spending: 34 percent of nonvoting Republicans opposed further cuts, while 23 percent of Republican voters opposed them.

On the foreign and defense items, we see almost no differences between groups of voters and nonvoters. Democratic voters are slightly more supportive of the idea of trying to get along with Russia than are nonvoters, but in general the similarities on these issues far outweigh the differences.

Thus on the whole—and leaving aside the question of preferential representativeness—we find relatively few differences between those who vote in primaries and those who do not. In terms of general orientations toward politics, in ideology, and in opinions on basic political issues, the primary electorate is fairly representative of those who do not vote in primaries. Demographically, the primary electorate is somewhat skewed toward older, wealthier, and better-educated individuals when compared with the group of nonvoters, but it looks very much like the group that votes in general elections.

---

*All issues were originally measured with seven-point Likert scales; we recoded the items to three categories, retaining the middle position and collapsing the responses on each side of the middle into one category.

## DISCUSSION

Under the banner of democracy, party reformers in the 1970s created an electorally based nominating process. They sought to give control of the nomination to the party membership. Through primary elections, party rank-and-file are encouraged to participate in the selection of the nominee, and changed rules have sought to make the convention faithfully represent the sentiments expressed in the primaries.

We have examined several aspects of representation in the nominating contests. Convention delegates still do not look exactly like the party membership in miniature, but increasingly they must follow the instructions of the rank-and-file who selected them. If the delegates faithfully represent the primary voters, then who do the primary voters represent? Our data suggest that primary electorates are much like general electorates in terms of demographics, ideology, and opinions on issues. Primary voters are, like general election voters better-educated, better informed politically, and more interested in politics than nonvoters.

Assessing what these differences mean is difficult. Just as we did with convention delegates, we might conceive of primary voters either as "trustees" or as "instructed delegates," representing the rest of the party's rank-and-file which for one reason or another does not participate in the primaries. If they should be "instructed delegates," the differences we see are perhaps undesirable. The socioeconomic differences may sometimes lead to the selection of candidates unrepresentative of the party, as Lengle argues occurred in the 1972 Democratic nomination. On the other hand, if primary voters are "trustees," then their greater interest and higher levels of information and education could, by the standard of informed choice in elections, be seen as a virtue.

Since participants in the early delegate selection contests serve to winnow the field and sometimes to determine the nominee, assessing their representativeness of the broader party membership is perhaps even more important. The evidence reviewed here suggests that early primary electorates are often different from the national membership in political outlook and candidate preference. In the important New Hampshire primary, Democratic voters are more liberal than Democrats nationally, while Republican voters are more conservative than Republicans nationally. But no single summary statement about early states is possible, and the effects of such unrepresentativeness on the fortunes of different candidates will vary according to which states manage to come first, who the candidates are, how fast a particular wing of the party is able to consolidate to one candidate, and what sort of episodic and unpredictable events occur during the campaigns in those states.

More generally, representation in the nominating process is hard to assess because the participants—particularly those in the early contests—don't have much to represent. Public interest in and attention to the campaign is relatively low, and citizens in other places have little basis for judging the candidates. Later in our study, we will look at the process of citizen learning and opinion formation during the nominating contests. After examining evidence about the bases on which citizens form opinions of the candidates, we will return to the question of representation in our concluding chapter.

## NOTES

1. Madison's defense of representative government is found in "Federalist 10," *Federalist Papers*, Alexander Hamilton, John Jay and James Madison (New York: Mentor, 1961), pp. 77–84.

2. Joseph Schumpeter, *Capitalism, Socialism and Democracy* (New York: Harper, 1950), p. 269.

3. Jeane Kirkpatrick, "Representation in the American National Conventions: The Case of 1972," *British Journal of Political Science* 5 (July 1975), p. 274.

4. Hannah Fenichel Pitkin, *The Concept of Representation* (Berkeley: University of California Press, 1967), Chapters 4-6. Much of the discussion that follows borrows from her treatment.

5. Ibid., Chapter 7.

6. Jeane Kirkpatrick, "Representation in the American National Conventions: The Case of 1972," *British Journal of Political Science* 5 (July 1975), p. 275.

7. James I. Lengle, *Representation and Presidential Primaries: The Democratic Party in the Post-Reform Era* (Westport, Conn.: Greenwood Press, 1981).

8. A lucid discussion of how this may occur can be found in Thomas H. Hammond, "Another Look at the Role of 'The Rules' in the 1972 Democratic Presidential Primaries," *Western Political Quarterly* 33 (March 1980), p. 59. For a more general discussion of the problem of reaching a rational or fair consensus in a multi-candidate election, see Kenneth Arrow, *Social Choice and Individual Values* (New York: John Wiley and Sons, 1963).

9. One way to gauge the extent to which the rules may have a systematic effect on the outcome is to "replay" the nomination contests in the states under different systems of allocating delegates. Two interesting attempts at this are: James I. Lengle and Byron Shafer, "Primary Rules, Political Power, and Social Change," *American Political Science Review* 70 (March 1976), pp. 25–40, and Gerald M. Pomper, "New Rules and New Games in Presidential Nominations,"

*Journal of Politics* 41 (August 1979), pp. 784-805. Both studies find that certain candidates were helped by the rules in effect, while others were hurt. For instance, Pomper argues that under winner-take-all rules, Jackson might have been able to prevent Carter's bandwagon from rolling. However, both studies note that if the rules had been different, the fields of candidates and the strategies employed by them (and thus the outcomes) might have been different as well.

10. Barbara G. Farah, "The Representativeness of Direct Primaries: Linkage Between Partisan Voters and Convention Delegates 1972, 1976, and 1980," manuscript (Center for Political Studies, University of Michigan, 1982), p. 22.

11. Ibid., pp. 22-25.

12. David C. Paris and Richard D. Shingles, "Preference Representation and the Limits of Reform: the 1976 Democratic Convention," *Journal of Politics* 44 (February 1982), pp. 208-10.

13. Austin Ranney, "Turnout and Representation in Primary Elections," *American Political Science Review* 66 (March 1972), pp. 21-37.

14. James I. Lengle, *Representation and Presidential Primaries: The Democratic Party in the Post-Reform Era* (Westport, Conn.: Greenwood Press, 1981), Chapter 4-5.

15. Ibid., Chapter 7.

# 3

# INVOLVEMENT IN
# THE CAMPAIGN

A presidential election is many things. It is a nation choosing leadership, it is reaffirmation of the democratic process, it is spectacle. It is a time for citizens to become active participants in the political process.

There is no more fundamental decision we are called upon to make than to select the individuals who will govern us. The leadership we choose is empowered to make the decisions that directly affect the quality of our lives. In this chapter we seek to explore the context in which such critical decisions about leadership are made. How interested is the public in the nominating campaigns? Does interest grow over the primary election season? How attentive is the public to campaign developments? And, what sources of information do people turn to for information about the campaign? These questions are fundamental, for they go to the heart of the public's ability to make informed choices.

## INTEREST IN THE ELECTION

Speaking generally, we do not have a citizenry that takes an active role in government and politics. As Walter Lippman noted more than half a century ago, the common man has little time for, and little interest in politics.[1] Three decades of behavioral research have done little to challenge Lippman's assertions. If ever the public was to become engaged in politics in noncrisis times, however, presidential elections would appear to be the most likely stimulus. Starting with the Iowa caucus in January, the nominating season is a string of highly visible media-events. To kick off the 1980 campaign, the national network newscasts stationed their anchormen in Iowa; CBS alone had 150 people in the Hawkeye State. It was then off to New Hampshire, where the pundits asked if George Bush could build on his Iowa victory and deliver a knockout blow to Ronald Reagan, and whether Edward Kennedy could defeat a sitting president on Kennedy's home turf.

Despite the intense magnification by the media of the early campaign tests,[2] and despite the obvious importance of choosing a president, only a small proportion of the public can be said to have a high degree of interest in presidential nomination campaigns. About one third of the public reported having a great deal of interest in the 1980 election. This was true at the start of the campaign in January (after Iowa and before New Hampshire), it was true at the end of the primary season, and it was true through the general election. Table 3.1 displays public interest at various times during the 1980 campaign.

The serial nature of the primary contests, coupled with the horse race style of media coverage, might lead one to suspect that interest would grow throughout the primary season. However, this was clearly not the case. Moreover, the constancy of interest among the electorate as a whole was not unique to the 1980 election. Thomas Patterson found the same pattern in the 1976 election, based on panel studies conducted in Los Angeles and Erie, Pennsylvania.[3]

### TABLE 3.1

**Interest in the 1980 Election**
**(percentage)**

|  | February | April | June | September | November |
|---|---|---|---|---|---|
| Level of Interest |  |  |  |  |  |
| Not much | 20 | 22 | 19 | 26 | 26 |
| Somewhat | 46 | 43 | 46 | 44 | 44 |
| Very much | 34 | 35 | 35 | 30 | 30 |
| Total | 100 | 100 | 100 | 100 | 100 |
| (n) | (1003) | (962) | (841) | (1567) | (1567) |

*Source:* 1980 National Election Study, Center for Political Studies (CPS).

**TABLE 3.2**

**Individual Change in Interest in the Election, February to June**
**(percentage)**

|  | Level of Interest in June | | | | |
|---|---|---|---|---|---|
|  | Very | Somewhat | Not Very | Total | (n) |
| Level of Interest in February |  |  |  |  |  |
| Very | 69 | 25 | 7 | 101 | (162) |
| Somewhat | 18 | 67 | 15 | 100 | (378) |
| Not very | 12 | 38 | 51 | 100 | (298) |

*Source:* 1980 National Election Study, Center for Political Studies.

But while data from the national election study show an *electorate* that did not become more interested or attentive as the campaign progressed, a considerable number of *people* did become more—and less—interested in the election as the campaign progressed. About one third of the public reported a different level of interest from one interview to the next across the four waves of the national election study in 1980. Little appears to have changed since 1940 when Lazarsfeld and colleagues found the same rate of change in their Erie County panel study.[4] Patterson made the same observation about interest in the 1976 election.

As can be seen in Table 3.2, only half of those having little interest in the election in February were so classified in June. Two thirds of those having "some" interest in February maintained this level of interest in June, with the balance split between those having more and less interest in June. About seven-in-ten of those who were very interested in the election in February remained so in June. The volatility in interest at the individual level can easily be seen by looking at the proportion of people who reported having the same amount of interest in the campaign at each of their four interviews. Overall, only 41 percent maintained a constant level of interest, with 18 percent being "very interested" in January, June, September, and November. Another 18 percent were "somewhat interested" and 5 percent were "not very interested" at all four times.

There are a number of factors that could account for the wide variation in interest. First is the nature of the campaign itself. Not only does the campaign progress through a number of stages—primaries, conventions, and the general election—but each stage has greater and lesser periods of intrinsic interest. Interviewing on one of the panel waves, for example, ran from September 2 to October 1. With the general election campaign not really in full swing in early September but quite active in October, it is entirely possible that events of the campaign interacted with general interest in the campaign in different fashion. Those interviewed in September, for example, may have expressed less interest than those interviewed in October in reaction to campaign developments, despite similar underlying levels of interest in the campaign.

It is also possible that different stages of the campaign appeal to different groups. For example, most independents do not participate in the selection of the nominees, and might be largely uninterested in the primary contests only to perk up after the conventions as the general election phase of the campaign begins. Our analysis, however, suggests that this was not the case in the 1980 election. Interest levels appeared to be fairly stable when individuals were classified by the strength of their attachment to a political party. Fifty percent of strong Democrats and Republicans reported being very much interested in January, with 54 percent reporting this level of interest in April and 48 percent in September. Twenty-seven percent of independent voters who leaned toward neither party reported being very interested in January. This figure declined to 16 percent in April but rebounded to 24 percent in September.*

In 1980 there was less interest in the presidential election campaign than in general public affairs. In April, the middle of the primary season, 35 percent reported being "very interested" in the election, while 45 percent said they followed "what's going on in government and public affairs" "most of the time." The difference in question wording makes direct comparisons between the two types of

---

*Our inability to explain shifts in individuals' levels of interest with substantive reasons means that we must consider the possibility that a good deal of measurement error may exist in the data. Much survey data is "soft." Assume for the moment that a perfect quantitative measure of interest is possible, and that a respondent could be characterized as a "4" on a scale ranging from 1 (not interested) to 5 (very interested). Even if this person's interest in the election remained constant throughout the campaign she might well report being "somewhat" interested to an interviewer at one time and being "very" interested at another. And of course there is always a good bit of random error in survey data no matter how carefully it is collected.

interest hazardous. And it is worth remembering that public affairs during this time were exceptionally interesting, with U.S. citizens being held hostage in Iran. Yet in both 1972 and 1976 a slightly greater proportion of the public reported following public affairs "most of the time" than reported being "very interested" in the election.* Clearly then, presidential elections do not stimulate an expansion of interest on the part of the general public.

## ATTENTION TO THE CAMPAIGN

Accompanying the generally low level of interest in presidential elections, most of the public pays little attention to the campaign as the primary elections run their course. The monthly surveys conducted by the *New York Times* and CBS News in 1980 found only about 15 percent saying they had paid "a lot" of attention to the presidential campaign during January and February. Three times this number reported paying "not much" attention. Later in the primary season, in March, April, and June, the proportion of the public that could be considered highly attentive varied only from one-in-five to one-in-four, as seen in Table 3.3.

It is interesting to note that while the proportion of attentive citizens grew only slightly, the proportion of totally inattentive citizens diminished to a much greater degree. Whereas almost half of the public paid scant attention to the campaign at the beginning of the primaries in January, only about one quarter were so classified at the end of the primaries in June. The trends in interest and attention are something of a paradox; interest did not increase while attention did, particularly from the lowest level of attentiveness. One must wonder if this is not partially attributable to the constant coverage the primaries received from the mass media. People may have felt they were more attentive because they *had* in fact attended to a greater amount of campaign information as the primaries progressed—even if they had not meant to.

This is particularly easy to hypothesize in the case of television, the dominant source of election information. Television news does not allow individuals to choose the content to which they are exposed, unlike the print media where individuals may decide which stories to read. Moreover, it is precisely among the least interested

---

*Source:* CPS National Election Studies of 1972 and 1976.

**TABLE 3.3**

**Attentiveness to the Campaign**
**(percentage)**

|  | January | February | March | April | June |
|---|---|---|---|---|---|
| Level of Attention |  |  |  |  |  |
| A lot | 15 | 14 | 20 | 25 | 23 |
| Some | 39 | 41 | 41 | 43 | 50 |
| Not much | 46 | 45 | 39 | 32 | 27 |
| Total | 100 | 100 | 100 | 100 | 100 |
| (n) | (1468) | (1536) | (1468 | (1594) | (1503) |

*Source:* CBS/*New York Times*, 1980 Primary Election Surveys.

and attentive where unintentional exposure to political information would be most likely to occur. The fact that learning may be largely unintentional has important consequences to which we will return shortly.

## EXPOSURE AND ATTENTION TO THE MEDIA

Television was in fact the medium through which the great majority of the public followed all phases of the 1980 campaign, as it has in all presidential elections since 1952. On six waves of the national election study, between 60 and 65 percent of the public said that television was their primary information source. Slightly less than one quarter said they relied primarily on newspapers, with the remainder receiving most of their information from radio or magazine.

The dominance of television is hardly surprising; it is well suited to the publics' weak appetite for political information. Moreover, election television comes in many forms: national and local news, primary night coverage and election specials, spot advertisements, and candidate debates. National network news would appear to be the principal supplier of campaign information in the early stages of the process. Other forms of television coverage lag tremendously. A voter in California, for example, would not see advertisements for most of the candidates who began the race in Iowa and were long departed by California's June primary.

Exposure to national network news reaches almost a saturation point. While it must be kept in mind that respondents' self-report on opinion surveys generally overestimates exposure to news, when interviewed in January only 6 percent said they never watched television news. Forty-four percent reported nightly viewing, while almost two thirds could be classified as "regular viewers," watching the news at least three times a week.

Exposure to a medium is of course not tantamount to information acquisition. For many people exposure to television news is largely habitual—a way to unwind between work and dinner. Simple measures of exposure to the news commingle a number of very different motivations for viewing or reading politically relevant material. This well-documented finding is a hallmark of the "Uses and Gratifications" approach to political communication.[5] Unfortunately, we lack the measures necessary to disentangle "information-seeking" reasons from "social" and "habitual" reasons for viewing, among many others.

The national election study did, however, ask people how much attention they generally paid to "news about government and politics" when exposed to the mass media. The simple percentages are instructive. Generally speaking, just under half of those watching television news said they paid a great deal of attention to stories about politics and government.* Even among regular viewers, only 55 percent reported paying a great deal of attention to the news. The figure is even lower among newspaper readers, who exercise greater control over the information to which they are exposed. Among the 64 percent who reported reading a newspaper, only 36 percent said they paid a great deal of attention to news about government and politics. This works out to just under one quarter of the public that can be said to be highly attentive to newspapers for political information. In both 1980 and 1976,[6] the electorate could more accurately be described as information-receivers than as information-seekers.

As was the case with interest, neither exposure to the mass media nor attentiveness to political information increased during the campaign. Unlike 1976, the mass media did not stimulate interest in the 1980 campaign. Thomas Patterson found that television news exposure contributed to an upturn in election interest at the early stages of the

---

*The percentage varied between 43 and 50 percent over the five waves on which this question was asked.

1976 campaign, with exposure to newspapers being more modestly related.[7] Following Patterson, we performed a multiple regression of campaign interest in June on (a) exposure to newspapers, (b) exposure to television news, and (c) campaign interest in January. With interest in January removed as an explanation of later interest we can see the independent effects of the mass media. The standardized regression coefficients (betas) were quite unimpressive: television—.08, newspapers—.11.*

## DISCUSSION

There are three interrelated general observations we may draw based on the data presented in this chapter. First, people were not excited by the campaign. There was not a great deal of interest in the election; certainly not more interest than in general public affairs. Second, the electorate depends heavily on television as its primary source of information. This is quite consistent with our conclusions about interest. Television viewing can be a largely nonpurposive act, requiring little active involvement. And third, consistent with the interest and exposure findings, we note that a majority of those exposed to television and newspapers did not pay a great deal of attention to political news.

In the introduction to this brief chapter we said our purpose was to examine the context in which citizens make decisions about leadership. What have we learned by exploring public interest in and attention to primary campaigns? Speaking generally, simply that the general public does not care very much about the parade of primary elections and does not become engaged in them. About one-in-three is very interested in the primary campaigns; only about one-in-four pays close attention to them. And while interest in the primaries is neither higher or lower than interest in general elections, the difficulty of the choice that citizens face in primaries requires greater involvement. There are more candidates for the voter to become familiar with, and party labels are unable to provide informational cues or serve as a screening mechanism.

---

*The newspaper readership question simply asked people if they "regularly read" a newspaper. We have dichotomized responses to the television news variable into an isomorphic "regular viewers" (3 or more nights per week). This could account for some of the variation between the two sets of findings.

It would appear then, that the mass public is ill disposed to discharge its responsibility in the selection of leadership under the new system. But we must remember that participation in primaries is not a mass activity. Only one eligible citizen in five participates,[8] fewer than claim to be very interested. What about the segment of the public that does actively participate? If there were a sharp division in the electorate, with those who voted being highly motivated and involved, we would have more confidence in the collective decision.

However, the evidence is that those who voted were only slightly more interested than those who did not vote. Forty-four percent of primary voters and 45 percent of nonvoters reported being "somewhat interested" in the election. Interestingly, 12 percent of those who voted in a primary confessed to not being much interested, as did 23 percent of those who did not vote.* Thus while primary voters were more interested than nonvoters, the differences were small. With fewer than half of primary voters being very interested in the campaign, the generalizations about the entire electorate remain largely true of voters.

---

*The CPS study included a "vote validation" measure which identified primary election voters. The figures reported here are a composite of the April and June waves. The number of primary voters is 368. The number of primary nonvoters is 1,435.

## NOTES

1. Walter Lippman, *Public Opinion* (New York: Free Press, 1922).

2. Michael Robinson, "Media Coverage in the Primary Campaign of 1976," *The Party Symbol*, ed. William Crotty (New York: Freeman, 1980); Thomas Patterson, *The Mass Media Election* (New York: Praeger, 1980); Donald Matthews, "Winnowing: The News Media and the 1976 Presidential Nominations," in *Race for the Presidency*, ed. James David Barber (Englewood Cliffs, N.J.: Prentice-Hall; The American Assembly, Columbia University, 1978).

3. Thomas Patterson, *The Mass Media Election* (New York: Praeger, 1980).

4. Paul Lazarsfeld, Bernard Berelson, and Hazel Gaudet, *The People's Choice* (New York: Columbia University Press, 1944).

5. For a general review see Jack McLeod and Lee Becker, "The Uses and Gratifications Approach," in *Handbook of Political Communication*, ed. Dan Nimmo and Keith Sanders (Beverly Hills, Calif.: Sage, 1981).

6. Thomas Patterson, *The Mass Media Election* (New York: Praeger, 1980).

7. Ibid., p. 70.

8. Thomas Marshall, *Presidential Nominations in a Reform Age* (New York: Praeger, 1981), p. 119.

# 4

# AWARENESS OF
# THE CANDIDATES

Howard Baker rose to national prominence as a member of the Senate committee investigating the Watergate scandal. Time and again Baker would phrase the central question of the investigation in mellifluous tones: "What did the president know, and when did he know it?" Ten years later we are investigating Howard Baker and those who joined him in seeking the presidency, asking "What did the public know, and when did they know it?"

We are interested in the process of citizen learning, a topic that is virtually boundless both in its scope and importance. A systematic exploration of the learning process will allow us to address two central questions. First, assuming that information is necessary to produce "good" decisions, how much do people know about the candidates? What is the quality of public choice? Second, how do people acquire their information? In what ways is learning related to the structure of the nominating system? Does the serial nature of primaries, interacting with the current style of journalistic coverage, produce a media environment that helps or hinders learning?

Our examination of citizen learning in the 1980 election begins simply enough with awareness of the candidates. This is an obvious starting point. If citizens are unaware of candidates there is little more to be said. Later in this chapter we will explore what may be termed "subjective knowledge," or how familiar people felt they were with the candidates. Knowledge of the candidates' ideological leanings and issue positions, or what may be termed "objective knowledge" is considered in the following chapter. Many of the questions concerning candidate awareness are related to the structure of the nomination process. The specific questions to be addressed are:

—What proportion of the general public is able to name the contestants, or at least recognize their names at the onset of the campaign?

—Do people learn about candidates gradually throughout the nominating period, or do they learn mostly in response to prominent events of the campaign?

—Assuming that events boost awareness, how large are these increases? What are the benefits in awareness from "winning" vis-à-vis simply running?

—At different stages of the campaign, what are the upper and lower limits of awareness? Particularly, what portion of the population responds to the first campaign news, and what portion remains inert throughout the campaign?

—Do all active candidates (that is, candidates who remain in the race with at least a mathematical chance of success) attain the same level of public awareness? Are such differences as may remain a function of the competitive positions of the candidates?

These questions are vital, for they go to the heart of a larger question: How well do the structure and dynamics of the current nomination system contribute to informed choice? Ideally, the early campaign tests would serve to introduce a wide range of candidates to the electorate—not simply those men who were initially successful. Moreover, we would hope that the early campaign activity, mediated by journalistic reporting, would provide both an incentive and framework for further learning.

The evidence to date, however, is that the public begins the campaign with little information about the candidates. Most first-time presidential contestants are largely unknown, regardless of their background in elected or appointed office. In February of 1976, a sample of Pennsylvania and California residents found only about one-in-five saying they knew something about Jimmy Carter, Frank Church, Birch Bayh, and Morris Udall. Only slightly more reported knowing something about Henry Jackson, and fewer reported knowing something about Fred Harris.[1]

Moreover, relatively few people appeared to learn much about the candidates over the course of the campaign. Excluding Carter, the average increase in those feeling they knew something about the candidates was only 4 percentage points from the beginning of the primaries in February to their conclusion in June. Carter was propelled into the public consciousness in dramatic fashion, starting at 20 percent in February and rising to 77 percent by April after highly visible primary victories. By June, 81 percent felt they knew some-thing about Carter, putting him almost on the same plateau as the old war horses George Wallace, Gerald Ford, and Hubert Humphrey.

Thomas Marshall also describes a public of "limited knowledge" after studying the available evidence from the new system elections of 1972, 1976, and 1980. Most first-time candidates were largely invisible to voters; detailed knowledge was limited even about the candidates with whom voters were familiar. In 1976, for example, less than half the public placed George Wallace to the right of center; only 40 percent placed Hubert Humphrey to the left. Few knew the issue positions or ideological leanings of presidential candidates and just slightly over one-in-four, on the average, held either strongly favorable or unfavorable opinions about the candidates.[2]

So most people start a presidential campaign with a blank slate. Learning, or how things get written on those slates, is largely a func-tion of the relationship between the information environment and the motivation to learn. The importance of the media environment is virtually axiomatic. As Thomas Patterson has noted, presidential campaigns are essentially mass media campaigns: ". . . it is no exag-geration to say that, for the large majority of voters, the campaign has little reality apart from its media version."[3] Intuitively, citizen knowledge of candidates, their activities, and their attributes is in great measure a function of the amount and character of information available to the public.

However, any theory of the dynamics of learning must also account for the motivations of the public. As we noted in the last chapter, people differ considerably in both levels and types of polit-ical interest. Some constantly monitor the news media, others attend in episodic fashion, while still others ignore politics completely. A considerable amount of evidence supports the common sense notion that those who are more interested learn more.[4] But we suspect this is not a simple relationship for there are both upper and lower boundaries to learning. Even the most interested cannot be expected to be fully knowledgeable about all the candidates. As John Aldrich has noted, information costs in primary elections are quite high due in part to the large number of candidates commonly in the field.[5] It may well be that until the campaign comes to the front door, so to speak, few citizens are likely to expend special effort to learn about the candidates. Moreover, the lack of media attention given to candi-dates who fail to make strong early primary showings, and the tendency of the media to focus on electoral fortunes and strategies of those who have done well, makes learning difficult even for those who are actively seeking information about candidates' background or issue positions.[6]

Correspondingly, even the least interested may be expected to learn something about the candidates from the campaign. Motivation is by no means a precondition for learning. "Passive learning," the acquisition of information by those without the intention to acquire information, has been demonstrated in a wide variety of political settings.[7] Learning may be largely a process of osmosis for those lacking in interest. We suspect that the structure of the nomination process, a succession of highly visible and repetitive events with a running story line, constitutes an environment in which passive learning would flourish, particularly with regard to awareness of candidates.

## THE DEVELOPMENT OF CANDIDATE AWARENESS

Among the three data sources available to us the Eagleton data are best suited to the task of tracking awareness of the candidates in 1980. The experience of past years has been that public awareness of different candidates varies widely at the onset of the campaign and is strongly reactive to happenings in states holding early caucuses and primaries. The principal advantages of the Eagleton data are that interviewing began well before the first formal event of the campaign (the Iowa caucus) and observations can be grouped around significant events so as to determine their impact.* We first asked our respondents if they could name the candidates running for the parties' nominations. The ability to identify individuals as candidates in

---

*One disadvantage of the data is that they come from a single state, although public opinion in New Jersey has been found to closely mirror the nation as a whole. (See Cliff Zukin and J. Robert Carter Jr., "The Measurement of Presidential Popularity," *The President and the Public*, ed. D. Graber [Philadelphia: Institute for the Study of Human Issues, 1982], p. 217.) The fact that New Jersey holds its primary at the end of the process in June is both a disadvantage and an advantage. While we are unable to ascertain the effects of a direct campaign to shape public opinion, we are able to judge the effects of general news about the nomination campaign without the contamination of such a direct campaign. Finally, the data are from repeated cross-sectional surveys. The lack of panel data makes it impossible to speak with certainty about individual-level change. Further discussion of the strengths and weaknesses of these data can be found in Appendix A.

**FIGURE 4.1**

**Percentage Able to Volunteer Candidates' Names, New Jersey, 1980**

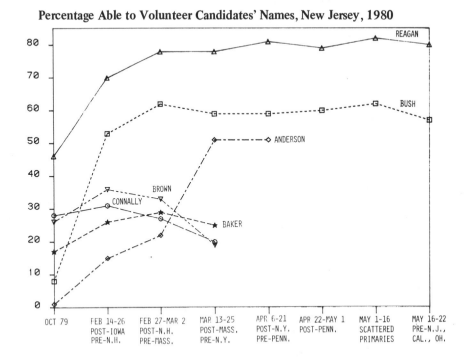

response to an open-ended question serves as our measure of *aware-ness.* Respondents were then read a list of candidates they had not named and asked if they "had heard of" each. Passing this easier test of aided recollection serves as our simple measure of name *recognition.* The data on awareness for six candidates are depicted graphically in Figure 4.1.*

---

*We have omitted some candidates from the figure to reduce clutter. Awareness of Phillip Crane increased from 2 to 7 percent from the October survey to the pre-New Hampshire measurement. Awareness of Robert Dole went from 5 to 3 percent over this same period. Carter and Kennedy have also been omitted from the figure. About 80 percent of the public was aware of each at the time of our first measurement in October 1979. The percentage aware of each fluctuated between 78 and 84 percent through May. Accordingly, most of our discussion of how the public *becomes* aware of candidates will focus on the contest for the Republican nominations. Numbers of cases may be found in Table 1 of Appendix A. Interviews were grouped by primary dates, also shown in the appendix.

The impact of a strong showing in the early contests on public awareness of candidates is dramatic. It is particularly evident in the case of George Bush after Iowa, and John Anderson after the Massachusetts and Vermont primaries. The percentage able to name Bush as a candidate for the Republican nomination jumped from 8 to 53 percent following his success in Iowa. This increase is particularly astounding considering that a CBS/*New York Times* survey taken at about the same time showed only 15 percent paying "a lot" of attention to the campaign. Truly, this is impressive prima facie evidence of passive learning. The initial measurement in October of 1979 is too far in advance of the Iowa caucus to rule out other causes of increased awareness. However, we know of no pre-caucus campaign activities that would have increased Bush's visibility while not affecting other candidates contesting the Republican nomination. Baker, Connally, and Anderson, for example, were present with Bush at the televised candidates' forum in Iowa, yet registered no such gains in public awareness.

Ronald Reagan was the second beneficiary of the Iowa caucus. While universally recognized before the caucus, the percentage able to spontaneously name Reagan as a candidate increased from 45 to 70 percent. We suspect that this is because Reagan, as the front-runner, served as the standard against which Bush's success was juxtaposed. Exposure from the Iowa campaign and the reporting of results did little to move the remaining candidates across the public's threshold of awareness. Fourteen percent more were aware of Anderson after Iowa, and about 10 percent more were aware of Baker and Brown. Connally, Dole, and Crane registered gains of less than 3 percent among the New Jersey electorate.

The other dramatic increase in awareness occurred with John Anderson. In the March 4 primaries, Anderson finished second to Reagan in Vermont by 700 votes out of 65,000 cast, and ran ahead of Reagan in Massachusetts, finishing behind Bush by three tenths of 1 percent. Anderson was the "media victor" of March 4; his unexpected strength commanded considerable attention from the press. The jump in public awareness of his candidacy was as dramatic as Bush's rise after the Iowa caucus. Awareness of Anderson more than doubled after these primaries, going from 22 to 51 percent.

There are three general observations to be made from the awareness patterns depicted in Figure 4.1. First, of course, is the impact of a strong showing in a campaign test. The attending media coverage, both on the Tuesday night election wrap-up and in the days that follow, introduces a previously little known candidate to a large portion of the public with great speed. The jumps in awareness are so steep as to suggest that a new segment of the public has been reached. Second, as a corollary to this first point, it is also apparent that not doing well in primaries carries no real benefits in public awareness. While not totally unexpected given Patterson's findings in 1976, the almost complete lack of learning is somewhat surprising when viewed from another perspective. Even weak candidates are reported in the box scores of the televised election specials and next day's newspapers. Yet awareness does not appear to grow over time from "just being in the news." Up until his Massachusetts breakthrough Anderson had only reached the awareness level of Baker and Connally—about one quarter of the electorate. We might consider the portion of the public aware of these candidates the "attentive" electorate. We suspect a strong motivation to follow politics among this segment. Awareness comes from simple exposure to the information present; the splash of coverage coming with victory (however defined) is not necessary for this group to become aware.

Third, we observe that once breakthroughs in awareness occur, when candidates do well in a contest and receive prominent coverage, a ceiling is reached quite quickly. The New Jersey public was no more aware of George Bush in May than in February, despite the increased attention given to him after Iowa, despite the fact that the Republican field was quickly winnowed to a Bush-versus-Reagan contest, and despite Bush's victories in Michigan and Pennsylvania. Nor did we observe any increase in awareness of John Anderson after his near-victories in Vermont and Massachusetts to the time he withdrew as an active candidate for the Republican nomination. Ronald Reagan also reached a ceiling of awareness quickly, after he pummelled Bush in the New Hampshire primary. After each quantum jump the candidates were simply playing on the margins.

As a final point concerning awareness, we wish to note the absence of strong partisan differences. When Democrats and Republicans were separated for analysis there were few important differences. On the average Republicans were just a few percentage points more likely to be aware of Republican candidates than other members of the public. Moreover, the learning pattern among Republicans was isomorphic to that depicted in Figure 4.1. Where we might have expected to see greater awareness and more evidence of gradual learning by partisans, based on a presumption of greater salience and interest, candidate awareness appears to be a nonpartisan affair.

Simply being able to *recognize* candidates' names is an easier test of knowledge than the ability to spontaneously volunteer the names of candidates. However, there is no guarantee that recognition is based on knowledge of *candidate-status*. Howard Baker might have been recognized for his participation in the Watergate hearings; Jerry Brown as governor of California; John Connally as a former Nixon cabinet official, defendant in a "milk-fund" trial, and former Democrat, among other roles. The percentage able to recognize each candidate is presented in Table 4.1, along with the percentage aware of each for comparative purposes.

The recognition patterns parallel the awareness patterns, although there is a ceiling effect as universal recognition accompanies the major jumps in awareness. We have noted that the group able to mention Bush as a candidate without prompting stabilized at about 60 percent and Anderson at about 50 percent (although one additional measurement would have been helpful to confirm this). In addition to those aware, another 30 percent were able to recognize both Bush and Anderson; this recognition must have come from campaign-related activities. Yet this third of the New Jersey population was unable to spontaneously recall these individuals as candidates. Thus we see evidence of learning by osmosis. A fair portion of the citizenry acquired some bits of information without really intending to do so, and perhaps not really knowing that they had done so. And while name recognition is likely to be the easiest bit of information to acquire passively, it is also one of the most fundamental.

Interestingly, there was a consistent difference between the proportion aware of, and the proportion only able to recognize those candidates who did not score well in the early primaries and dropped out of the campaign in March. Awareness of Baker, Brown, and Connally varied between one quarter and one third of the electorate, with an additional 60 percent able to recognize each of the three. Thus while the ceiling of *recognition* was the same for Anderson and Bush on the one hand, and Baker, Brown, and Connally on the other, the point at which *awareness* leveled was considerably different.

In summary, awareness and recognition of candidates in 1980 occurred in jumps, predicated on primary successes and attending media coverage. Simply running in primaries, without making a strong showing, seemed to be sufficient to bring candidates to the attention of between one quarter and one fifth of the electorate in New Jersey. Over and above this, a strong primary showing appeared to have a "hypodermic" effect, introducing the candidate—as a candidate—to another 30 to 40 percent of the electorate, as was the case with Bush and Anderson. Parallel to this in time, and on top of this stratum, another third of the electorate gained a vague familiarity with the candidates. This group learned only the names of the actors, probably in a very passive fashion as they were unable to recall the context surrounding the name. Finally, about one fifth of the electorate was totally inattentive to presidential politics. Even at the end of the primary campaign this group could not volunteer Jimmy Carter, Ronald Reagan, or Edward Kennedy as presidential aspirants.

The picture that has been sketched by these data is one of strata, thresholds, and breakthroughs. Specifically, based on our observations of these learning patterns we hypothesize an electorate existing in various layers, with different levels or intensities of media coverage necessary to reach each layer. We believe that these layers, or *strata* of public opinion, may be differentiated largely by their interest in political affairs and attentiveness to political information.

The notion of a public that may be classified by interest and information-seeking behavior is certainly not novel. V. O. Key spoke of a top layer of activists and a bottom layer of "apoliticals," but did not attempt to differentiate the strata between these extremes.[8] Public opinion researchers commonly distinguish between "attentive" and "nonattentive" publics, and, of course the "two-step" flow of mass communication where opinion leaders pass information along with their interpretations to less interested members of the public, is based on a segmentation of the public.[9]

Support for the existence of strata and the notion of thresholds is not confined simply to the data collected in 1980. Thomas Patterson observed the same phenomenon in the 1976 election both with regard to knowledge about the candidates and interest in the campaign. Patterson first observed that the amount of news coverage a candidate received was strongly related to public recognition. He went on to note:

> Importantly, though, the relationship was not strictly linear. Small amounts of coverage resulted in stable or even declining recognition, a moderate amount contributed modestly to the public's awareness of the candidate receiving it, and intense coverage led to a dramatic increase in the public's familiarity with a candidate. In other words, within the relationship were thresholds at which the impact of news coverage on public awareness changed significantly. Below a certain level of news coverage, the effect was muted; above that level the effect was magnified.[10]

Patterson's conclusions about the 1976 election and our observations about learning in the 1980 election are in accord: in neither

# TABLE 4.1

## Comparison of Percentages of Those Aware and Able to Recognize Candidates

| | Oct 1979 Pre-Iowa | Feb 14-26 Post-Iowa Pre-N.H. | Feb 27-March 2 Post-N.H. Pre-Mass. | Mar 13-25 Post-Mass. Pre-N.Y. | Apr 6-21 Post-N.Y. Pre-Penn. | Apr 22-May 1 Post-Penn. | May 1-16 Scattered Primaries | May 16-22 Pre-N.J. Cal., Ohio |
|---|---|---|---|---|---|---|---|---|
| **Reagan** | | | | | | | | |
| Aware | 46 | 70 | 78 | 78 | 81 | 79 | 82 | 80 |
| Recognize | 99 | 99 | 99 | 99 | 99 | 99 | 99 | 99 |
| Difference | 53 | 29 | 21 | 21 | 18 | 20 | 17 | 18 |
| **Bush** | | | | | | | | |
| Aware | 8 | 53 | 62 | 59 | 59 | 60 | 62 | 57 |
| Recognize | 53 | 86 | 90 | 90 | 94 | 94 | 95 | 94 |
| Difference | 45 | 33 | 28 | 31 | 35 | 34 | 33 | 37 |
| **Anderson** | | | | | | | | |
| Aware | 1 | 15 | 22 | 51 | 51 | | | |
| Recognize | 27 | 48 | 54 | 85 | 86 | 88 | 88 | |
| Difference | 26 | 33 | 32 | 34 | 30 | | | |

| | | | |
|---|---|---|---|
| Connally | | | |
| Aware | 28 | 31 | 27 |
| Recognize | 88 | 91 | 91 |
| Difference | 60 | 60 | 64 |
| | | | |
| Baker | | | |
| Aware | 17 | 26 | 29 |
| Recognize | 72 | 82 | 82 |
| Difference | 55 | 56 | 53 |
| | | | |
| Brown | | | |
| Aware | 26 | 36 | 33 |
| Recognize | 87 | 91 | 92 |
| Difference | 61 | 55 | 59 |

*Note*: Recognition is the percentage either spontaneously mentioning the candidate or able to recognize the candidate's name. Carter and Kennedy began the campaign with universal recognition and about 80 percent aware of their status as candidates. These figures did not change over the course of the campaign. In October, 4 percent were aware of Dole with 68 percent recognizing his name. Recognition of Crane increased from 20 to 31 percent between October and February; awareness of him went from 2 to 6 percent over this same period. Numbers of cases are as displayed in Table 1 of Appendix A. Anderson had ceased his pursuit of the Republican nomination, making the "awareness" question, focused on knowledge of candidates for the *nomination*, invalid. Eagleton continued to track his recognition.

*Source*: The Eagleton Poll, New Jersey Sample.

case does the evidence fit a pattern of gradual learning. Rather, once a certain threshold of media attention was reached, an entire stratum of the public that was previously uninformed became knowledgeable. These findings have led us to conceptualize the public as residing in four discrete strata, which we have labeled the *attentive, latent, inadvertent,* and *apathetic* publics.[11] We believe this conceptualization provides a framework through which the process of citizen learning may be fruitfully viewed and will employ a measure of "opinion-strata" in the following analysis of citizen learning.

## SUBJECTIVE KNOWLEDGE: PUBLIC FAMILIARITY WITH THE CANDIDATES

The data collected by the Center for Political Studies (CPS) in 1980 included one basic question designed to tap citizens' knowledge of political candidates. In February, April, June, and September-October respondents were asked to indicate whether they had (1) never heard of a candidate, (2) had heard of him but felt they did not know much about him, or (3) had heard of him and felt they knew something about him. While the general pattern of responses to this question over time offers an independent contribution to our knowledge of "citizen learning," it is the panel design of the data that make them attractive for *analytic* purposes.

The *descriptive* value of the CPS data is considerably less for three reasons. First, there is the long time interval between survey waves in February, April, and June. From the analysis presented earlier in this chapter it is clear that knowledge was heavily reactive to specific primary events, a number of which are commingled in the February to April period. This makes it difficult to link causes and consequences. Second, George Bush and John Anderson were the newcomers who rose from obscurity to play prominent roles in the 1980 election. As such they are the most interesting cases to track. Yet the CPS data are seriously deficient with regard to these two candidates. Questions about Anderson were not asked on the February interview schedule. Anderson was first asked about in April— after awareness of him had risen from 1 percent and stabilized at 50 percent according to the Eagleton data. Similarly, the CPS data also missed the rise of George Bush. The Eagleton data show substantial changes in the public's view of Bush due to his "victory" in the Iowa caucus, and lesser, but still significant, changes in the public's images of other candidates. The first wave of the CPS election study was conducted after Iowa.

Finally, we note that this measure of knowledge about the candidates relies on respondents' self-assessment of what they knew and their honesty in reporting that knowledge. Judging from responses to the least-known candidate, Philip Crane, no serious overreporting appeared to occur: only 6 percent of the respondents in February claimed to know something about Crane, while nearly two thirds admitted that they had never heard of him. More serious is the problem of determining what a respondent meant by claiming to know something about a candidate. This category undoubtedly includes individuals with widely differing amounts of knowledge, particularly about the prominent and long-standing candidates such as Reagan or Kennedy. Thus, much of the learning in the campaign is invisible to us.

Despite these limitations, the measure of knowledge does permit an examination of the initial stages of learning about political figures, especially among those citizens with less political knowledge to begin with. And we can compare the picture of learning presented in cross-sectional data with that revealed by panel data. We will first present the candidate knowledge items for the interviews conducted in February, April, and June, and then present changes in individuals' knowledge of candidates from February to June. Finally, we will look at knowledge as it relates to the hypothesized strata of public opinion.

The percentage feeling they "knew something" about each candidate is presented in Figure 4.2. The overall picture is one of little learning during the course of the campaign. George Bush was the only candidate about whom the electorate felt substantially more knowledgeable in April than in February. While Reagan was already well known at the time of the first interview, the average increase in knowledge about the remaining candidates was only five percentage points. An even more discouraging picture of learning is painted by the April-to-June comparisons. The percentage feeling they knew something about Baker, Brown, Connally, and Dole actually declined to their February levels. As these declines were confined to those candidates who had ceased their active pursuit of the nomination, they may be due as much to measurement artifact as to real change. "Knowing something" about the candidates in April may have simply reflected knowledge that a particular candidate was seeking his party's nomination. With this no longer true in June a portion of the public were less able to report "knowing something." But even if this explanation is correct it means that citizens failed to learn much about the candidates' issue positions, ideological makeup, or character

**FIGURE 4.2**

**Percentage Feeling They "Knew Something About Candidates," 1980**

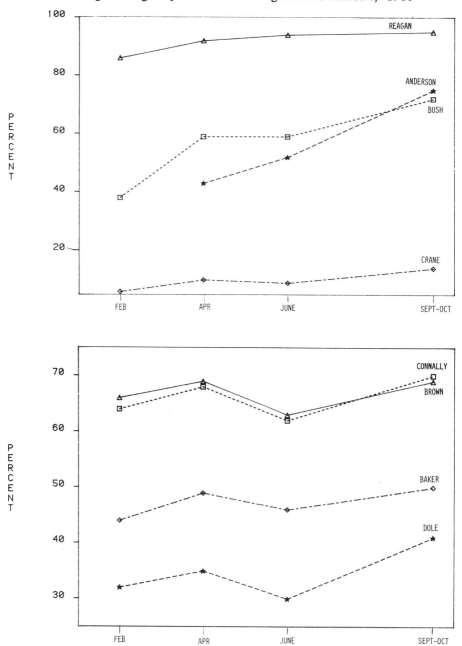

while they were active contestants. In either case, what the general electorate felt it knew about these candidates in April was not made of very lasting stuff.

Citizens also appeared to learn little about Anderson and Bush during the April-to-June period. However, the public felt significantly more knowledgeable about each as the campaign progressed from the primary season to the general election. The percentage saying they knew something about Anderson rose from 43 percent in April to 52 percent in June to 75 percent in September-October. Just under 60 percent felt they knew something about Bush in both April and June, despite his intervening primary victories in Pennsylvania and Michigan. However, as Reagan's running mate, 72 percent said they knew something about Bush when questioned in September-October.

We may entertain three explanations for the relative stability between April and June coupled with the growth in knowledge between June and September. First, a subset of the electorate that was largely inattentive through the primary season may have "tuned in" during the general election campaign. However, we find that it was not the same "group" that learned about Anderson and Bush between June and September. Only 7 percent of those interviewed in September had become more knowledgeable about both candidates than they had been in June, while 14 percent became more knowledgeable only about Bush and 9 percent became more knowledgeable only about Anderson. Moreover, we were unable to locate any particular group where learning was concentrated. Increases in knowledge were roughly proportional across partisans grouped either by their party allegiance or strength of identification, by interest and attentiveness to the campaign, and by educational attainment.

Republicans were slightly more knowledgeable about all candidates—including Democrat Jerry Brown—than Independents and Democrats. However, partisan similarities rather than differences characterized *patterns* of learning. Only in the cases of John Anderson and George Bush were there traces of partisan differences, and even these were not of substantial magnitude. As shown in Figure 4.3, similar proportions of Democrats, Independents, and Republicans felt they knew something about Anderson in April. By June, Democrats were no more knowledgeable about Anderson, while the percentage feeling they knew something about him increased 12 points among Independents and 16 points among Republicans. Knowledge about Anderson then increased by about 25 percentage points among all groups between June and September.

**FIGURE 4.3**

Percentage Feeling They "Knew Something About Candidates," by Party, 1980

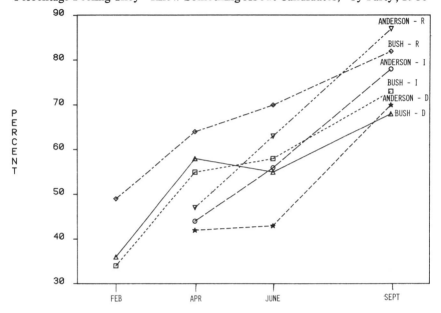

Republicans were significantly more familiar with Bush than were Independents and Democrats in the early stages of the campaign. Almost half said they knew something about Bush in February, compared to about one third of Democrats and Independents. Differences moderated slightly by April, with Republicans being an average of 7 percentage points more knowledgeable than others. No group really became more knowledgeable about Bush by the end of the primary season in June, with the observed changes all within the range of sampling error. And the proportion feeling they knew something about Bush increased between 12 and 15 percentage points among all groups between June and September. Thus there is little in the data to suggest that knowledge about candidates interacts heavily with partisanship or that different models for partisan groups are necessary to explain the learning process.

The second explanation focuses on the weakness of the indicator of knowledge being used. As noted earlier, it does not take much in the way of information for respondents to say they "know something about" the candidates. We suspect that of the 20 percent or so that became more knowledgeable about Bush, many were simply aware that he had been chosen as Reagan's running mate. Similarly, the attention given to the issue of whether Anderson would be invited to join Carter and Reagan in the League of Women Voters debates informed some citizens that Anderson was running for the presidency as an independent.

Finally, we note that knowledge of *all* candidates increased between June and September, even for those who had withdrawn early in the campaign. The September figures presented are from an independent survey rather than the panel, so activation as a result of earlier interviews may be ruled out as an explanation. However, it may be that the September sample was simply a more knowledgeable group than those interviewed earlier.

The panel design of the study allows us to compare each respondent's knowledge of candidates prior to the primaries (but after the Iowa caucuses) with their knowledge at the conclusion of the primaries in June. The data are presented by way of a "learning" typology. Any respondent who moved from a "lower" category of knowledge in February to a "higher" one in June was said to have "learned." Conversely, a respondent who moved from a higher to a lower category was said to have "forgotten." The remaining respondents did not change from February to June, and are categorized according to the level of knowledge at which they remained. Schematically, the typology has the following form:

### How the Learning Typology Was Created

|  | June | | |
|---|---|---|---|
| **February** | Doesn't recognize | Doesn't know much about | Knows something about candidate |
| Doesn't recognize | Stayed the same: Doesn't recognize | Learned | Learned |
| Doesn't know much about | Forgot | Stayed the same: Doesn't know much about | Learned |
| Knows something about the candidate | Forgot | Forgot | Stayed the same: Knows something about candidate |

**TABLE 4.2**

**Learning About the Candidates—February to June**

|  | Learned | Forgot | Stayed Same: Doesn't Recognize | Stayed Same: Doesn't Know Much About | Stayed Same: Knows Something About | (n) |
|---|---|---|---|---|---|---|
| Candidate |  |  |  |  |  |  |
| Reagan | 9 | 1 | 0 | 3 | 86 | (838) |
| Kennedy | 3 | 2 | 0 | 1 | 93 | (838) |
| Bush | 35 | 7 | 4 | 21 | 33 | (838) |
| Crane | 25 | 10 | 42 | 20 | 3 | (838) |
| Brown | 12 | 16 | 5 | 13 | 54 | (838) |
| Connally | 13 | 14 | 4 | 15 | 53 | (838) |
| Baker | 18 | 15 | 9 | 21 | 36 | (838) |
| Dole | 19 | 18 | 15 | 28 | 20 | (838) |

*Note:* Entries are percent of respondents in each category for each candidate (sums to 100 percent across row).
*Source:* CPS National Election Study, 1980.

Little movement is noted in Table 4.2 for the two best known candidates, Reagan and Kennedy. Around 90 percent of the respondents said they knew something about these candidates in both surveys. Brown and Connally were the next-best-known in February, but neither made a serious run at his respective party's nomination. For each candidate, as many respondents "forgot" or moved downward in the knowledge categories as "learned" or moved up. A similar pattern was apparent for Howard Baker. Crane was hardly known in February but one fourth of the sample moved up by June (most of them into the "don't know much about" category). The greatest movement was seen for Bush. Over one-third of the sample was in a higher category of knowledge in June than in February.

In order to investigate actual "learning" over the course of the campaign we removed those feeling they knew something about the candidates in both February and June from the base of percentages (data not shown here). Since this group had reached the ceiling of the CPS knowledge measure there was no "room" to learn during the course of the campaign. With these respondents removed we are in effect looking at the percentage of those that moved to a higher position on the knowledge scale over the base of those who had the opportunity to become more knowledgeable. With the ceiling effect removed it is clear that the electorate learned only about Reagan and Bush. Sixty-four percent of those who could have become more knowledgeable about Reagan did so, while 52 percent became more knowledgeable about Bush. The figures for the remaining candidates were remarkably similar, and paint a bleak picture of citizen learning: on the average, only about one-in-four felt they knew more about Baker, Brown, Connally, Crane, or Dole in June than in February.

## LEARNING WITHIN OPINION STRATA

Based on the patterns of awareness and recognition described earlier in this chapter we have developed a set of expectations for each of the hypothesized strata of public opinion.[12]

The *attentive* public, perhaps one fifth of the electorate, is aware of candidates and issues when the media first devote attention to these subjects. Intense media coverage is not necessary for awareness, in that stories need not be on the front page or considered sufficiently important to be aired on the evening news. Both originating and sustaining motivations for acquiring political information rest with the individual.

The *latent* public would lack the motivation to actively seek information about political affairs. They would in essence be activated by events accorded prominence in the mass media, as indicated by front page newspaper stories or repeated and/or heavy emphasis on national television news. Once activated, the latent public would act much as the attentive public in tracking information. Thus the originating motivation comes from the media while the sustaining motivation is individually based. We suspect the latent public comprises about one third of the electorate.

The *inadvertent* public is also expected to be about one third of the electorate. This segment is basically uninterested in the world of politics, depending largely, if not solely, on television for information about political events and issues. Lacking both originating and sustaining self-motivation for acquiring political information, learning would be largely a passive process, as described in the preceding chapter. Moreover, we suspect persons in this stratum would not learn very well. The inadvertent public would over time be expected to learn the "labels" of current political debate and rhetoric but would have little or no informational base associated with those labels. We suspect this group could be reached only by prominent and intense media coverage.

The *apathetic* public has no interest in politics and would make little use of the mass media for informational reasons. Included in this stratum, for example, would be those unable to name Carter and Reagan as candidates at the conclusion of the primaries—between one fifth and one seventh of the New Jersey public.

Citizens have been classified as belonging to one of the four groups depending on their interest in politics—both interest in the election and in general public affairs—and their attentiveness to the mass media.* The top and bottom groups were assigned solely on the basis of interest: those having been "very much interested" in the political campaign and being interested in government and public affairs "most of the time" were classified as the *attentive* public. Those who had "not much" interest in the presidential election and who followed public affairs "only now and then" or "hardly at all" were classified as the *apathetic* public.

The remainder of the sample was classified as belonging to one of the two middle layers by their attentiveness to the mass media. In essence, attentiveness serves as a surrogate measure of purposive motivation for acquiring information. Those saying they paid a great deal of attention to news about government and politics from the mass media may be considered *active* consumers. Those paying only some or no attention to political information may be though of as more *passive* consumers, and are expected to engage in a greater amount of what we have termed passive learning. In operational terms those who paid a great deal of attention to either television or newspaper stories about public affairs were considered to be the latent public. Those who did not pay a great deal of attention to either were classified as the inadvertent public.

The distribution of the public according to strata assignments is displayed in Table 4.3. About one quarter of the public was found to be very interested both in the presidential election and general political happenings, and classified as attentives. The latent public in February comprised one third of the electorate. Despite having less interest than the top stratum, this group is generally attentive to the mass media for public affairs information. Equal in size to this group is the inadvertent public. Among this third of the public politics is less salient. They are less attentive to the media and less likely to be

---

*See Appendix B for a more extensive discussion of the character of the strata and how they were operationally defined.

**TABLE 4.3**

**Distribution of Opinion Strata**
**(percentage)**

|              | February | April | June  |
|--------------|----------|-------|-------|
| Attentives   | 24       | 26    | 24    |
| Latents      | 33       | 30    | 45    |
| Inadvertents | 33       | 31    | 20    |
| Apathetics   | 10       | 12    | 11    |
| Total        | 100      | 100   | 100   |
| (n)          | (999)    | (961) | (832) |

*Source:* CPS National Election Study, 1980.

information-seekers. Finally, 10 percent of the public can be labeled as clearly apathetic, displaying little interest in the election and in general public affairs. It is comforting to note that the predictions of group sizes, made from the patterns of awareness in the New Jersey data, are within a few percentage points of the CPS strata measure based on interest and attentiveness.

We have employed the measure of opinion strata to help explain the patterns of "learning" and "forgetting" about presidential candidates. The percentage of each stratum saying they "knew something about" each candidate has been plotted in Figure 4.4.* A first observation to be made is simply that there are clear differences in knowledge by stratum. Moreover, they are monotonic. In all cases, attentives were more knowledgeable than latents, who were more knowledgeable than the inadvertents, who in turn were more knowledgeable than apathetics. The median percentages of the strata saying they knew something about the candidates in June were: attentives, 76 percent; latents, 63 percent; inadvertents, 50 percent; and apathetics, 29 percent.†

---

*Panel respondents in June have been held to the stratum to which they were first assigned in February.

†This includes the six candidates depicted in Figure 4.4 and three others: Edward Kennedy, Robert Dole, and Philip Crane.

**FIGURE 4.4**

**Percentage Feeling They "Knew Something About Candidates," by Opinion-Strata, 1980**

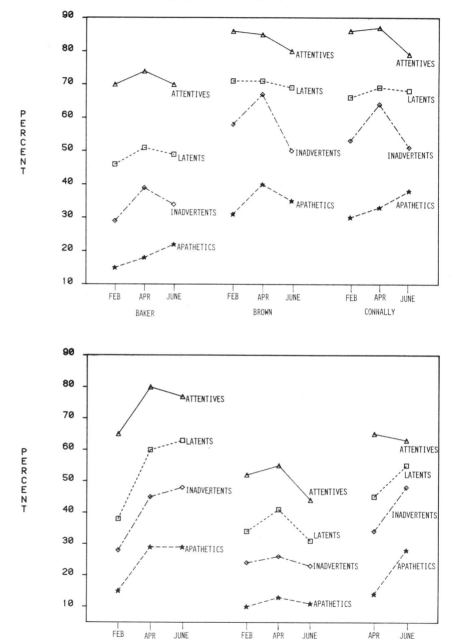

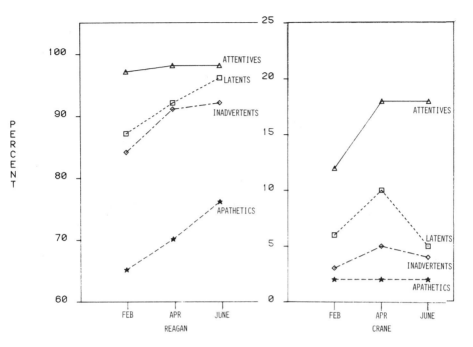

Some, but not all of the expected variations in learning patterns are evident. For example, we note that all of the learning among attentives took place between February and April. In none of the cases shown in Figure 4.4 was a greater proportion of attentives knowledgeable in June than in April, as per our expectation. At the other extreme, among the apathetics, we note that learning did take place as the campaign progressed, somewhat contrary to expectations. While it is important to keep in mind that less than 30 percent of this stratum felt they knew something about Bush and Anderson in June, these figures represent sizeable gains from earlier measurements. This attests to the phenomenon of "passive learning," as individuals in this stratum had little interest both in the election and in general public affairs. Remarkably, fully three quarters of apathetics felt they "knew something" about Reagan by June despite their total disinterest in political affairs.

The inadvertents and latents are more difficult to disentangle. What seems to differentiate these two strata more than anything else (beyond general level of knowledge) is "forgetting." In regard to Brown, Connally, and Baker, who all gave up active pursuit of the nomination before the April survey, there are sharp drops in the proportion of inadvertents saying they knew something about each. In contrast, "forgetting" among the latents (and attentives) was modest. This pattern conforms to expectations that inadvertents would be more likely to learn passively. Under such conditions information would be less well integrated into an individual's store of political knowledge and would more easily be "lost."

## DISCUSSION

A few concluding observations are in order before leaving this chapter on the development of candidate awareness and recognition. The politicians' conventional wisdom about the impact of a strong showing in one of the early campaign tests could not be truer. Anderson and Bush catapulted from obscurity to prominence because of their successes, which bought the more important element—intense media attention devoted to their candidacies. Those who could not achieve a victory, real or media-determined, were doomed to obscurity, their campaigns simply doomed. At the time these win-less candidates withdrew due to the lack of financial or political support, two thirds of the New Jersey public were unaware of their candidacies. This is true not only of Philip Crane, but of men with long records who had even at some point commanded the spotlight— Howard Baker, John Connally, Robert Dole, and Jerry Brown.

Even those who achieved a victory—with the exception of Reagan who began the campaign quite well known—did little after their breakthroughs. There was no evidence of gradual learning over the course of the campaign in either the New Jersey or national survey data. Anderson and Bush stabilized where their "wins" had placed them. And it is worth remembering that despite their breakthroughs, about half of the electorate emerged from the primaries feeling they knew little about either man.

These results can hardly be comforting to those placing their trust in a wise selection of leadership by an informed public, and to those trusting the mass media to educate the citizenry. While there is clear evidence of the existence of different layers of public opinion based on interest and attentiveness, it is important to note that the measure of opinion strata employed here is far more successful in differentiating *knowledge* than *learning*. Citizens generally learned that which was prominent in the information environment. In 1980, as in 1976, such information appeared to make only a meager contribution to what would be considered "informed choice" by ideal democratic standards. However, too pessimistic a conclusion is premature; those participating in primaries may be substantially better informed than passive spectators. Moreover, we have not yet looked at learning in terms of "objective knowledge"—how much citizens actually knew rather than what they felt they knew. It is to these questions that we now turn.

## NOTES

1. Thomas Patterson, *The Mass Media Election* (New York: Praeger, 1980), p. 109.

2. Thomas Marshall, *Presidential Nominations in a Reform Age* (New York: Praeger, 1981), pp. 118–56.

3. Thomas Patterson, *The Mass Media Election* (New York: Praeger, 1980), p. 3.

4. Angus Campbell, "Has Television Reshaped Politics?" *Columbia Journalism Review* 6 (Fall 1962–63).

5. John Aldrich, *Before the Convention* (Chicago: University of Chicago Press, 1981), p. 81.

6. Thomas Patterson, *The Mass Media Election* (New York: Praeger, 1980); Michael Robinson and Margaret Sheehan, *Over the Wire and on TV: CBS and UPI in Campaign '80* (New York: Basic Books, 1983).

7. Examples include (a) national elections, (b) network news, (c) television documentaries, and (d) the televised Watergate hearings. See (a) Jay Blumler and Denis McQuail, *Television in Politics* (Chicago: University of Chicago Press, 1969); (b) Gary Wamsley and Richard Pride, "Television Network News: Rethinking the Iceberg Problem," *Western Political Quarterly* 25 (1972), pp. 434–50; (c) Steven Fitzsimmons and Hobart Osburn, "The Impact of Social Issues and Public Affairs Television Documentaries," *Public Opinion Quarterly* 32 (1969), pp. 379–97; (d) Michael Robinson, "The Impact of the Televised Watergate Hearings," *Journal of Communication* 24 (1974), pp. 17–30.

8. V. O. Key, Jr., *Public Opinion and American Democracy* (New York: Alfred A. Knopf, 1961), p. 15.

9. Paul Lazarsfeld, Bernard Berelson, and Hazel Gaudet, *The People's Choice* (New York: Columbia University Press, 1944). See also Elihu Katz and Paul Lazarsfeld, *Personal Influence* (New York: The Free Press, 1955).

10. Thomas Patterson, *The Mass Media Election* (New York: Praeger, 1980), p. 110.

11. Cliff Zukin, "Mass Communication and Public Opinion," *Handbook of Political Communication*, eds. Dan Nimmo and Keith Sanders (Beverly Hills, Calif.: Sage, 1981), pp. 376–78. In work published simultaneously, David Paletz and Robert Entman also identify four public opinion groupings: elite, attentive, mass, and apolitical publics. The elite public is only 1 percent of the public. Their attentive and apolitical publics are in substantial agreement with our formulation. The main difference between the two conceptualizations is that we have further broken down Paletz and Entman's mass public (estimated to be about 60 percent of the electorate) into two discrete groups—the latent and

inadvertent publics. However, we are in substantial accord with Paletz and Entman's treatment. See David Paletz and Robert Entman, *Media Power Politics* (New York: The Free Press, 1981), pp. 185–86.

12. For a more extended discussion and rationale, see Cliff Zukin, "Mass Communications and Public Opinion," in *Handbook of Political Communication*, ed. Dan Nimmo and Keith Sanders (Beverly Hills, Calif.: Sage, 1981).

# 5

# KNOWLEDGE ABOUT
# THE CANDIDATES

Knowledge about the candidates has been narrowly defined up to this point, focusing on simple awareness of candidates and people's subjective feelings that they "knew something" about them. Such knowledge is only the first step on a path of decision making that leads to the selection of leadership. We would hope, of course, that citizens know a great deal more about the individuals seeking the presidency by the time they are ready to participate in the electoral process. This chapter is about the next step in the journey: How much do people actually know about candidates? What and when do people learn, and how does the structure of the nomination system contribute to learning?

Political scientists, social commentators and private citizens hold many ideas about what is "good" or "useful" knowledge. Some would argue that citizens should be well versed in where the various candidates stand on issues of the day and should be able to locate candidates on an ideological spectrum. This information allows citizens to choose the person who best represents their positions and values. Others would argue that citizens could more profitably expend their energies seeking information about the "type of person" each candidate is. The gap between what a *candidate* wants or promises to do, and what a *president* is able to do, is often quite wide. As it is impossible to predict the issues and crises a president will face in his four year term, the argument continues, information about the character of the man who will be leading us through these crises is more important than knowing specific issue positions.

We see merit in both these views and offer no prescriptions about which type of information is "better" than the other. What constitutes "useful" knowledge is best left to the individual. We are less reticent about arguing that however knowledge is defined, more information will produce better decisions. The amount of information citizens hold about presidential candidates, is an important concern, for it bears directly on the quality of citizen choice. If citizens felt well informed about the policy preferences and character of the candidates by the end of the nominating process, there would be evidence that the system had worked well and contributed to the ideal democratic standard of informed choice. Correspondingly, a system that concluded with citizens having only the vaguest understanding of what the candidates were about could be considered desirable only by standards quite perverse to democratic intentions.

In this chapter we examine three kinds of information citizens may find useful in evaluating and choosing between candidates: ideology, issues, and character. Ideology is important for it involves information about a candidate's philosophy or world view. Knowledge of a candidate's ideology may provide citizens with a clear idea of the general policy goals and direction a president will take once entrusted with the responsibility to govern. Similarly, knowledge of where candidates stand on issues of the day is also important if elections are to be a meaningful device for citizen control over public policy. Finally, when we look over our last two presidencies we see the failings of Richard Nixon's character and public disenchantment with the quality of Jimmy Carter's leadership. Clearly, there is useful information to be gained about the character of the men who seek the presidency.

In the analysis that follows our focus is not simply on *knowledge*, the amount of information people have about candidates. We are equally concerned with learning, the growth of knowledge over the primary election campaign, and how learning is related to the structure of the nominating system. In investigating ideological, issue, and candidate knowledge our primary focus will be on those candidates in the 1980 election with whom the electorate developed some familiarity—Ronald Reagan, George Bush, and John Anderson. As the incumbent, Jimmy Carter was well known to the public and is less interesting to study in terms of the development of knowledge and opinions. Yet data on Carter is valuable for it presumably represents "full knowledge," a standard against which knowledge of other candidates may be measured. We will consider only briefly the candidacies of those who did not emerge from the primary season as central figures—Baker, Brown, Connally, Crane, and Dole.

## MEASUREMENT CAVEATS

The data collected by the Center for Political Studies (CPS) included three sets of questions that allow us to trace the development of these different types of knowledge about the candidates over the 1980 campaign. The specific measures we have used are described in the appropriate sections below. Unfortunately, questions about the candidates' ideological stances, issue positions, and character traits were not asked of all respondents. The CPS employed two different filters for determining which people would be asked the questions. First, only those saying they "knew something" about the candidates were asked follow-up knowledge questions. While this sounds reasonable, there is clearly some proportion of those who recognized the candidates but said they "don't know much about them" who would have given correct responses to the follow-up knowledge questions if asked. As we shall see in the following chapter, the Eagleton Poll data reveal that a good number of those New Jerseyans who were only able to recognize candidates' names had in fact formed opinions of them. Because of this measurement strategy knowledge about issues, ideology, and character is operationally defined as building on the base of those feeling they knew something about the candidates. While this is probably an accurate assessment in most cases, these measures will underestimate the amount of actual knowledge.

The CPS used a second filter on questions about candidates' ideologies and issue positions. Respondents who could not describe themselves in ideological terms were not asked about candidate ideology; respondents who took no position on an issue were not asked if they knew the various candidates' positions on the same issue. Thus there is an assumption in the survey design that all of those who were unable to rate themselves would be unable to rate the candidates. This circumstance has led to a dilemma in the choice of an appropriate analysis strategy. Statements may be made either about a subset of the electorate that is disproportionately knowledgeable by analyzing only those respondents who were actually asked the questions; or, about the entire public by accepting the assumptions inherent in the screening questions. Because our focus is on the general public we have chosen the latter alternative.*

---

*We know the assumptions made by the CPS knowledge screens are not true in all cases, but feel this to be the path with the least amount of error. The

**TABLE 5.1**

**Ideological Perceptions of Candidates in April 1980**
**(percentage)**

| Candidate | Extremely Liberal | Liberal | Slightly Liberal | Moderate Middle-road | Slightly Conservative | Conservative | Extremely Conservative | Don't Know | Total |
|---|---|---|---|---|---|---|---|---|---|
| Carter | 2 | 7 | 10 | 20 | 11 | 9 | 2 | 39 | 100 |
| Kennedy | 16 | 16 | 11 | 7 | 4 | 4 | 1 | 41 | 100 |
| Reagan | 1 | 3 | 7 | 6 | 10 | 20 | 10 | 43 | 100 |
| Connally | 1 | 3 | 5 | 11 | 9 | 7 | 3 | 60 | 99 |
| Bush | 0 | 2 | 4 | 13 | 11 | 5 | 1 | 64 | 100 |
| Anderson | 1 | 4 | 8 | 9 | 5 | 3 | 0 | 70 | 100 |
| Brown | 8 | 13 | 10 | 7 | 4 | 2 | 0 | 57 | 101 |

*Note:* Box indicates responses scored as "correct" (n = 946).

## KNOWLEDGE AND LEARNING OF IDEOLOGY

Those respondents who were able to describe themselves in ideological terms* were asked to locate many of the candidates on an ideological scale at various points in the campaign. The scale had seven positions, ranging from "extremely liberal" at one end of a continuum to "extremely conservative" at the other. While this measure appears to be fairly straightforward, what constitutes "ideological knowledge" is far from clear. We have a great deal of hesitation in grading responses as "right" or "wrong." The terms liberal and conservative may mean different things to different people, depending on their world views. One individual might consider Jimmy Carter to be a liberal while another considers him to be conservative, with both being able to articulate reasons for their beliefs. Because we do not wish to superimpose our views on our respondents we have accepted a wide range of answers as accurate for each candidate in evaluating the correctness of responses. Table 5.1 shows how the public perceived the candidates' ideologies in April, the middle of the primary season. Boxed responses indicate which were considered correct.

Jimmy Carter was the best known "candidate" in ideological terms as the 1980 campaign began. This is hardly surprising given that the electorate had been able to observe his actions as president for the preceding three years. However, just over half of the electorate—57 percent—could place Carter on the ideological scale. Ronald Reagan and Edward Kennedy, both of whom had been on the political scene for some time, and who represented the clearest ideological extremes of "conservative" and "liberal" candidates, were correctly identified by 43 and 49 percent, respectively. The public did far less well in labeling other candidates, none of whom were ideologically known by more than one third of the electorate (see Table 5.2).

Despite the media's discussion of the candidates in ideological terms, for this is a convenient shorthand way to label and organize candidates, there was virtually no growth in the proportion of the

---

practical effects of the screens are discussed in notes in the appropriate sections which follow.

*This screen had the practical effect of filtering out between one fourth and one third of respondents on the various interview waves. These individuals have been grouped with those unable to identify candidates' ideological leanings in subsequent analyses.

**TABLE 5.2**

**Percentage Able to Give Candidate's Ideological Labels—
February to September
(percentage)**

| Candidate | February | April | June | September |
|---|---|---|---|---|
| Carter | 57 | 59 | 63 | 56 |
| Kennedy | 49 | 50 | 56 | 49 |
| Reagan | 43 | 46 | 53 | 49 |
| Brown | 33 | 35 | 35 | 33 |
| Connally | 28 | 30 | 32 | 27 |
| Bush | 21 | 29 | 32 | 35 |
| Anderson | – | 28 | 34 | 43 |
| Number of respondents | (999) | (946) | (832) | (1577) |

*Source:* CPS 1980 National Election Study.

public able to correctly ascribe an ideological label to any candidates as the campaign progressed to the later primaries through the conventions and into the general election period. While there appeared to be some growth in ideological identification from February to June, upon closer examination this may largely be attributed to the activating effect of the initial interviews conducted in February rather than real change in the population.* The proportion able to classify the Democratic candidates correctly—Carter, Kennedy, and Brown—was identical in February and September. Only 6 percent more were able to describe Reagan as a conservative in September than in February. There were minor changes in the proportion able to label the

---

*This explanation is supported by a comparison of the September cross-sectional and panel waves. The panel figures are higher than the cross-sectional figures in all cases and are at the level of the June panel figures. The panel figures not presented in Table 5.2 are as follows: Carter (63 percent), Kennedy (56 percent), Reagan (56 percent), Brown (42 percent), Connally (34 percent), Bush (41 percent), and Anderson (51 percent). Thus we suspect that knowledge did not really decrease. However, neither set of figures allows for a conclusion of increased knowledge.

two candidates who did well in the early primaries and became widely recognized. The proportion identifying Bush as a conservative increased from 21 percent in February to 35 percent in September. Anderson rose from 28 percent in April to 43 percent in September.

Ideological knowledge was not related to partisan loyalty in 1980. It was not the case, for example, that partisans were more knowledgeable about the ideological leanings of their own candidates and less knowledgeable of the opposition. In fact, Republicans were slightly more likely to ideologically label all candidates—Democrats and Republicans alike—than others. However, there was virtually no difference in the learning patterns of Democrats, Independents, and Republicans. Republicans did not learn proportionately more about Republican candidates than others.

The failure of the electorate to learn ideological positions cannot be solely attribted to deficiencies in the structure of the electoral system or the information conveyed by the mass media. We suspect the data attest more to the relative uselessness of the concept "ideology" as a means of organizing information for much of the general public. This is not due to "inherent cognitive limitations" of the mass public, as was once argued.[1] Rather, increased use of an ideological framework and integration of beliefs occurs to a greater extent on topics that are salient to individuals.[2] Given the levels of interest and attentiveness to the campaign we observed in Chapter 3, this condition is not well met in nomination politics. Thus two interrelated conclusions are in order. First, in this particular context, the concept of ideology holds little meaning to about half of the electorate. Second, the 1980 campaign did not serve to increase the salience or utility of this concept to the electorate, even for candidates such as Reagan and Kennedy.

## KNOWLEDGE AND LEARNING OF ISSUE POSITIONS

The level of ideological awareness is so low, and evidence of learning so sparse as to make further analysis pointless. But the failure of the public to employ an ideological yardstick in evaluating the candidates does not necessarily mean that candidates' stands on issues of the day were unclear to members of the electorate, nor that the electorate failed to learn where the candidates stood as the campaign progressed. In looking back on the 1980 election we are interested in a number of questions:

—How much did people feel they knew about candidates' issue positions at the onset of the campaign?

—Did issue-knowledge grow over the course of the campaign?

—How was knowledge related to characteristics of the electoral system and campaign; in particular, were people living in states having held primaries more knowledgeable than their counterparts in states without primaries?

—How was knowledge related to individuals' attitudes—did partisans learn more about "their" candidates than others; did different opinion-strata manifest different levels of knowledge or learning tendencies?

Respondents were asked to identify candidates' issue positions a number of times during the 1980 campaign. We have selected four items for study, all of which were central themes of the 1980 primary season. While we have no assurance that the four issues selected were salient to individual voters in 1980,[3] these concerns—whether unemployment should be used to halt inflation, reduced government spending on social programs, increased military spending, and a "get tough" policy with the Soviet Union—have structured political and social discussion since the 1980 election.* These themes rode with

---

*Respondents were read an introductory statement and asked where they would place candidates on a seven-point scale. The statements and endpoints are:

A. Some people feel it is important for us to try very hard to get along with Russia. Others feel it is a big mistake to try too hard to get along with Russia.
   1. IMPORTANT TO TRY VERY HARD TO GET ALONG WITH RUSSIA
   7. BIG MISTAKE TO TRY TOO HARD TO GET ALONG WITH RUSSIA
B. Some people think the government should provide fewer services, even in areas such as health and education, in order to reduce spending. Other people feel it is important for the government to continue the services it now provides even if it means no reduction in spending.
   1. GOVERNMENT SHOULD PROVIDE MANY FEWER SERVICES; REDUCE SPENDING A LOT
   7. GOVERNMENT SHOULD CONTINUE TO PROVIDE SERVICES; NO REDUCTION IN SPENDING
C. Some people believe that we should spend much less money for defense. Suppose these people are at one end of the scale at point number 1. Others feel that defense spending should be greatly

Ronald Reagan from the campaign trail to bring changes in government policy. How many people felt they knew what Reagan and the other candidates wanted to do about these important issues when the campaign began, and how many learned where the candidates stood as the campaign progressed?

In order to investigate these questions we have created a scale of *felt issue-knowledge*. Scores on the scale range from "0," indicating an inability to attribute a position to a candidate on any of the four issues asked about, to "4," indicating perceptions of a candidate's position on all four issues.* It is important to note that we have not classified answers as "right" or "wrong." Our concern with "felt knowledge" does not penalize "guessing" candidates' positions and

increased. Suppose these people are at the other end, at point 7. And, of course, some other people have opinions somewhere in between at points 2, 3, 4, 5, or 6. Where would you place yourself on this scale, or haven't you thought much about this?
1. GREATLY DECREASE DEFENSE SPENDING
7. GREATLY INCREASE DEFENSE SPENDING
D. Some people feel the federal government should take action to reduce the inflation rate, even if it means that *un*employment would go up a lot. Others feel the government should take action to reduce the rate of *un*employment, even if it means that inflation would go up a lot.
1. REDUCE INFLATION EVEN IF UNEMPLOYMENT GOES UP A LOT
7. REDUCE UNEMPLOYMENT EVEN IF INFLATION GOES UP A LOT

*The CPS screen excluded respondents who did not themselves express positions on issues. Respondents not taking a position on the inflation-unemployment tradeoff, for example, were not asked what they perceived the candidates' position to be on that issue. For the purposes of being able to make statements about the entire public we have grouped those screened out in this manner with the proportion unable to identify a candidate's position.

Our rationale is based partly on the reasons why respondents were unable to place themselves on issue scales. On the one hand we have individuals who responded that they had "not thought much" about an issue or ideological position. We have little objection to not asking this subset to rate candidates on matters to which they have devoted little thought. On the other hand, there are those individuals who simply "have not taken a position," or "don't know." It is entirely possible that these individuals would have been able to identify a candidate's position on various issues had they been asked. However, as is apparent from the data collected in February, the uninformed "haven't thought about it" response was given far more frequently than the possibly-informed "don't

**FIGURE 5.1**

**Average Number of Issue Positions Ascribed to Candidates, 1980**

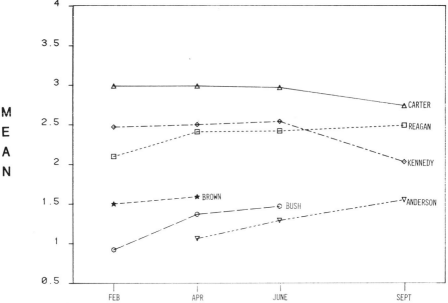

may allow answers that many of us would consider incorrect. However, whatever biases this measure has have been held constant over time, allowing us to observe change and learning during the campaign despite its imperfections.

The mean issue scores for all candidates are presented in Figure 5.1. As the graph shows, the practical ceiling of the scale is

know" response. The percentages giving each response to the four issues and ideology questions are:

|  | Haven't thought | Don't know |
|---|---|---|
| a. unemployment-inflation | 21% | 10% |
| b. government services/spending | 14 | 3 |
| c. defense spending | 13 | 3 |
| d. relations with USSR | 8 | 3 |
| e. ideology | 32 | 3 |

marked by knowledge of Carter's positions. The average member of the public felt knowledgeable about Carter's positions on three of the four issues asked about. Knowledge about Reagan and Kennedy could be considered moderate at best. In February the average citizen knew where Kennedy stood on an average of two and one-half issues and could identify Reagan's positions on two of the four issues asked about. As was the case with ideology, there is a further jump between Kennedy and Reagan and the remaining candidates in the extent of citizens' issue-knowledge. Knowledge of Connally and Brown, with whom the electorate had some prior familiarity, averaged about one and one-half issues, while for Baker and Bush the average was about one issue.

The issue-knowledge figure for George Bush is particularly interesting, for the February CPS survey occurred after the dramatic surge in awareness of Bush. Despite a first place finish in the Iowa caucus, propelling awareness of him from 8 to 52 percent (in the Eagleton data), Bush's position on slightly less than one of four issues asked about was known by the average member of the public. The same is true of the other candidate the public became aware of overnight—John Anderson. The proportion of the New Jersey public spontaneously identifying Anderson as a candidate jumped from 22 to 52 percent in early March, well before the CPS April interviews were conducted. Yet the average member of the public knew Anderson's position on only one of four issues.

Knowledge about Bush and Anderson continued to grow slowly through the primaries. But at the end of the primary season, after Bush had won primaries in Pennsylvania and Michigan, and at the end of the general election campaign, after Anderson ran the strongest third-party candidacy since 1968, the average member of the public felt they knew where Bush and Anderson stood on only one-and-one-half issues out of four. This is hardly impressive evidence of learning. In fact, this is about the same level of issue familiarity seen for Connally and Brown at the beginning of the 1980 campaign.

Knowledge about the eventual winner of the Republican nomination was somewhat higher. The average person knew Reagan's positions on two-and-a-half of the four issues in September. This is the same level of knowledge the public had in April, and is not that much above what they brought with them to the campaign in February. It is no exaggeration to say that the largest change depicted in Figure 5.1 is one of confusion rather than clarity. The public actually

TABLE 5.3

**Comparisons of Average Issue Scores by Status of Primary Election**

| | Issue Scores | | | |
|---|---|---|---|---|
| | April | | June | |
| Candidate/Group | Mean | Std. Dev. | Mean | Std. Dev. |
| Carter | | | | |
|   Total–had primary | 3.08 | 1.28 | 2.94 | 1.28 |
|   Total–no primary | 2.90 | 1.31 | 2.99 | 1.28 |
|   Dem–had primary | 3.04 | 1.30 | | |
|   Dem–no primary | 2.93 | 1.28 | | |
| Kennedy | | | | |
|   Total–had primary | 2.67 | 1.53 | 2.49 | 1.54 |
|   Total–no primary | 2.40 | 1.57 | 2.44 | 1.56 |
|   Dem–had primary | 2.59 | 1.63 | | |
|   Dem–no primary | 2.38 | 1.59 | | |
| Reagan | | | | |
|   Total–had primary | 2.55 | 1.59 | 2.39 | 1.56 |
|   Total–no primary | 2.32 | 1.60 | 2.39 | 1.54 |
|   Rep–had primary | 2.76 | 1.37 | | |
|   Rep–no primary | 2.61 | 1.48 | | |
| Anderson | | | | |
|   Total–had primary | 1.19 | 1.67 | 1.27 | 1.67 |
|   Total–no primary | 0.99 | 1.56 | 1.34 | 1.68 |
|   Rep–had primary | 1.12 | 1.59 | | |
|   Rep–no primary | 1.05 | 1.57 | | |
| Bush | | | | |
|   Total–had primary | 1.46 | 1.73 | 1.48 | 1.71 |
|   Total–no primary | 1.31 | 1.69 | 1.31 | 1.72 |
|   Rep–had primary | 1.56 | 1.73 | | |
|   Rep–no primary | 1.55 | 1.74 | | |
| Brown | | | | |
|   Total–had primary | 1.69 | 1.69 | | |
|   Total–no primary | 1.45 | 1.67 | No June | |
|   Dem–had primary | 1.32 | 1.64 | measurements | |
|   Dem–no primary | 1.39 | 1.68 | | |

*Note:* Entries in the table are the average number of issue positions a respondent ascribed to a candidate (of the four asked about), and the accompanying standard deviations. "Total had primary" includes all respondents living in states that had held primaries prior to their being interviewed. The numbers of cases are: April (278), June (679). "Total no primary" includes those living in states not having had primaries prior to their being interviewed. The numbers of cases are: April (687), June (153). Further categories divide the electorate both by whether their state's primary had been conducted and by party identification. The numbers of cases are: April, Dems had (105), not had (304), Reps had (71), not had (173). The June partisan breakdowns are not included as there were less than 50 cases in the cells of partisans in states not having held primaries.

*Source:* CPS 1980 National Election Study.

felt less knowledgeable about both Carter and Kennedy between June and September.*

Despite the fact that people were not very knowledgeable about the candidates' issue positions, the question of what accounts for knowledge about the candidates—and how the current system contributes to knowledge and learning—remains. Since we are primarily concerned with the relative strengths and weaknesses of the nominating system it is a fair question to ask what difference the actual campaign makes. Do people, for example, learn about the candidates by being directly exposed to the campaign in their state? Earlier we stipulated that learning must be in large measure a function of the individual's motivation to acquire information interacting with the information environment. The information environment is in turn a product of the output of both candidate and journalistic organizations. It is virtually impossible to separate messages in the environment by their original source, especially for the less attentive. But we may assume that messages from the national media—television and wire service—are constant across all population groups. Candidates of course localize their efforts, concentrating their resources on achieving strategic goals. Local news organizations also devote more attention to the campaign when it is close to home.

If a richer information environment was a sufficient condition for learning we would expect those living in states having had primaries to be more knowledgeable than those not having had primaries, at the same point in time. If, on the other hand, motivation is the key element in learning we could not expect large differences between those having been exposed to the campaign and those not exposed. There would be a sufficient amount of data in the general information environment for those with the motivation to learn to become knowledgeable without direct exposure to the campaign. In Table 5.3 we have organized the issue-awareness scores by whether or not respondents lived in a state where a primary had taken place prior

---

*Average knowledge of Kennedy's issue positions decreased from 2.54 to 2.03 while Carter's declined from 2.97 to 2.74. The decline occurred among all segments of the public but was more pronounced for Independents and Democrats. The mean issue scores about Kennedy (June/September) for partisan groups were: Democrats (2.43/1.97), Independents (2.60/2.01), and Republicans (2.53/2.20). For Carter: Democrats (2.93/2.65), Independents (2.98/2.72), Republicans (3.06/2.93).

# TABLE 5.4

## Comparisons of Average Issue Scores by Opinion-Strata

| | Mean | | | | Standard Deviation | | | |
|---|---|---|---|---|---|---|---|---|
| | Feb. | April | June | Sept. | Feb. | April | June | Sept. |
| Carter | | | | | | | | |
| Attentive | 3.50 | 3.41 | 3.36 | 3.35 | 0.84 | 0.98 | 0.98 | 0.87 |
| Latent | 2.99 | 3.11 | 3.10 | 3.07 | 1.21 | 1.11 | 1.13 | 1.17 |
| Inadvertent | 2.87 | 2.90 | 2.79 | 2.71 | 1.27 | 1.31 | 1.33 | 1.35 |
| Apathetic | 1.96 | 1.74 | 1.90 | 1.83 | 1.49 | 1.54 | 1.53 | 1.58 |
| Reagan | | | | | | | | |
| Attentive | 2.80 | 3.06 | 2.95 | 3.18 | 1.40 | 1.35 | 1.35 | 1.03 |
| Latent | 2.07 | 2.58 | 2.56 | 2.84 | 1.62 | 1.49 | 1.47 | 1.37 |
| Inadvertent | 1.86 | 2.15 | 2.17 | 2.39 | 1.64 | 1.58 | 1.56 | 1.48 |
| Apathetic | 1.04 | 1.11 | 1.18 | 1.48 | 1.52 | 1.52 | 1.55 | 1.59 |
| Anderson | | | | | | | | |
| Attentive | – | 1.80 | 1.72 | 2.20 | – | 1.73 | 1.76 | 1.67 |
| Latent | – | 1.13 | 1.39 | 1.87 | – | 1.65 | 1.70 | 1.67 |
| Inadvertent | – | 0.68 | 1.07 | 1.66 | – | 1.37 | 1.58 | 1.60 |
| Apathetic | – | 0.16 | 0.48 | 1.03 | – | 0.71 | 1.19 | 1.49 |
| Kennedy | | | | | | | | |
| Attentive | 3.05 | 3.02 | 3.00 | 2.89 | 1.22 | 1.34 | 1.32 | 1.36 |
| Latent | 2.45 | 2.65 | 2.62 | 2.44 | 1.50 | 1.43 | 1.45 | 1.52 |
| Inadvertent | 2.31 | 2.33 | 2.26 | 2.03 | 1.53 | 1.58 | 1.59 | 1.59 |
| Apathetic | 1.41 | 1.31 | 1.46 | 1.29 | 1.60 | 1.55 | 1.60 | 1.56 |
| Bush | | | | | | | | |
| Attentive | 1.74 | 2.26 | 2.25 | – | 1.75 | 1.71 | 1.75 | – |
| Latent | 0.78 | 1.37 | 1.53 | – | 1.46 | 1.72 | 1.69 | – |
| Inadvertent | 0.64 | 0.95 | 1.06 | – | 1.30 | 1.53 | 1.58 | – |
| Apathetic | 0.20 | 0.39 | 0.32 | – | 0.78 | 1.02 | 0.96 | – |
| Brown | | | | | | | | |
| Attentive | 2.19 | 2.13 | – | – | 1.63 | 1.67 | – | – |
| Latent | 1.41 | 1.60 | – | – | 1.62 | 1.70 | – | – |
| Inadvertent | 1.29 | 1.29 | – | – | 1.63 | 1.61 | – | – |
| Apathetic | 0.56 | 0.56 | – | – | 1.27 | 1.21 | – | – |

*Note:* The September data are from the September panel study. Not all of the questions needed to create the strata measure were asked on the September cross-sectional wave. Numbers of cases may be found in Appendix C.
*Source:* CPS 1980 National Election Study.

to their being interviewed. The scores are displayed by respondents interest and motivation, the measure of opinion-strata, in Table 5.4.*

Those living in states having had primaries before being interviewed in April were slightly more knowledgeable about the candidates' issue stances than others. However, the differences are not substantively significant. The average score, across the six candidates listed in Table 5.3, for those already touched by the campaign was 2.1 issues, compared to 1.9 for all those living in states that had not held primaries. The difference is even smaller when partisanship is controlled. Moreover, even this small difference vanishes by the end of the primary campaign. While there is less variation to explain in June, as four-in-five respondents have been exposed to a primary (however meaningful) in their state, the mean figures for the two groups were identical. Summing across all candidates, the average member of the general public living in a primary state could identify candidates' positions on 2.04 issues and on 2.02 issues in nonprimary states. Thus from this measure it is hard to argue that the campaign itself contributed to citizen learning.

There is a much clearer differentiation of knowledge by the motivation to learn, as indicated by the interstrata differences shown in Table 5.3. In all cases attentives were more knowledgeable about candidates' issue positions than latents, who were more knowledgeable than inadvertents, who in turn were more knowledgeable than apathetics. By the end of the primary campaign in June the impact of both interest and purposive motivation for acquiring information were obvious. The average issue-awareness score for individuals in the attentive public, defined by strong interest in the campaign and general political affairs, was 2.3 across the five candidates asked about in June. The mean score for members of the latent public, who were less interested but paid a good deal of attention to the mass media, was 1.9. The average issue-awareness score for the less attentive member of the inadvertent public was 1.5. Members of the apathetic public trailed far behind, averaging only .85 in their ability to identify candidates' positions on the four issues asked about.

It is both interesting and important to note that while the strata are quite successful in differentiating the electorate in terms of *knowledge*, they are not nearly as successful in differentiating *learning*. There were small gains among all strata, contrary to our

---

*The numbers of cases are not sufficient to present simultaneous controls.

## TABLE 5.5

### Knowledge of Reagan's and Bush's Issue Positions
### in June by Predictor Variables

|  | Knowledge in June | | | |
|  | Reagan | Bush | Reagan | Bush |
|---|---|---|---|---|
| Issue knowledge in February | — | — | .52 | .48 |
| National TV news exposure | -.05 | -.04 | -.06 | -.06 |
| Regular newspaper reading | .10 | .13 | .05 | .07 |
| Primary held in state | .00 | .04 | .00 | .04 |
| Opinion-strata | .30 | .33 | .16 | .19 |

*Note:* Entries are beta coefficients from regression equations in which people's knowledge of issue positions of Reagan and Bush in June was the dependent variable. The entries show the effect of each independent variable, controlling for the effects of other dependent variables. The higher the number the stronger the impact of the independent variable on knowledge. Negative numbers mean that as scores on the independent variable go up scores on the dependent variable go down, and vice versa.

The equation on the right includes people's knowledge of Reagan and Bush's issue positions in February. With that variable in the equation what people knew in February is removed from what they knew in June. By removing people's initial knowledge we can get a clear picture of how the other independent variables relate to learning. The equation on the left omits what people knew in February, and shows how the different independent variables are related to knowledge of issue positions in June.

expectations that different groups would learn about different candidates at different times. In fact, very little appears to differentiate individuals who felt they knew more about candidates' issue positions at one time than another. Through regression analysis we are able to remove the variation in issue-knowledge in June that is due to knowledge in February, and to observe the impact of the campaign, the mass media, and individual motivation on learning.

The campaign's contribution to learning is represented by whether or not there had been a primary held in the respondent's state. The contribution of the mass media is represented by exposure to national network news and a dichotomous variable of whether the individual regularly read a newspaper. The contribution of individual motivation is represented by the opinion-strata variable, encompassing interest and attentiveness. Regression equations are presented for Reagan and Bush in Table 5.5, both with and without the contribution of issue-knowledge in February included.

The first set of equations shows the impact of the independent variables on knowledge. Only motivation made a substantial contribution to knowledge of Bush's and Reagan's issue positions. The standardized slopes (betas) are comparable for both candidates, and of modest strength. Exposure to the mass media made minor offsetting contributions to knowledge. The beta for newspaper reading was small, but at least positively related to issue-knowledge. It is apparent that people learned nothing from simple exposure to national network news. The contribution of television to issue awareness was on balance negative, although small. As in the 1976 election, the medium on which most citizens rely for their election information did little to inform them about candidates' stands on the issues.[4] Nor does it appear that the campaign itself served as an information source. Although the measure is weak, those living in primary states appeared to be no more issue-knowledgeable than those living in states that had not had a primary.

The second set of equations in Table 5.5 seeks to explain learning, rather than knowledge, by controlling for the issue-knowledge respondents held in February. Motivation is again the strongest predictor in relative terms. However in absolute terms none of the factors appears to have much to do with learning. The simplest explanation for this set of relationships is that since little learning took place over the course of the campaign, there was little variation in issue-knowledge left to be explained in June once the variation due to initial knowledge in February was removed.

We may consider three explanations for the dearth of issue-knowledge and absence of learning over the course of the campaign. These are by no means exclusive and are complimentary in some cases. First is the motivation of the public. People did not learn about the candidates' issue positions because they did not need or want to. Some people simply are not interested in public affairs; others become involved in the electoral process only to the extent of voting for the candidate nominated by their party. Public motivation, or the lack thereof, is clearly in part responsible for the scant amount of issue-knowledge. Yet, we have already seen evidence that people may learn despite lacking the motivation to do so. If factual "tidbits" about candidates' policy positions were plentiful in the information environment we would have expected to see more evidence of learning than is present in the data.

Second is the behavior of the candidates. The first rule of politics is to get elected. Candidates may not want to take positions that give clear and accurate signals to the electorate. Politicians prefer general stands that have broadest popular appeal; this is the nature of coalition-building. Yet in primary elections candidates must seek a unique identity—something that sets them apart from the rest, and this acts as incentive for *some* candidates to take clear positions on *some* issues. John Anderson's media strategy in 1980 was built around the use of "the issues" as a means to set himself apart from the others. The central theme of his primary election advertisements drew attention to "the Anderson difference." Upon having lost the primaries as a vehicle for making the evening news, Anderson turned to a "Daniel in the Lion's Den" strategy for his free media. While the wisdom of espousing gun control before the National Rifle Association may be questionable, the issue-orientation is not.

Anderson was not alone in running an "issues" campaign. Edward Kennedy competed with Jimmy Carter to define the Democratic party's very soul and identity. Nor was Ronald Reagan hiding as a conservative-in-moderate's-clothing. Reagan proclaimed his conservatism, particularly during the primaries, claiming that he was at the center of a New American Politics. This is particularly true with the four issues chosen for study. In sum, it is hard to argue that the lack of information and learning about candidates' issue positions is attributable to the behavior of the candidates. The campaign of 1980 may have been atypical in this regard, but the candidates appeared to be willing to put information about their issue positions into the information environment.

Most of the communication between candidates and voters is indirect, however, being filtered by the mass media. As the public's chief source of information about politics and government the media must to some extent be responsible for the information held (and not held) by the public. We have no measures of content, so we cannot directly address the adequacy of media performance in 1980. However, the evidence from prior elections is that the mass media—particularly television—make little in the way of a contribution to an informed citizenry.[5] The focus of the media is on the campaign as a "horserace." The focus of stories is on the "game" aspects of the campaign: winning, setting expectations, strategy, and pageantry. In 1976, only 18 percent of the stories broadcast on the evening news focused on issues and matters of policy.[6] Data from 1980 are comparable.[7]

It is not our intention to point a finger at the mass media—or citizens or candidates—over the failure of people to learn policy-relevant information from the campaign. It is a *system* that we are describing. In general we have an electorate that is not issue-oriented; although one must slyly add that this depends on what the issue is. In general we do not have candidates who wish to raise salient position-issues; yet this happens from time-to-time. And, in general we do not have an information system that is conducive to citizen learning about issues. The media have no formal responsibility to educate the public. They are, after all, profit-making institutions and seek mainly to expand their audience. However, there is a small "prestige press" in the print community which does take seriously this responsibility, and this serves as an example to the nonprestige press. There is variation in the behavior of each of the three actors—the public, the candidates, and the media—over time. But as different as the 1980 election may have been from 1976, the basic characteristics of the system seemed quite similar. By the end of the primaries the public had little idea of what candidates stood for.

## KNOWLEDGE AND LEARNING
## OF CHARACTER TRAITS

While people learned little about the candidates' ideological or issue positions we suspect it is considerably easier to feel knowledgeable about "what kind of man" the candidate is. And, as we have argued, information about character is more than mere fluff. Television conveys images more clearly and more forcefully than policy-relevant information. Simply viewing a 20 second film clip of the candidate addressing a rally may allow insight—accurate or not—about the candidate's character. Television, after all, is a medium far better suited to transmit style than substance. Glimpses of "leadership" may come from mannerisms or firmness of voice. The ability to inspire may be viewed from the reactions of supporters at a campaign rally.

In this section we trace the development of *felt character-knowledge* about the candidates. How well did members of the public feel they knew Ronald Reagan, George Bush, and the others at the beginning of the campaign and at the end of the primaries in June? Were citizen judgments reactive to events in the campaign? Or, as was the case with issue-knowledge, did the public learn little about the character of presidential aspirants from the campaign?

**FIGURE 5.2**

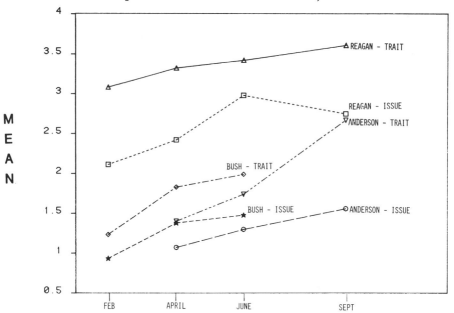

Comparison of Issue and Trait Awareness, 1980

Respondents were read a list of traits and asked if each described a candidate "extremely well," "quite well," "not too well," or "not well at all." As we are more concerned with whether citizens came to feel they knew the candidates, rather than with how their specific impressions changed during the course of the campaign, we have collapsed these four options to a single "yes" response. Four items, representing a cross section of character traits, were selected from those asked about: (1) a strong leader, (2) knowledgeable, (3) inspiring, and (4) moral. As with the issue scale, respondents were given a score of 1 for each trait they ascribed to a candidate, resulting in a scale ranging from "0" to "4." Unfortunately, questions about character traits were not asked about all candidates. Still, the cases of Ronald Reagan, George Bush, and John Anderson provide a sufficient sampling for our purposes.

A comparison of issue and trait-awareness (Figure 5.2) shows that respondents began the campaign relatively more knowledgeable about the character of the candidates, and learned more about character than issues as the campaign progressed.* The public had a fairly well-developed image of Ronald Reagan even in February—the average person could ascribe three of the four traits asked about to him. Scores on this measure averaged a full point higher than issue-awareness scores at all points of the campaign. There were also partisan differences in trait knowledge and learning, which we did not observe in the case of issue awareness. Republicans felt considerably more familiar with Reagan (3.40) than Independents (2.89) or Democrats (3.04) in February. This gap narrowed as the campaign progressed through the latter half of the primaries and the summer convention into the fall general election campaign. Where there had been a .51 difference between Republicans and Independents in February, the mean difference was only .11 in September. While all partisan groups felt quite knowledgeable about Reagan's character in September, Democrats (3.47) trailed Independents (3.66) and Republicans (3.77).

We are unable to fully trace changes in how much members of the public felt they knew about the character of George Bush and John Anderson. The candidate-trait questions were not asked about Bush in September or about Anderson in February. However, it is clear that as the campaign progressed the public gained a stronger impression of what these two men were like than where they stood on issues of the day. As with Reagan, trait-awareness scores were consistently higher than issue-awareness scores. But the differences were not large, averaging about .40. By the end of the primary season the electorate had only a vague impression of both men. The average member of the public could attribute two of four characteristics to Bush and slightly less to Anderson. As with issue-awareness the standard deviations associated with these means are high, indicating a segmentation of the public with some having full knowledge and others having heard nothing about the candidate.

The public felt far more familiar with Anderson's makeup during the general election campaign. The mean trait score shot from about

---

*Some of the difference in the absolute levels of the two types of knowledge is spurious. While the knowledge screen of whether respondents "knew something about" candidates was the same for both scales, the issue scale had a further screen, excluding those respondents who themselves took no position on a given issue. However, the second screen does not explain all the difference between the two scales, and is of course irrelevant to the difference in rates of *learning* as the same filter questions were used from one interview to the next.

1.73 in June to 2.67 in September. This is partly a function of an increase in the percentage feeling they "knew something" about Anderson (Figure 4.2) and becoming eligible to be asked about Anderson's character. Yet issue awareness posted a far more modest net increase of .26 during this same period. If we assume that the motivation to acquire information was the same for both traits and issues—that is that individuals did not seek trait information about Anderson while avoiding issue information—the difference between these two lines must largely be due to the information environment and the degree to which people can learn trait information through visual representation. Bolstering this interpretation, we note that learning about character traits occurred in all opinion-strata groups, which are defined largely by motivation. We have been unable to find any measure that differentiates those having learned about Anderson between June and September from those not having learned more about his character.

## KNOWLEDGE AND THE VOTING PUBLIC

The conclusions drawn so far are distressing as they relate to the quality of citizen choice. In neither 1976 nor 1980 did we see an electorate that learned much about candidates' ideologies, issue positions, or character traits over the course of the primary campaign. By June citizens knew little about the prominent newcomers who remained active throughout the primaries. While the public was more knowledgeable about Reagan than Bush, Anderson, and other candidates who withdrew after early campaign tests, there was little *learning* about Reagan in the true sense of the word. Greater knowledge of Reagan was based on information the public brought with them to the campaign, not information *acquired* during the campaign.

While it is clear that the current nomination system does not lead to a more informed *public*, it is premature to conclude that the choices *voters* make are uninformed. Participation in primaries and caucuses is not widespread. Only about 20 percent of the eligible adult population actually participates in the nomination process. We would certainly expect participants to be more interested and informed than nonparticipants, but *how much* more informed is a central question. Should voters be found to be highly knowledgeable we would reach a very different conclusion about the adequacy of the system. In essence, the relative lack of participation would be seen as a virtue. Informed choice, as Berelson and colleagues argued,

**TABLE 5.6**

### Ideological, Issue, and Trait Knowledge by Participation in Primaries (June)[a]

|  | Knowledge | | |
|---|---|---|---|
|  | Ideology[b] | Issue[c] | Trait[d] |
| **Reagan** | | | |
| Voters | 63 | 2.56 | 3.59 |
| Nonvoters | 50 | 2.34 | 3.31 |
| **Anderson** | | | |
| Voters | 40 | 1.44 | 2.00 |
| Nonvoters | 32 | 1.23 | 1.63 |
| **Bush** | | | |
| Voters | 44 | 1.62 | 2.35 |
| Nonvoters | 28 | 1.38 | 1.84 |
| **Kennedy** | | | |
| Voters | 68 | 2.63 | — |
| Nonvoters | 53 | 2.43 | — |
| **Brown** | | | |
| Voters | 43 | — | — |
| Nonvoters | 33 | — | — |
| **Connally** | | | |
| Voters | 38 | — | — |
| Nonvoters | 30 | — | — |

[a]Voter n-size (186), nonvoter n-size (656).

[b]Percentage able to correctly identify ideology.

[c]Mean number of candidates' issue positions described.

[d]Mean number of candidates' traits described.

would be accomplished by self-selection, with those less knowledgeable voters not muddying the waters of rational decision making.[8]

The vote validation study conducted by the Center for Political Studies allows us to identify those who voted in primaries and those who did not. The ideological, issue, and trait knowledge held by voters and nonvoters is compared in Table 5.6. The data presented are from the June wave of the panel study and allow us to contrast levels of knowledge at the end of the primary season. With only 186 primary election voters included in this sampling it is not feasible to analyze Democratic and Republican voters separately.

On a relative level, voters were clearly more knowledgeable about candidates' ideology, issue stances, and character traits than nonvoters. All differences between the two groups were statistically significant at the .05 level or better. However, on an absolute level, even voters were not terribly knowledgeable about the candidates. Even among this elite fifth of the population only about four-in-ten accurately described Bush or Anderson's ideology after the primaries had concluded. On the average, two-and-one-half of Reagan's four issue positions were known to primary election voters; knowledge of Bush and Anderson's positions was considerably less. Even the general images of Bush and Anderson were not well defined in voters' minds by the end of the primary season.

Thus the conclusions drawn about the character of the eligible electorate held for those actually voting in primaries in 1980. We are of course limited by our measures, and different measures might reveal a better informed public.* But despite the millions of dollars spent in a period lasting over half a year and despite the considerable attention paid to the campaign by the mass media (or at least to the "horserace" aspect of it), the electorate knows and learns little about the candidates running for their party's nomination for president.

---

*While some "artificial ignorance" is imposed on some respondents by the screens built in to the CPS study design, it is worth remembering that our measures within these confines were quite generous and "tilted" toward finding a knowledgeable public. One could have called both Edward Kennedy and Ronald Reagan "moderates" and been scored correct by our measure of ideology (although few did). Similarly we did not test to see whether respondents had accurate views of candidates' policy positions, only if they *felt* they knew where candidates stood.

## NOTES

1. Philip Converse, "The Nature of Belief Systems in Mass Politics," in *Ideology and Discontent*, ed. David Apter (New York: The Free Press, 1964), pp. 206–61. For a critical discussion of this issue see J. Harry Wray, "Comment on Interpretations of Early Research into Belief Systems," *Journal of Politics* 41 (November 1979), pp. 1173–1181.

2. See Norman Nie and Kristi Andersen, "Mass Belief System Revisited: Political Change and Attitude Structure," *Journal of Politics* 36 (1974), pp. 540–87; John Pierce, "1970 Party Identification and the Changing Role of Ideology in American Politics," *Midwest Journal of Political Science* (February 1970), pp. 25–42; Stephen Bennett, "Consistency Among the Public's Social Welfare Policy Attitudes in the 1960s," *American Journal of Political Science* (August 1973), pp. 544–70.

3. See Peter Clarke and Erick Fredin, "Newspapers, Television and Political Reasoning," *Public Opinion Quarterly* 42 (1978), pp. 143–60; Rebecca Quarles, "Mass Media and Voting Behavior: The Accuracy of Political Perceptions Among First-Time and Experienced Voters," *Communication Research* 6 (1979), pp. 407–36; Jack McLeod, Carl Bybee, and Jean Duvall, "Equivalence of Informed Participation: The 1976 Presidential Debates as a Source of Influence," *Communication Research* 6 (1979), pp. 463–87.

4. Thomas Patterson, *The Mass Media Election* (New York: Praeger, 1980), chapter 11.

5. Ibid.

6. Ibid., chapter 3.

7. Michael Robinson and Margaret Sheehan, *Over the Wire and on TV: CBS and UPI in Campaign '80* (New York: Basic Books, 1983).

8. Bernard Berelson, Paul Lazarsfeld, and William McPhee, *Voting* (Chicago: University of Chicago Press, 1954).

# 6

# THE FORMATION OF
# OPINIONS ABOUT CANDIDATES

There is a simple question that becomes more important and more curious the more one thinks about it: How did we, as a public, come to trust with our lives someone who was a total stranger only six months before? The process by which a citizenry that is generally cynical and untrusting of politicians comes to feel comfortable ceding tremendous power to an individual they know little about, and know only indirectly, must indeed be a fascinating one.

This intrigue is what we have called the process of *opinionation*— how opinions of candidates form and develop. Opinionation is not, of course, unique to the new system of presidential nomination. But it is now a more significant concern with the public having formal power over candidate selection. Despite the low public esteem in which parties have historically been held, we suspect voters did indeed trust them to serve as a screening mechanism for qualified individuals, a tapping of the reservoir of diffuse trust in the system. Today, party responsibility has given way to individual responsibility. Now citizens must learn about a greater number of candidates than in the past, must learn earlier in the election process, must learn independently of party organization, and their opinions carry greater weight.

This process of opinionation is crucial to our understanding of citizen behavior in nomination politics and eventual conclusions about the utility of the new system. In this chapter we will explore a number of key questions:

—**What is the nature of opinion formation about presidential candidates?** Do early campaign successes bring a steep increase in the proportion of the public holding opinions of the candidates? Or, does opinion formation occur substantially after awareness? Evidence for the former could suggest that people formed opinions based largely on limited information about the candidates' electoral fortunes. To the degree that opinion formation lagged behind awareness, and was found to change with issue or ideological knowledge, there would be evidence of a greater degree of "informed choice."

—**Are the patterns of opinion formation similar in 1976 and 1980?** If so, how can these regularities be explained? Is it the structure of the system of primaries that is most responsible for the pattern of opinion formation? Or, do personal characteristics such as partisanship and attention to the campaign (motivation) offer a more satisfactory explanation of when and why people form opinions of presidential candidates.

—**How do opinions develop over the course of the campaign?** If citizens were acquiring useful information from the nominating system we would expect that opinions about the candidates would intensify, becoming more strongly held as the campaign progressed from the events of January to June. A pattern of selective reinforcement would offer evidence that citizens had come to feel they knew the candidates better through media coverage of their campaign activities, and could be considered a positive attribute of the new system.

—**Do primary voters and nonvoters differ in how many hold opinions of the candidates, or in how quickly they come to form opinions?** We would certainly expect voters to be more opinionated than nonvoters. But, does each group have the same essential character, or are they fundamentally different? A large disparity between participants and nonparticipants would be symptomatic of alienation in the system and raise questions about the unrepresentativeness of the process. Somewhat paradoxically, however, it may also be argued that the greater the discrepancy between voters and nonvoters, the healthier one can say the system is on other grounds. If 40 percent of the public expressed an opinion about George Bush at the conclusion of the primaries in June, for example, we might be quite alarmed if this included 40 percent of both voters and nonvoters alike. However, if the 40 percent with opinions comprised 80 percent of primary voters we might be far more sanguine about the implications for "informed choice" and confident in the wisdom of the new system. In offering opinions, voters would have demonstrated they had in some way evaluated Bush by the end of the nomination period.

While undeniably important, there has been little in the way of prior research to inform us about the process of opinionation in primary elections. The early studies conducted by the team of researchers from Columbia University focused mainly on the vote decision and social correlates of the vote.[1] The national election studies conducted by the University of Michigan's Survey Research Center focused exclusively on general elections until the 1980 study. In 1972, the first "new system" election, Patterson and McClure also focused on the general election,[2] as did others.[3]

Thomas Patterson's analysis of the 1976 election is the first major work that began early in the primary election period and furnished some evidence on the general question of opinionation. Patterson, however, was largely concerned with the formation and development of "images," which he defined as voters' subjective impressions of candidates, rather than opinions. In 1976 these impressions tended to be stylistic rather than substantive. The images voters held focused on candidates' mannerisms and performance in primary election contests.[4] Images, however, may be neutral in affective content, whereas opinions must have an evaluative component. Thomas Marshall does deal explicitly with opinions about candidates, but his treatment is brief and limited to the proportion of the public holding intense opinions about candidates rather than the more general question of opinion formation.[5]

The lack of attention to the question of how opinions* of candidates form and develop is due more to problems collecting adequate information than to minimization of its importance. If the data presented earlier on candidate awareness is a harbinger of the general dynamics of the campaign, it is apparent that samplings of opinion should be closely tied to the formal events of the campaign. Our data are well suited for this purpose. In this chapter we examine the nature of opinion formation during the 1980 campaign, and then look to see if these same patterns were evident in 1976. After tracing the general dynamics of opinionation we examine how individual moti-

---

*We use the term "opinion" rather than "attitude" to indicate feelings and beliefs of a more transitory nature. As noted earlier, most people were not terribly interested in the campaign and learned little about the cast of characters as the campaign progressed. As the impact of new information should vary inversely with the amount of stored information we would expect opinions about the candidates to be fairly volatile.

vation (measured by attentiveness to the campaign) was related to opinion formation and then show how opinions about the candidates became weaker—rather than stronger—as the 1980 campaign progressed. Finally, differences between primary voters and nonvoters are analyzed.

## OPINION FORMATION IN THE 1980 PRIMARIES

We initially rely on the New Jersey data to describe the dynamics of opinion formation. These data can be grouped around significant events of the primary season to serve as a sensitive barometer of the campaign's impact. Respondents who were at least able to recognize the names of candidates were asked, "Is your general impression of him favorable or unfavorable; or don't you have an opinion about him?" At this point in the analysis we are only concerned with opinion-holding rather than with the direction of opinions.* We have displayed the percentage of the New Jersey public *not* holding opinions about the candidates in Figure 6.1.

The data presented in this figure make it difficult to argue that the public became increasingly familiar with the candidate through the primaries, insofar as this should be reflected in opinion formation. The commanding feature of this graph is the flatness of the candidate lines. Candidates of course differed in how well known they were to the public in October of 1979 before the campaign began; about as many people held opinions about Ronald Reagan (and Edward Kennedy) as President Carter. Far fewer offered opinions about the lesser-known candidates, particularly John Anderson and George Bush. What is more surprising, and more significant, is that even as these candidates became better known through primary breakthroughs, New Jerseyans felt no more comfortable expressing opinions about them.†

---

*We assume that opinion-holding is the next step in a logical progression after awareness. In this sense opinion-holding is a further indicator of knowledge. However, we do not assume that not having an opinion is necessarily due to a lack of information. Some knowledgeable individuals will simply be undecided about the candidate and will answer interviewers' questions with an "informed don't know" when asked for their views.

†It is also worth remembering that these figures overstate the actual amount of opinion-holding in the entire electorate. The proportion with opinions is based on the subset of the New Jersey public able to recognize the candidates. In

**FIGURE 6.1**

**Percentage Not Expressing Opinions About Candidates,
New Jersey, 1980**

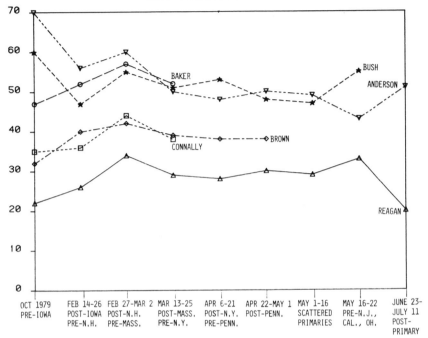

Take first the case of George Bush. In October of 1979, 60 percent of those recognizing him were unable to offer an opinion about
him. His strong showing in the Iowa caucus lowered this figure only
to 47 percent. Yet over this same period awareness of Bush had
increased substantially—from 8 to 53 percent. Moreover, at no time
did a larger portion of the electorate express opinions about Bush
than immediately after his Iowa victory; this was his high mark of
the campaign. By the final measurement in mid-May, 55 percent

─────────────

the case of a universally recognized candidate such as Reagan there is no practical difference between those able to recognize him and the electorate as a
whole. In the case of a little-known candidate such as John Anderson, however,
there is a considerable difference. Whereas 30 percent of those able to recognize
Anderson in October expressed an opinion this represented only 8 percent of
the entire electorate.

expressed no opinion about Bush—almost exactly where he began the campaign. Thus despite dramatic growth in name recognition of Bush, from 53 to 94 percent between October of 1979 and May 1980, the electorate was not better able to offer an evaluation of him.

We see the same pattern of public response to John Anderson. The proportion not holding an opinion of Anderson declined from 70 percent in October to 57 percent after Iowa and before the New Hampshire primary. Despite awareness shooting from 22 to 51 percent, and name recognition climbing from 43 to 85 percent as a result of his strong showing in the Massachusetts and Vermont primaries on March 4, the proportion without opinions of Anderson declined only to 50 percent. After these primaries there was no additional reduction in the size of the group without opinions of Anderson.

There was even less evidence of opinion formation about the other candidates running in the 1980 primaries. The upper and lower bounds for John Connally ranged from 34 to 44 percent unable to offer an opinion of him; across the same four measurements the proportion without an opinion of Howard Baker varied only between 47 and 58 percent. There was a similar 10 point range in readings on Jerry Brown between October and May. Moreover, in none of these three cases did the proportion of the public holding opinions consistently increase over time. We suspect that what little variation we observed is largely due to differences in sample means rather than to real change in the population.

The trend line of the proportion unable or unwilling to express an opinion about Ronald Reagan is also flat, varying between 20 and 32 percent over the 10 month period, despite continuous media coverage of Reagan's convincing primary election successes. Still, a substantial portion of the public felt they knew Reagan well enough to offer an opinion. However, it is clear that opinions about Reagan were not *generated* by events of the campaign so much as citizens *began* the campaign with impressions about him. The foundation of his 1980 campaign was built by his efforts to secure the Republican nomination in 1976. Reagan appears to have begun the 1980 campaign at the threshold where informed and uninformed "no opinions" meet. The proportion without an opinion of Carter, about whom the entire sample should be sufficiently knowledgeable to hold an opinion, varied only from 14 to 24 percent from October to June, a range only slightly below Reagan's. The proportion without an opinion of Kennedy ranged only from 20 to 23 percent, about 10 points under Reagan.

Thus the evidence from 1980 is that the public did not gradually form opinions about the candidates through the campaign. The public never came to form opinions of those men who were early victims in 1980, or even late victims. While primary successes appeared to have led some citizens to form opinions of various candidates, further opinionation of the electorate did not occur after these successes. In sum, there was no real evidence of learning over the course of the campaign, insofar as this would be reflected in the growth of opinions about presidential aspirants.

There are, however, two factors that could forestall this conclusion. First, the figures presented in Figure 6.1 are calculated on the base of those who could either spontaneously mention each contestant as a candidate for his party's nomination *or* who could recognize the candidate's name. It is possible that as the base of people eligible to be asked the question increased due to the growth in recognition of previously little known candidates, the composite figures mask countervailing trends. Those "aware" of the candidates may be more able to offer opinions while those only able to recognize the candidates may not be more able to do so. This would fit with many notions of a tiered public. As the group who only "recognized" the candidate became larger relative to the group "aware" of the candidate, evidence of learning may be partially hidden.

To examine this contingency, those "aware" of and those only "recognizing" each candidate are shown separately in Table 6.1. As one would expect, fewer of those simply able to recognize the candidates' names were able to offer opinions about them. However, the patterns across time are exactly the same. Awareness and recognition lines would be parallel, and nearly straight if graphed. We also observe the same layering with opinion formation as we saw with candidate awareness. About 15 percent more of those aware of Reagan were able to offer an evaluation of him than of those who were simply able to recognize Reagan's name. The comparable figures for Bush and Anderson average out to about 20 percent, with little individual variation.*

---

*The relatively small difference in opinion-holding between those mentioning and those aware of candidates points out a weakness of the CPS data. We suspect that a fair proportion of those filtered out in the CPS study because they only "had heard of" the candidates also held opinions about them.

## TABLE 6.1

### Opinion Holding by Familiarity with Candidates

(Cell entries are percentages *unable* to offer an opinion.)

| | Oct 1979 Pre-Iowa | Feb 14-26 Post-Iowa Pre-N.H. | Feb 27-Mar 2 Post-N.H. Pre-Mass. | Mar 13-25 Post-Mass. Pre-N.Y. | Apr 6-21 Post-N.Y. Pre-Penn. | Apr 22-May 1 Post-Penn. | May 1-16 Scattered Primaries | May 16-22 Pre-N.J., Cal, Ohio |
|---|---|---|---|---|---|---|---|---|
| **Reagan** | | | | | | | | |
| % Aware | 18 | 22 | 32 | 25 | 25 | 26 | 27 | 30 |
| % Recog. | 25 | 35 | 43 | 42 | 37 | 39 | 41 | 50 |
| n Aware | 515 | 1184 | 598 | 252 | 493 | 500 | 775 | 647 |
| n Recog. | 601 | 505 | 163 | 66 | 112 | 121 | 157 | 157 |
| **Bush** | | | | | | | | |
| % Aware | 52 | 38 | 50 | 45 | 45 | 42 | 42 | 47 |
| % Recog. | 62 | 62 | 72 | 63 | 63 | 58 | 62 | 67 |
| n Aware | 88 | 906 | 474 | 192 | 361 | 380 | 587 | 466 |
| n Recog. | 509 | 550 | 208 | 98 | 213 | 214 | 308 | 297 |
| **Anderson** | | | | | | | | |
| % Aware | * | 35 | 43 | 45 | 40 | | | |
| % Recog. | 72 | 65 | 60 | 65 | 60 | | | |
| n Aware | 13 | 263 | 168 | 166 | 313 | | | |
| n Recog. | 288 | 569 | 239 | 109 | 219 | | | |

*Only 13 cases.

**FIGURE 6.2**

**Percentage of Republicans Not Expressing Opinions About Candidates, New Jersey, 1980**

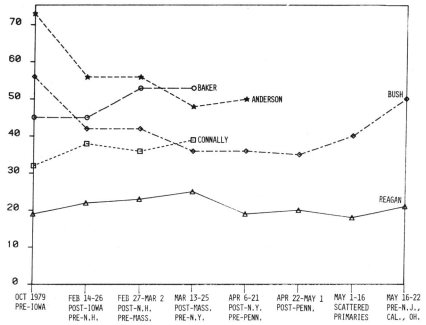

We also tested a second factor that could dilute evidence of learning (as indicated by the degree of opinion formation). Primaries are of course partisan affairs. It is not necessary for Democrats to become knowledgeable about Republican candidates, nor for Republicans to learn about Democratic candidates, at least not until the general election. It may be that evidence of opinion formation and citizen learning is more impressive when viewed from a "need-to-know" perspective. Figure 6.2 displays the pattern of opinion-holding about Republican candidates among New Jersey Republicans.* The

---

*Independents who "leaned" toward the Republican party were included with other Republicans in the New Jersey data to bolster the number of cases. Behaviorally, leaners bear a close resemblance to partisans. See, among others, Herbert Asher, *Presidential Elections and American Politics* (Homewood, Ill.: The Dorsey Press, 1976), Chapter 3.

basic pattern is clearly isomorphic to that in Figure 6.1. Republicans were slightly more likely to have opinions about their candidates, but not by much. Moreover, this is largely explained by the fact that Republicans were generally more knowledgeable about all candidates in New Jersey. Except for a few more "don't knows" about Bush after he had all but conceded to Reagan, Republicans were no different from other members of the electorate in forming opinions about the candidates.

Thus despite our attempts to find a more flattering perspective from which to view opinion formation in the new system the basic conclusions to be drawn from these data remain unchanged. To restate: very little in the way of opinion formation took place during the primary election season in 1980. There was no evidence of gradual learning, where the mass electorate became more familiar with candidates as the campaign progressed. The changes in opinion formation that did occur were closely tied to individual candidate successes in specific primaries.* Finally, we wish to note the absolute level of opinion-holding among New Jerseyans at the conclusion of the primaries in June. It is a telling comment about the nomination system that among those able to recognize Anderson and Bush, one half or more emerged from the primaries expressing no opinion about them.

## OPINION FORMATION IN THE 1976 PRIMARIES

We have described the general happenings of the 1976 nominating campaigns in Chapter 1. The contest for the Democratic nomination provides the more interesting case study of opinion formation, as it featured a host of unknown candidates vying for the nomination. We are relying on the monthly surveys conducted by CBS News and the *New York Times* to illuminate the dynamics of opinionation during these primaries.

In the baseline survey taken in early February, 90 percent expressed no opinion of Morris Udall and Fred Harris, while three quarters expressed no opinion of Henry Jackson and Jimmy Carter

---

*Such a pattern comports well with the notion of opinion-strata advanced earlier and will be examined more fully later in this chapter. The differences in opinion-holding between those fully aware and those only able to recognize candidates' names also lends credence to this view.

**FIGURE 6.3**

Percentage Not Expressing Opinions About Candidates, 1976

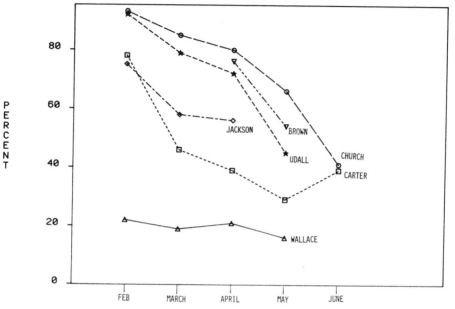

(see Figure 6.3). We suspect that Carter actually began at the same level as Udall and Harris but benefited from the publicity he received by doing well in January's Iowa caucus. While "uncommitted" led the field in Iowa at 39 percent, Carter received the next highest delegate total of 29 percent and was accorded "winner" status by the media.[6]

There was a major change in the proportion holding opinions of Carter between the February and March surveys and lesser changes in opinions of Jackson and Udall. The percentage without opinions of Carter took a precipitous drop from 78 to 46 percent. The proportion without opinions of Udall and Jackson declined by 17 and 13 percentage points respectively. During this time period Carter had finished first in New Hampshire with 28 percent of the vote to Udall's 23 percent. Jackson "won" the Massachusetts primary with only 22 percent of the vote while Udall again finished second with 18 percent. The changes in opinion-holding, which occurred equally among

Democrats and others,* were basically proportionate to the amount of media attention the winner was accorded, and quite disproportionate to the size of the victories. By March, 54 percent expressed an opinion of Carter, but only 21 percent of Udall. The overemphasis of the mass media on primary "victors"[7] had clear effects on the nature of public opinions about the candidates.

As the campaign continued Udall reinforced his bridesmaid's image by finishing second to Jimmy Carter in Wisconsin by 1 percent and losing to Carter in Michigan by three tenths of 1 percent. Unable to shake the tag of "second place Mo," the Udall campaign acknowledged defeat. With Udall's challenge fading California Governor Jerry Brown and Idaho Senator Frank Church began active pursuit of the nomination with A-B-C campaigns—anybody but Carter. Their late primary successes are also clearly reflected in changes of opinion-holding. As Brown beat Carter in Maryland by 48 to 37 percent the proportion not holding an opinion of him decreased from 76 to 54 percent between April and May. Church's success in the Oregon primary, where he bested Carter by 34 to 27 percent, was followed by a 25 percentage point decrease in the proportion without opinions of him between the May and June surveys.

There are a number of similarities between the Democratic race of 1976 and the Republican contest in 1980. Foremost among them is that opinions about candidates are largely formed on the basis of primary successes, to the extent they are formed at all. It is somewhat discomforting to put this finding together with conclusions of the two preceding chapters: Primary successes led to increased awareness of candidates and, to a much lesser extent, to the formation of opinions about candidates, but they did not lead to greater knowledge about the candidates. The pieces do not easily fit together to form a picture of informed choice.

So what accounts for the shape of the pieces? How can the patterns of opinion formation in 1976 and 1980 be explained, within the context set by the last two chapters? We again turn our attention to the nature of the information available to the public. There is no doubt the news media focus primarily on the game—winning and losing.[8] This after all is "the story," of a nomination contest. It is critical to remember that, as a collectivity, the news media define

---

*See Appendix C, "Chapter 6: Points of Information," for partisan breakdowns and opinionation about Republican candidates.

their job as reporting the story; not as informing the public. The latter may or may not be a residual consequence of the former. If citizens are to become educated they must sift through the media's preoccupation with the horserace aspect of the campaign to mine nuggets of information about candidate characteristics and views. A question arises as to whether that information is even available. If not, citizens must form opinions on the information that is available—success or failure in campaign tests—or be unable to form opinions about presidential candidates. If other information is available, we would expect more attentive citizens to use that information in developing opinions. In this next section we return to the 1980 Republican campaign to look at the role of motivation in opinion formation and to look at a case study of changes in public opinion based on primary outcomes.

## THE ROLE OF MOTIVATION IN OPINION FORMATION

The monthly CBS/*New York Times* surveys are useful for examining how attentiveness to the campaign was related to opinion formation in 1980. Respondents can be grouped according to whether they said they paid "a lot," "some," or "not much" attention to the campaign.* This grouping also allows us to probe a pattern found in the New Jersey public. The differences in opinion-holding between those fully aware of a candidate and those only able to recognize his name are well tailored to the notion of a stratified public advanced earlier. Our attention will be focused on the three most consequential actors in the Republican drama—Ronald Reagan, George Bush, and John Anderson.

Before proceeding with the analysis we wish to note that the New Jersey and national data find similar levels in opinion-holding in the electorate.† The national surveys show a greater impact of strong

---

*See the discussion of Table 3.3.

†When the percentage holding opinions in New Jersey is put over the base of all respondents rather than those able to recognize the candidates, so as to make the data set comparable to the CBS/*Times* data, the level of opinion-holding is quite close. In October of 1979, 92 percent of New Jerseyans had no opinion of Anderson, 79 percent had no opinion of Bush, and 23 percent expressed no opinion about Reagan. Nationwide, the percentages expressing no opinion of Anderson, Bush, and Reagan were 82, 70, and 20 percent respectively. As the CBS/*Times* survey was concluded only one week prior to the Iowa caucus

## TABLE 6.2

**Percentage Without Opinion by Level of Attention to Campaign**

|  | January | February | March | April | June |
|---|---|---|---|---|---|
| Candidate/Attention |  |  |  |  |  |
| Reagan |  |  |  |  |  |
| —a lot | 11 | 11 | 15 | 13 | 14 |
| —some | 12 | 9 | 24 | 23 | 27 |
| —not much | 30 | 24 | 46 | 42 | 42 |
| Bush |  |  |  |  |  |
| —a lot | 53 | 29 | 30 | 32 | 31 |
| —some | 66 | 43 | 42 | 48 | 41 |
| —not much | 79 | 62 | 61 | 68 | 70 |
| Anderson |  |  |  |  |  |
| —a lot | 73 | 61 | 35 | 32 | 28 |
| —some | 82 | 80 | 51 | 48 | 54 |
| —not much | 87 | 83 | 68 | 65 | 69 |
| Numbers of cases |  |  |  |  |  |
| —a lot | 220 | 215 | 294 | 399 | 346 |
| —some | 573 | 630 | 602 | 685 | 751 |
| —not much | 675 | 691 | 573 | 510 | 406 |

*Source:* CBS News/*New York Times* monthly surveys.

primary showings on opinion-holding. Bush's success in Iowa was reflected in a 20 percentage point increase in opinion-holding, while Anderson's success in the Massachusetts and Vermont primaries was followed by a 25 point increase. However, as in New Jersey, after these breakthroughs, the level of opinion-holding remained constant throughout the remainder of the primary season. Interestingly, the percentage not expressing an opinion of Reagan increased from 16 to 31 percent after Anderson's success, and remained at this level through

---

the actual differences may be less, since pre-caucus media attention should have had some informational effects on the CBS/*Times* sample. The proportion not expressing opinions in the late May New Jersey study and the June CBS/*Times* study are in quite close agreement: Anderson, 52 percent in New Jersey and 53 percent nationwide; Bush, 55 percent in New Jersey and 52 percent nationwide; Reagan, 34 percent in New Jersey and 29 percent nationwide.

June. Evidently, Anderson's good fortune was taken as a sign of Reagan's weakness and caused some to be less certain about the GOP front-runner, a point to which we will return later. In the national data, as in the New Jersey data, Republicans did not differ significantly from the larger public in patterns of opinion-holding.*

The role of motivation in opinion formation is illuminated by the data displayed in Table 6.2, which divides the electorate by how much attention individuals said they paid to be campaign. Not surprisingly, there is a clear and strong positive relationship between attentiveness and opinionation. However, we also note that increases in opinion-holding occurred in jumps among *all* groups, not just among highly motivated individuals. Again, there is no evidence of gradual learning. In fact, outside of the changes associated with primary successes there is no evidence of any of the three groups becoming more comfortable forming opinions about any of the three candidates from March to June. Without panel data this conclusion must remain an inference, as the size of the groups changed over the course of the campaign (see Table 3.3). This pattern, however, is consistent with other evidence presented thus far.

The impact of George Bush's success in the Iowa caucus affected all groups roughly to the same extent. Opinion-holding about Bush increased 23 percentage points among those who paid either a lot or some attention to the campaign and by 17 points even among those who had not been paying much attention to the race. After Iowa no real change occurred in the proportion of any of the groups holding opinions about Bush through the rest of the primary season. In this case, motivation was not related to opinion formation. How attentive people had been to the campaign was incidental. Evidently the splash of Bush's victory in the waters of the media was enough to drench everybody, whether or not they wanted to get wet.

With John Anderson we discern a greater role played by attentiveness in opinion formation. Between January and February, after minimal exposure in the Iowa caucus but before Anderson had made his own splash in Massachusetts and Vermont, opinion-holding increased 12 points among the most attentive. However, the benefits of campaigning in Iowa, without winning, were confined to this upper stratum. It should also be noted that even among the most attentive group only four-in-ten expressed an opinion about Anderson

---

*See Appendix C for partisan breakdowns.

after Iowa. After Anderson's strong runs in Vermont and Massachusetts there was a dramatic increase in the proportion of all three groups with opinions about him. Opinion-holding increased by 26 percentage points among those paying a lot of attention to the campaign, by 31 points among those paying some attention, and by a small 15 points among the least attentive. A good number of people appear to have formed opinions about Anderson based on his electoral success. But as with Bush, after the threshold accompanying the breakthrough was reached the process of opinionation ground to a halt.

We earlier noted that concomitant with Anderson's success was a decline in the proportion with opinions about Reagan. This decline occurred entirely among the two less attentive groups. Between February and March there was a 13 percentage point decrease among the somewhat attentive and a 22 point decrease among the least attentive in opinions of Reagan. Opinionation remained at this less-formed level for the balance of the campaign. Opinions held by the less attentive are likely to be based on scant information and more susceptible to change. Evidently Reagan's third place showing in Massachusetts and 1 percent margin over Anderson in Vermont on March 3 introduced an element of doubt into the thoughts of those who knew little about Reagan save that he had been an effective campaigner and had formed opinions on that basis.

This point is important for it allows a glimpse into how easily opinions come to be held and disregarded by passive followers of the campaign. It takes on even greater importance with the realization that we are not talking about an inconsequential or even modest portion of the electorate. The great majority of the public follows the campaign as largely disinterested spectators. At the time that opinions of Reagan "backed up" only one-in-five was paying a great deal of attention to the campaign. There was no real decline in opinion-holding among this highly attentive segment of the public. There was a 15 point reversal among the two fifths of the public paying "some attention" to the campaign. Among the least attentive there was a 22 point decline in the percentage expressing opinions about Reagan. This represented another 40 percent of the public at the time the survey was conducted in March. Overall, the investigation into attentiveness leads to the following generalization: while individual characteristics such as motivation and involvement are important in explaining how and when people form opinions of candidates, the structure of the nominating system is itself a more important explanation for the dynamics of opinion formation.

## OPINION DEVELOPMENT: CHANGE
## IN THE INTENSITY OF OPINIONS

While the proportion of the public not expressing opinions about the various candidates shows the basic contours of the electorate's involvement, we are also interested in examining those who did have opinions about the candidates. In this section we are concerned with how those opinions developed over the course of the campaign; in the next chapter we turn our attention to changes in the direction of opinions about the candidates. In opinion development we focus on the intensity with which opinions were held and the degree to which citizens came to feel more strongly about candidates as the campaign progressed. Intensity is a clue to the salience of candidates to the individual and to the informational underpinning of opinions.

As citizens become more familiar with the candidates, especially in the case of the eventual victors such as Carter in 1976 and Reagan in 1980, there is reason to believe opinions would come to be more firmly held. As incoming information was selectively interpreted consistent with prior beliefs and expectations opinions would presumably be strengthened.[9] In particular, we would expect to see a greater proportion of citizens expressing more strongly positive and negative opinions about Reagan as his status as the Republican nominee became evident in late spring. As an individual about whom Democrats and Republicans alike would have to make a decision in the coming fall, we would expect even those who had not participated in the primaries to become more opinionated about Reagan. Familiarity may not always breed contempt, but it should at least breed a stronger reaction rather than a weaker one.

The panel study data collected by the Center for Political Studies, where the same individuals were interviewed on two occasions, allows us to observe the development of opinions about candidates.* The

---

*Respondents were asked to rate candidates on a "feeling thermometer" ranging from 0 (coldest or the most intense dislike) to 100 (warmest or the most positive feeling). We have grouped respondents according to the intensity of their opinions. Those giving a candidate a score of 0 to 24 or 76 to 100 were said to hold strong opinions. Those rating a candidate between 25 and 49 or 51 and 75 were defined as having weak opinions. A score of 50 indicated neither warm nor cold feelings toward the candidate. These respondents are categorized as having "no opinion."

In the accompanying analysis we generally refer to this measure as an indicator of the intensity with which opinions are held. This is certainly one dimension that is tapped. A respondent giving Reagan a score of 10 has stronger

## TABLE 6.3

### Changes in Intensity of Opinions, February to June

| February | June | | | Row total | (n) | Percentage in February |
|---|---|---|---|---|---|---|
| | No opinion | Weak opinion | Strong opinion | | | |
| **Reagan** | | | | | | |
| —weak opinion | 13% | 63% | 24% | 100% | (364) | 69% |
| —strong opinion | 9 | 32 | 59 | 100 | (161) | 31 |
| **Connally** | | | | | | |
| —weak opinion | 46 | 45 | 8 | 99 | (237) | 74 |
| —strong opinion | 22 | 33 | 35 | 100 | (85) | 26 |
| **Baker** | | | | | | |
| —weak opinion | 44 | 48 | 8 | 100 | (199) | 75 |
| —strong opinion | 34 | 34 | 32 | 100 | (65) | 25 |
| **Bush** | | | | | | |
| —weak opinion | 34 | 55 | 11 | 100 | (168) | 66 |
| —strong opinion | 11 | 50 | 40 | 101 | (86) | 34 |
| **Dole** | | | | | | |
| —weak opinion | 58 | 36 | 6 | 100 | (139) | — |
| —strong opinion* | | | | | | |
| **Kennedy** | | | | | | |
| —weak opinion | 25 | 60 | 15 | 100 | (329) | 61 |
| —strong opinion | 14 | 35 | 51 | 100 | (210) | 39 |
| **Brown** | | | | | | |
| —weak opinion | 53 | 40 | 7 | 100 | (265) | 75 |
| —strong opinion | 40 | 42 | 18 | 100 | (88) | 25 |
| **Reagan-Among Republicans Only** | | | | | | |
| —weak opinion | 4 | 60 | 36 | 100 | (104) | 63 |
| —strong opinion | 5 | 16 | 79 | 100 | (61) | 37 |

*Only 29 cases.

*Note:* Entries are percentage of respondents in June at each level of intensity, based upon the intensity of their opinion in February. Entries in the column "Percentage in February" show the distribution of opinions for each candidate in February.

data in Table 6.3 show how those persons having opinions about the various candidates at the beginning of the primaries in February felt about them at the end of the campaign in June. The first observation to be made comes from simple inspection of the marginal percentages. Few citizens held intense opinions about any of the candidates at the start of the campaign. Strongly held opinions, *as a percentage of all persons with opinions*, ranged only from a high of 39 percent in the case of Edward Kennedy to a low of 25 percent in the cases of Howard Baker and Jerry Brown.* The second important observation to be made from these data is that a greater number of people actually came to feel *less* strongly about candidates than came to feel more strongly about them from the beginning to the end of the primaries. This is particularly dramatic among those candidates who ceased their quest for the nomination in the middle of the primaries. Among those who had held opinions about Howard Baker and John Connally in February, about 45 percent expressed no opinion in June. Another 45 percent continued to hold weak opinions of each, while only 8 percent came to feel more strongly about them. Just one-in-three of those with strong opinions about either man in February continued to hold strong opinions in June. The same pattern is true with regard to George Bush and Democrat Jerry Brown. Fully half of those with weak opinions of Brown in February expressed no opinion at all in June. Fewer than one-in-ten of those with a weak opinion of Brown in February had developed a more intense opinion of him by June. Indeed, only about one-in-five with strong opinions about Brown in February continued to feel strongly about him in June.

This pattern of "reverse development" is not only true of minor candidates and eventual losers. Even in the case of Ronald Reagan we notice more weakening than strengthening of opinion. Only about one fourth of those with weak opinions of Reagan in February graduated to holding strong opinions about him in June. This increase was more than offset by corresponding movement. Forty-one percent of those with strong opinions about Reagan in February either offered

---

feelings about him than another respondent giving him a rather ambivalent score of 45. However, the measure undoubtedly taps other concepts related to intensity, such as the certainty with which opinions are held.

*The small number of respondents (under 100) with strong opinions about the candidates in February imposes limits on the depth of analysis and cautions against overinterpretation of figures.

TABLE 6.4

Changes in Intensity of Opinions by Partisanship and Voting Status

| February | June No opinion | Weak opinion | Strong opinion | Total | (n) |
|---|---|---|---|---|---|
| By Partisanship[a] | | | | | |
| All Partisans | | | | | |
| —weak opinion | 28% | 55% | 17% | 100% | (526) |
| —strong opinion | 16 | 29 | 55 | 100 | (302) |
| Republicans | | | | | |
| —weak opinion | 22 | 59 | 20 | 101 | (295) |
| —strong opinion | 13 | 26 | 61 | 100 | (144) |
| Democrats | | | | | |
| —weak opinion | 36 | 51 | 13 | 100 | (231) |
| —strong opinion | 20 | 31 | 49 | 100 | (158) |
| By Voting Status[b] | | | | | |
| Weak Opinion | | | | | |
| —primary voters | 35 | 51 | 14 | 100 | (422) |
| —nonvoters | 38 | 50 | 12 | 100 | (1238) |
| Strong Opinion | | | | | |
| —primary voters | 22 | 34 | 44 | 100 | (204) |
| —nonvoters | 22 | 36 | 42 | 100 | (524) |

[a]In order to have a sufficient number of cases on which to base generalizations, responses have been summed across candidates. "All partisans" includes Republicans' reactions to Reagan, Bush, Baker, and Connally and Democrats' reactions to Kennedy and Brown. This is a composite of the "Republican" and "Democratic" figures below.

[b]This is a summation of responses given by primary voters and nonvoters to Reagan, Bush, Baker, Connally, Dole, Crane, Kennedy, and Brown.

*Note:* Entries are the percentage of respondents in June at each level of intensity, based upon the intensity of their opinion in February.

no opinion or were found to have a weakly held opinion of him when re-interviewed in June. We suspect that much of the tempering of opinions about Reagan is due to Democrats and Independents becoming less extreme in their hostility. While the sample size of Republicans with opinions about Reagan in February is quite small, 36 percent of partisans with weak opinions in February came to hold stronger views in June, compared to 21 percent of those who had a strong opinion of Reagan in February and expressed a less intense sentiment about him in June.

It is difficult to test the hypothesis that evidence of opinion development is masked by partisan forces. The even smaller number of partisans with strong opinions about candidates other than Reagan makes it impossible to reliably trace changes in the intensity of opinions held by partisans about specific candidates. Accordingly, we have aggregated responses given by partisans about six candidates so as to bolster statistical validity (see Table 6.4).* However, even with partisanship controlled in this fashion it is clear that the campaign contributed little, or perhaps negatively, to the development of more strongly held opinions about candidates. Overall, only 17 percent of those with weak opinions in February came to hold strong opinions in June. In fact, a slightly greater proportion, 28 percent, went from holding a weak opinion in February to holding no opinion in June. Only about half of those partisans with strong feelings about their candidates in February continued to have strong feelings in June.

We also note that primary voters were no different from nonvoters in terms of opinion development. Across a more extensive set of eight candidates, only about 13 percent of both primary voters and nonvoters went from holding weak opinions in February to holding strong opinions in June. Moreover, only about four-in-ten of those beginning the campaign with intensely held opinions about candidates ended the campaign in the same fashion. The greater destabilization of opinions when the number of candidates considered is expanded by the inclusion of "early failures" (Dole and Crane) illustrates a clear dynamic of the primary system: as candidates do poorly and withdraw, people become less certain of them.

---

*We will be examining Republican partisans' responses to four Republican candidates—Reagan and Bush as the central contestants for the Republican nomination, and Baker and Connally, who were at least recognized by a significant portion in February. We have also included the responses of Democrats to President Carter's two challengers, Edward Kennedy and Jerry Brown.

The lack of opinion development runs contrary to the expectations set forth at the beginning of this section. Part of the explanation for this is a tendency for the public to react very positively to new candidates upon being introduced to them through caucus or primary success. But as candidates then lose and are shown to be human this new romance sours quickly and opinions become more temperate. The *new romance* phenomenon is discussed in greater depth in the following chapter, as part of the nature of attitude change in response to campaign successes and failures.

## SUMMARY

The foregoing analysis leads to two general conclusions. First, it is discouraging to note the relative lack of knowledge and opinions about candidates at the end of a campaign that lasts for six months. In 1976, 40 percent of the public emerged from the primary season having formed no opinion of Jimmy Carter; even fewer had formed opinions of other candidates. By the end of the primaries in 1980 almost one third expressed no opinion about Ronald Reagan, with fully half of the public expressing no opinion of George Bush and John Anderson. As a vehicle by which the electorate becomes familiar with those who wish to lead them, the new system is a failure.

Second, to the extent that opinionation occurred, it was solely based on candidates' successes in early campaign tests. Opinionation and awareness occurred together, and only for the perceived "winners." Losers, whether by 30 points or one point, remained largely invisible to most of the public. And, it appears that information about the candidates' electoral fortunes was the only information the great majority of the public had when called upon to offer their evaluations of the candidates, for we noted no increase in knowledge about the candidates' issue positions or ideological leanings. Moreover, once impressed by a candidate's breakthrough the public did not become activated to the point of learning more about the candidate. This view of the electorate can hardly be comforting to those placing their trust in an informed citizenry wisely selecting leadership.

Some of the responsibility for this state of affairs clearly rests on the shoulders of the individual citizen. Many are not interested in politics. They do not feel they have a stake in the outcome and are unwilling to take the time to be informed. Some responsibility clearly rests with the mass media as well. The data indicate that even a good many of those who were motivated to follow the campaign received information that was not particularly useful in helping them form opinions. The "horserace" style of media—and particularly television—coverage has been widely documented in all elections conducted under the new system.[10] With this bias of coverage about the only choice citizens were offered was between forming opinions based mostly on the candidates' fortunes or not being able to easily form impressions of the men they must judge. This Hobson's choice clearly does little to inspire confidence in the system, or in the men who emerge victorious from it.

## NOTES

1. Paul Lazarsfeld, Bernard Berelson, and Hazel Gaudet, *The People's Choice* (New York: Columbia University Press, 1944); Bernard Berelson, Paul Lazarsfeld, and William McPhee, *Voting* (Chicago: University of Chicago Press, 1954).

2. Thomas Patterson and Robert McClure, *The Unseeing Eye* (New York: G. P. Putnam's Sons, 1976).

3. Harold Mendelsohn and Garrett O'Keefe, *The People Choose a President* (New York: Praeger, 1976).

4. Thomas Patterson, *The Mass Media Election* (New York: Praeger, 1980), pp. 133–52.

5. Thomas Marshall, *Presidential Nominations in a Reform Age* (New York: Praeger, 1981), pp. 131–32.

6. Thomas Patterson, *The Mass Media Election* (New York: Praeger, 1980), p. 44.

7. Ibid., pp. 43–53.

8. Michael J. Robinson and Margaret Sheehan, *Over the Wire and on TV: CBS and UPI in Campaign '80* (New York: Basic Books, 1983).

9. Among many studies, see C. Richard Hofstetter, "Perceptions of News Bias in the 1972 Presidential Campaign," *Journalism Quarterly* 56 (1979), pp. 370–74; Churchill Roberts, "Media Use and Difficulty of Decision in the 1976 Presidential Campaign," *Journalism Quarterly* 56 (1979), pp. 794–802. For a general review, see Garrett O'Keefe and L. Erwin Atwood, "Communication and Election Campaigns," in *Handbook of Political Communication*, eds. Dan Nimmo and Keith Sanders (Beverly Hills, Calif.: Sage, 1981), pp. 329–47.

10. See C. Richard Hofstetter, *Bias in the News* (Columbus: Ohio State University Press, 1976); Thomas Patterson and Robert McClure, *The Unseeing Eye* (New York: G. P. Putnam's Sons, 1976); Thomas Patterson, *The Mass Media Election* (New York: Praeger, 1980); Michael Robinson, *Over the Wire and on TV: CBS and UPI in Campaign '80* (New York: Basic Books, 1983).

# 7
# POPULARITY OF
# THE CANDIDATES

Wisconsin figured prominently in Morris Udall's plans to capture the 1976 Democratic nomination. Long known for its progressive politics, it seemed like the sort of state that would be responsive to an intelligent liberal like Udall. Wisconsin's primary was relatively early in the season—it would be held on April 6, only the seventh of twenty-seven to be held in 1976. But by the end of March Jimmy Carter had already become the "front-runner" by virtue of his good showing in the Iowa caucuses and five of the previous primaries. Udall expected to do well in Wisconsin, given the kind of state it was and the effort he had made there. But he was in for a surprise:

> I'd been there thirty times and I had organization, newspaper endorsements, and all the congressmen and state legislators. Well, I take a poll and he's [Carter] ahead of me, two to one, and he has never been in the state except for a few quick visits.

Udall had discovered firsthand the role played by "momentum" in the serial primary system, and he didn't like it:

> It's like a football game, in which you say to the first team that makes a first down with ten yards, "Hereafter, your team has a special rule. Your first downs are five yards. And if you make three of those you get a two yard first down. And we're going to let your first touchdown count twenty-one points. Now the rest of you bastards play catch-up under the regular rules."[1]

The experience of Mo Udall in 1976 raises important questions about the basis upon which the public judges candidates for presidential nominations. This chapter addresses some of those questions, including the following:

—Given the way campaign events have been shown to affect the level of awareness, recognition, and opinionation of candidates, what are the effects of candidate performance in campaign tests on their popularity?
—What role do traditional bases of opinion—in particular, partisanship and ideology—play in the popularity of candidates for nomination?
—How does the popularity of candidates differ for citizens who are directly exposed to a primary campaign and those who only hear about the campaign via the national news media?
—Do vigorous battles for the nomination lead to intraparty polarization?
—What role do the parties' conventions play in public opinion about the candidates?

For two reasons, we are especially interested in citizen reaction to the new candidates who figured in the nominations of 1976 and 1980. First, the new nomination process encourages relatively unknown candidates to run. Some—McGovern, Bush, and Anderson—succeeded in becoming nationally prominent, and one—Carter—won the presidency. This openness to "outsiders" was extolled as an important virtue of the new system, and was one of the chief rationales put forth by the turn-of-the-century Progressives who "invented" the primary. Thus an understanding of regularities in how the public greets "outsiders" may be useful in predicting the future shape of our politics and in evaluating the quality of the selection process.

A second reason for a close examination of opinion formation and change about new candidates is that social scientists know little about the genesis of attitudes toward politicians and public figures. A great deal is known about how attitudes affect voting in general elections, and dynamic processes such as presidential popularity have been well studied. But relatively little research has focused on how the public first meets and comes to like or dislike politicians, perhaps because the process is irregular and temporally unpredictable. Presidential nominations present a convenient opportunity to study this phenomenon.

The most useful tool for explaining citizen behavior in elections is partisanship, but given the fact that nominations are *intra*party affairs, we expect that partisanship will influence public opinion during nominations differently than during the general elections.

Partisanship reduces information costs, and helps voters make rational choices. If a party is known to stand for a particular policy, then voters who support that policy need not be informed about the views of the candidates; they may choose a candidate on the basis of party and have some assurance that their vote is consistent with their policy interest. Of course, elections in America fall far short of this ideal for a variety of reasons noted by political scientists,[2] including resistance of candidates to party discipline, the presence of other motives by voters (such as the desire to elect an honest candidate, rather than one who necessarily agrees with the voter on issues), or the deliberate avoidance of clear stands on important issues by one or both candidates. Nevertheless, party identification remains the single most important factor in voter decisions.[3] Yet the so-called responsible party model is not even applicable in theory to the public's participation in presidential nominations. Where the model assumes that the party will find and promote appropriate candidates, the new system of nomination has shifted this task to the public.

## THE PARADOX OF CANDIDATE POPULARITY

Conventional wisdom holds that the public is generally suspicious of politicians, their character, motives, and competence. Indeed, the decline in public trust of government officials over the past twenty years or so is substantial and has been well chronicled.[4] A majority of survey respondents in recent years agreed that quite a few public officials: Don't know what they're doing; can't be trusted to do what's right most of the time; and don't care what the average citizen thinks or wants. A 1981 Eagleton Poll found that nearly two thirds of New Jersey residents surveyed said that their overall impression of politicians was unfavorable rather than favorable, and that most people are in politics for personal gain rather than public service.[5]

Given this generally negative view of politicians, public reaction to new and little-known presidential candidates is surprisingly positive. To be sure, not all aspirants are greeted by the public with open arms, but over half of the newcomers in 1976 and 1980 were at some point during the nomination campaign regarded favorably by a majority of citizens holding opinions. The better-known candidates (often those who had tried for the presidency before) were on the whole less favorably regarded than the newcomers—unless they prevailed in the nomination contests. Opinions about the candidates during the nomination tend to be ephemeral and the public's judgments are based on criteria peculiar to nomination politics. Taking an obvious cue from journalists, the public's most important criterion is success. Since most of the candidates must ultimately be unsuccessful in securing the nomination, most candidates lose popularity over the course of the nomination.

The warm greeting given to newcomers who have early successes is, despite the public's suspicion of politicians as a class, not as paradoxical as it might seem. Political psychologists have long noted a phenomenon labeled the "positivity bias," in which individual politicians are generally rated favorably by the public. Sears and Whitney note that this bias is quite strong in the United States and speculate that it may have its roots in a general tendency of people to rate other individuals positively (a so-called "leniency effect"), and a specific national intolerance for political conflict or partisanship.[6] A familiar example of this is Fenno's observation that while Congress may be unpopular, individual *members* of Congress are usually well regarded.[7] Thus politicians as a *class* may be seen as loathsome, but individual politicians are people, and eligible for the same break accorded any other person. The New Jersey sample mentioned above provides support for this notion, for while over 60 percent had unfavorable impressions of politicians overall, less than 40 percent had unfavorable impressions of their own New Jersey politicians (despite the fact that several important New Jersey officials had been convicted of crimes in the last two decades).

Another reason for the warm reception accorded some candidates may be a political kind of wishful thinking. Despite—or perhaps because of—the low regard for politicians as a class, the public retains hope that someone better may come along. These hopes can be more easily projected on new candidates about whom little is known. Public attitudes toward the Republican candidates after the well-publicized first round of the Iowa caucuses provide a clear example of this phenomenon, and offer some evidence about the basis on which early public responses to the candidates are made.

The precinct-level party caucuses held on January 26, 1980, were the first round of a multi-stage process leading to the selection of delegates to the parties' national nominating conventions. Though relatively insignificant in terms of the numbers of delegates eventually selected, the Iowa caucuses attracted a disproportionate amount of journalistic attention. As shown by our analysis in Chapter 4, the caucuses were prominent enough that quite a large portion of the New Jersey public became aware of the candidacies of Ronald Reagan and George Bush, despite the fact that New Jersey residents

## TABLE 7.1

### Opinion of Republican Candidates Before and After the 1980 Iowa Precinct Caucuses

|  | October 1979 | February 1980 |
|---|---|---|
| Bush |  |  |
| Republicans | 65% | 85% |
| Democrats | 49 | 74 |
| Anderson |  |  |
| Republicans | 53 | 67 |
| Democrats | 47 | 77 |
| Baker |  |  |
| Republicans | 80 | 73 |
| Democrats | 66 | 61 |
| Connally |  |  |
| Republicans | 49 | 34 |
| Democrats | 27 | 21 |
| Reagan |  |  |
| Republicans | 69 | 56 |
| Democrats | 40 | 31 |

*Note:* Entries are percent favorable, based on those respondents willing to judge. Party groups include "leaners."
*Source:* Eagleton Poll of Rutgers University.

would not have to vote in their own primary for nearly five months. Of all the Republican candidates, only Bush and Anderson enjoyed increases in the proportion of citizens with favorable impressions of them.* They were also the only two for whom the level of opinion-

---

*In the New Jersey surveys, respondents who were able to name or to recognize the candidates were asked: "Is your general impression of him favorable or unfavorable; or don't you have an opinion about him?" In the CBS News/*New York Times* surveys, respondents were instructed: "If you haven't heard much about someone I name, just tell me," and then asked: "Do you have a favorable or unfavorable opinion about [name], or don't you know enough about him to have an opinion?" These questions are our basic measures of candidate popularity throughout this chapter. The percentage of respondents with a favorable impression of a particular candidate is based upon all respondents who said they had an opinion of that candidate.

ation increased. Nationwide surveys conducted by CBS News and the *New York Times* show essentially the same phenomenon, except that opinionation rose only 4 percent for Anderson and (perhaps consequently) his popularity declined slightly. Table 7.1 shows the Eagleton data for the Republican candidates, and Table 7.2 shows the national data. The January interviews were completed before the caucuses were held. Bush received slightly more caucus votes than Reagan, but his success was proclaimed a "surprising victory" by journalists who had expected Reagan to do better. As seen in Chapter 5, relatively few respondents in the CPS National Election Study's February survey knew much about Bush. But the prominent coverage of the caucuses ensured that many citizens knew who had been successful and who had not. Those candidates who had not done well lost popularity. Every Republican candidate except Bush (and in the

**FIGURE 7.1**

**Opinion of Reagan and Connally by Party, 1980**
**(New Jersey Data)**

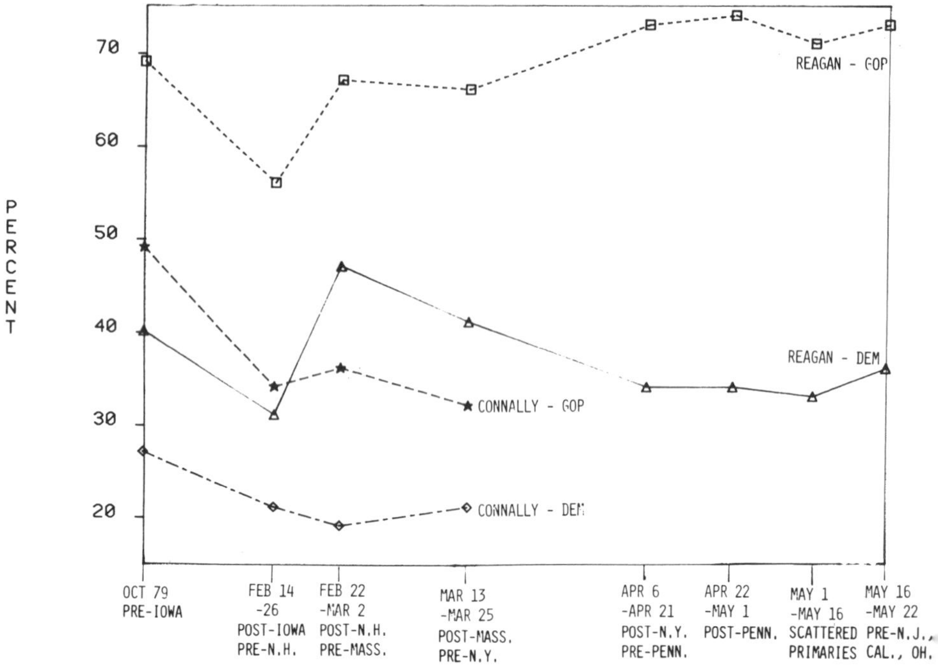

**FIGURE 7.2**

**Opinion of Carter and Anderson, 1980, by Party**
**(New Jersey Data)**

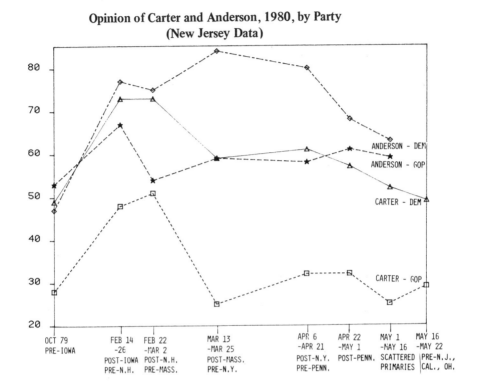

New Jersey sample, Anderson) declined in popularity from interviews conducted before the caucuses to those conducted afterward.

## THE DYNAMICS OF OPINION
## DURING THE PRIMARIES

The responsiveness of public opinion to success and failure in the
Iowa caucuses is characteristic of the primaries as well, in both 1976
and 1980. The effect is greater in the early contests, when opinions
are still being formed, but is also seen in the later Democratic primaries in 1976 when Carter was being challenged by Brown and
Church. Public judgments about the candidates are partially dependent on the context in which they are made. Having joined the battle,
candidates are judged on their effectiveness. In virtually all cases,

losers declined in popularity until they quit the race. Winning brought gains in popularity, although the relationship was not a direct one but was dependent on *how* the candidate's performance was depicted by journalists. To facilitate discussion of those dynamics, we will refer to one set of figures and two tables showing the changes in candidate popularity through the nomination period: Figures 7.1 through 7.4 show the popularity of eight candidates in 1980 among our New Jersey samples, and Table 7.2 shows their popularity for national samples. Table 7.3 shows the popularity of the candidates in 1976 for national samples.

Although Reagan's popularity dipped after Iowa in 1980, the decline did not prevent him from registering a strong first place finish in New Hampshire. Figure 7.1, showing the response of the New Jersey samples, indicates that Reagan's success restored to him the popularity he had lost after Iowa. Bush's decline (Figure 7.4) after

**FIGURE 7.3**

**Opinion of Kennedy and Baker, 1980, by Party
(New Jersey Data)**

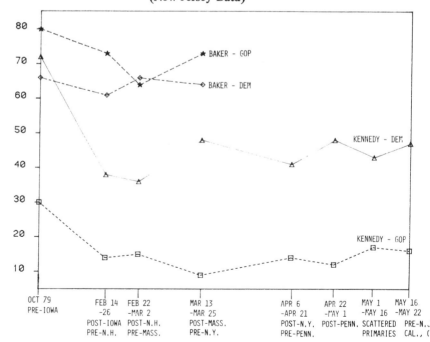

**FIGURE 7.4**

**Opinion of Bush and Brown, 1980, by Party**
**(New Jersey Data)**

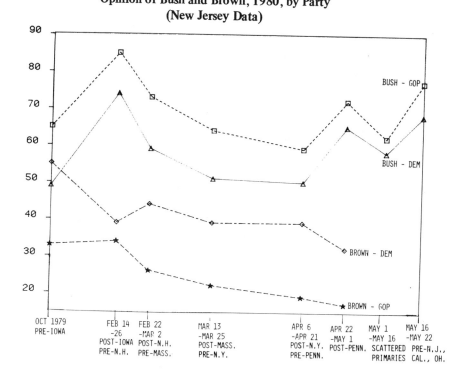

New Hampshire was almost as sharp as his rise before it. One week after New Hampshire, primaries were held in Massachusetts and Vermont. Reagan finished first in Vermont and Bush finished first in Massachusetts, but Anderson was a close second in both states. Bush's "win" was not well publicized as journalists chose instead to speculate about Anderson's chances in the wake of his surprisingly strong showing. Bush's popularity declined further, and Anderson's was boosted (Figure 7.2).

National surveys conducted by CBS News and the *New York Times* do not permit a primary-by-primary analysis, but the overall patterns for 1976 and 1980 support the generalizations made so far. Table 7.2 shows national data for 1980. Dole, Baker, Crane, and Connally were considered losers in the Iowa caucuses. The popularity of all four men declined from the January to the February interviews. Dole dropped out before the first round of primaries,

**TABLE 7.2**

**Opinion of Candidates, January–June 1980, by Party**

|  | January | February | March | April | June |
|---|---|---|---|---|---|
| **Carter** | | | | | |
| Republicans | 39% | 45% | 34% | 32% | 23% |
| Democrats | 70 | 76 | 66 | 56 | 46 |
| **Reagan** | | | | | |
| Republicans | 70 | 56 | 69 | 75 | 85 |
| Democrats | 40 | 38 | 35 | 43 | 40 |
| **Bush** | | | | | |
| Republicans | 55 | 74 | 56 | 53 | 62 |
| Democrats | 31 | 55 | 39 | 38 | 44 |
| **Anderson** | | | | | |
| Republicans | 40 | 33 | 46 | 40 | 38 |
| Democrats | 31 | 29 | 53 | 45 | 44 |
| **Kennedy** | | | | | |
| Republicans | 25 | 15 | 16 | 17 | 16 |
| Democrats | 57 | 40 | 40 | 40 | 47 |
| **Dole** | | | | | |
| Republicans | 39 | 28 | — | — | — |
| Democrats | 28 | 21 | — | — | — |
| **Baker** | | | | | |
| Republicans | 64 | 62 | — | — | — |
| Democrats | 60 | 53 | — | — | — |
| **Crane** | | | | | |
| Republicans | 38 | 36 | — | — | — |
| Democrats | 46 | 21 | — | — | — |
| **Brown** | | | | | |
| Republicans | 21 | 22 | 15 | — | — |
| Democrats | 31 | 30 | 21 | — | — |
| **Connally** | | | | | |
| Republicans | 49 | 35 | — | — | — |
| Democrats | 28 | 27 | — | — | — |
| **Ford** | | | | | |
| Republicans | — | — | 82 | — | — |
| Democrats | — | — | 59 | — | — |

*Note:* Entries are percent favorable, based on those respondents willing to judge. Party groups in all months except June include "leaners."
*Source:* CBS News/*New York Times* monthly surveys.

and these contests provided further discouragement to the other three. Baker and Connally dropped out in early March, while Crane waited until April. Thus all four were winnowed out before even 10 percent of Republican primary voters were able to pass judgment on them. Questions about them were not even included on the March national survey.

On the Democratic side in 1980, Brown campaigned until April 1. The 12 percent of the vote he received in the Wisconsin primary that day was his best showing. Even at the start of the primaries he was very unpopular, and his lack of success led to a further decline in public approval of him. Kennedy did poorly in the Iowa caucuses and encountered hostility when he suggested that Carter might be using international events as an excuse not to campaign. Kennedy's popularity declined sharply from January to February, while Carter's increased. Although given little chance to win the nomination, Kennedy campaigned vigorously and finished first in several primaries, including Connecticut, New York, and Pennsylvania. Carter's popularity was declining during this period, speeded perhaps by Kennedy's campaign against him and by international events, but Kennedy was able only to hold his own popularity steady.

The Democratic race in 1976 provides many parallels to the experiences of 1980. Table 7.3 shows Carter's popularity already very high in February 1976 (the February survey, the first of the year, was conducted after Carter's "introduction" in the Iowa caucuses). His chief rivals, Jackson and Udall, were relatively popular among the few Democrats and Independents who had opinions about them in February. Jackson finished first in Massachusetts, but did not contest New Hampshire and finished third in the highly-publicized Florida primary. From February to March, he was able only to maintain his popularity. Udall had no first-place finishes during this period, and while he became slightly better known he was less well regarded in March than in February, losing nearly 20 percent in favorable impressions among Democrats and Independents. He finished only 1 percent behind Carter in Wisconsin but this failure to win in a progressive state was much discussed by the press. The CBS News/*New York Times* poll one week later found that his popularity had slipped another 10 percent; at this point, more Democrats held unfavorable than favorable opinions of him. If everybody loves a winner, it appears that the converse is also true.

Although Carter was generally conceded the 1976 nomination by May (as Hubert Humphrey chose not to wage a campaign), he began to come under greater scrutiny by journalists and was challenged in

**TABLE 7.3**

**Opinion of Candidates, February–June, 1976**

| | February | March | April | May | June |
|---|---|---|---|---|---|
| Carter | | | | | |
| Republicans | 57% | 59% | 43% | 47% | 62% |
| Democrats | 81 | 80 | 66 | 63 | 87 |
| Ford | | | | | |
| Republicans | 77 | 84 | 79 | 75 | 80 |
| Democrats | 45 | 50 | 47 | 40 | 48 |
| Wallace | | | | | |
| Republicans | 39 | 40 | 35 | 31 | — |
| Democrats | 42 | 31 | 29 | 26 | — |
| Humphrey | | | | | |
| Republicans | 28 | 31 | 28 | 26 | — |
| Democrats | 60 | 65 | 63 | 61 | — |
| Church | | | | | |
| Republicans | — | 28 | 27 | 24 | 71 |
| Democrats | — | 55 | 45 | 44 | 76 |
| Brown | | | | | |
| Republicans | — | — | 53 | 52 | — |
| Democrats | — | — | 56 | 64 | — |
| Reagan | | | | | |
| Republicans | 77 | 67 | 72 | 72 | 69 |
| Democrats | 43 | 46 | 43 | 49 | 52 |
| Udall | | | | | |
| Republicans | 34 | 26 | 17 | 29 | — |
| Democrats | 73 | 54 | 44 | 54 | — |
| Shriver | | | | | |
| Republicans | 25 | — | — | — | — |
| Democrats | 60 | — | — | — | — |
| Bayh | | | | | |
| Republicans | 31 | — | — | — | — |
| Democrats | 75 | — | — | — | — |
| Jackson | | | | | |
| Republicans | 38 | 40 | 33 | — | 49 |
| Democrats | 62 | 68 | 52 | — | 56 |
| Harris | | | | | |
| Republicans | 19 | 24 | 21 | — | — |
| Democrats | 70 | 24 | 36 | — | — |

*Note:* Entries are percent favorable, based on those respondents willing to judge. Party groups do not include "leaners."

*Source:* CBS News/*New York Times* monthly surveys.

the late primaries by Governor Jerry Brown of California and Senator Frank Church of Idaho. Carter's popularity declined in April and May from its March high. Meanwhile, Church had four first-place finishes: Nebraska on May 11 (though this had no effect on his popularity in the CBS/*New York Times* poll taken a week later), Idaho and Oregon on May 25, and Montana on June 1. The latter three contests were prominently covered, and Church's popularity in June had jumped an amazing 37 percentage points.

Brown in 1976 was an enigmatic newcomer to national politics. Being governor of the nation's largest state accorded him a modicum of public credibility though most people knew relatively little about him. His perceived eccentricities were assets rather than liabilities in 1976. The CBS News/*New York Times* poll of April 1976 found him favorably regarded by a majority of those with opinions, including 53 percent of Republicans. The poll taken in May came immediately following Brown's first-place finish in Maryland. About twice as many respondents as in April had an opinion of him, and his popularity had risen among Democrats, though it had fallen among Independents. It was unchanged among Republicans. Brown also finished first in Nevada May 25, and received 59 percent of the vote in California on the last day of primaries, June 8. Unfortunately, the June CBS News/*New York Times* poll did not include a question on impressions of Brown, so we cannot determine the impact of his late successes on opinion about him.

## CANDIDATE SUCCESS AS A BASIS OF PUBLIC OPINION

The positive reaction of citizens—even those identifying with the opposite party—to a candidate's early successes in nominating contests suggests that the public longs for better leadership. New candidates, about whom little is known except that they have done well in the early tests, are the objects of considerable public affection. The political "new romance" that citizens have with these candidates is facilitated by the lack of information about them. Initially, citizens may easily project their hopes upon promising newcomers; but with the passage of time and the availability of new information, blemishes that were overlooked become apparent, and the public's ardor cools. The popularity of all candidates, including the victors, eventually declines.

The tendency of public opinion to shift with the fortunes of the candidates in the various campaign tests (and the way those fortunes are depicted by the press) is a fairly strong one, but in itself does not determine the eventual course of the nomination. Reagan's popularity fell a lot after Iowa, but he was still able to win a majority of votes against a crowded field in the New Hampshire primary, perhaps in part because he started the campaign as a well-known figure. Opinion shifts may have been more important in the better-balanced 1976 Democratic race in which much attention was paid to the notion of "momentum." The reaction of the spectators (who are most of the public, since 80 percent don't vote in primaries) to the early contests is consequential for two reasons: Wherever the next contest is held, the public there is thought to be more receptive to the previous contests's winners and more skeptical of its losers (as Udall colorfully noted); and shifts of opinion as reflected by the polls have a direct impact on fund raising, recruitment of volunteers, and general morale of the candidate's organization. The latter result is perhaps most important as a means of winnowing the field, effectively producing the early death of the more impecunious candidates.

Yet momentum is not inexorable. The phenomenon of momentum, or its extreme form, the "bandwagon," has been widely discussed in the literature on public opinion and elections.[8] In general elections, the "underdog effect" appears as often as the bandwagon. In primaries, the consequences of ephemeral bandwagons are more noteworthy (the winnowing effect) but they still can be checked. Patterson suggests that the likelihood of bandwagons varies according to the strength of initial commitment by citizens to the candidates. In the 1976 Republican race, very little attitude change occurred as a result of campaign events, and in fact citizens' attitudes toward the candidates had a greater impact on their perceptions of the competitive standing of the candidates than vice-versa.[9] In 1980, long standing attitudes toward Reagan undoubtedly minimized the effects of the early assault on him by Bush and Anderson.

As we have noted, momentum is a function not only of the objective situation, but also of how the situation is portrayed. In particular, the salience of campaign events is highly manipulable by journalists, whose greatest power is, as Bernard Cohen put it, to tell people what to think *about* rather than what to think.[10] News organizations have received a great deal of criticism for the heavy emphasis on early contests, and for interpretations that have the effect of fueling bandwagons. Michael J. Robinson argues in his analysis of the media in the 1980 election that journalists consciously strove to lessen their impact on the nomination campaign. Though the early contests still received disproportionate attention, Robinson observed a phenomenon he calls the "new tentativeness" in interpreting results. Further, journalists more quickly turned on their own creations. As soon as Bush and Anderson faltered, the positive themes of the coverage became negative.[11] This tendency to attack front-runners may thus serve as a check on bandwagons, though if closure of the nomination process continues to occur as early as it has in most of the postreform contests, the only result may be marital discord with the hastily chosen partner who now cannot be divorced.[12]

A citizen's decision to like or dislike a candidate might logically be based upon the candidate's performance in campaign tests, but such a criterion for judgment is not what the reformers had in mind when they ceded new power to the party rank-and-file. Much of the public's approval or disapproval of candidates, particularly in the early part of the campaign, appears to be based upon how effective the candidates are in playing the game. Yet the game is being played in places that are not necessarily representative of the nation as a whole, and the changing field of candidates introduces a generous portion of luck into the outcomes. That citizens would base their opinion of a candidate on how he did in, say, New Hampshire (or more correctly, how journalists said he did) and not on his character, intelligence, or position on issues, would seem to undermine an important rationale for the new nominating system.

This negative interpretation might be tempered if only a portion of the public—in particular, the less interested and less attentive public—was influenced by the candidates' early fortunes. But both Patterson's 1976 panel study and our 1980 data show that all citizens, regardless of the amount of attention paid to the campaign, were affected by candidate performance and the most attentive were often the most affected.[13]

Table 7.4 shows the proportion of respondents with favorable impressions of candidates in the 1980 CBS News/*New York Times* surveys, divided according to how much attention they said they had been paying to the campaign. The jump in favorable impressions for Bush, the one Iowa "winner," is about as large for the most attentive group as for those who paid less attention. On the other hand, the popularity of all the Iowa losers except Crane declined more among the attentive than the nonattentive. Similarly, Anderson's splash in the early March primaries made a bigger impression on the attentive than the nonattentive.

We point out the fact that attentive citizens respond to candidate success and failure not to rebuke the citizenry but rather to comment on the information environment. Those citizens who by virtue of

# TABLE 7.4

## Opinion of Candidates 1980 by Attention to the Campaign

| | Amount of Attention | January | February | March | April | June |
|---|---|---|---|---|---|---|
| Carter | A lot | 52% | 62% | 41% | 44% | 29% |
| | Some | 60 | 63 | 54 | 45 | 41 |
| | Not much | 58 | 67 | 57 | 49 | 37 |
| Dole | A lot | 32 | 16 | — | — | — |
| | Some | 28 | 23 | — | — | — |
| | Not much | 39 | 29 | — | — | — |
| Baker | A lot | 64 | 55 | — | — | — |
| | Some | 64 | 56 | — | — | — |
| | Not much | 55 | 57 | — | — | — |
| Crane | A lot | 30 | 27 | — | — | — |
| | Some | 43 | 28 | — | — | — |
| | Not much | 54 | 28 | — | — | — |
| Reagan | A lot | 49 | 40 | 49 | 57 | 56 |
| | Some | 53 | 43 | 47 | 54 | 59 |
| | Not much | 53 | 50 | 51 | 58 | 60 |
| Brown | A lot | 17 | 14 | 11 | — | — |
| | Some | 26 | 25 | 21 | — | — |
| | Not much | 33 | 33 | 19 | — | — |
| Bush | A lot | 48 | 71 | 49 | 45 | 56 |
| | Some | 36 | 66 | 49 | 45 | 52 |
| | Not much | 39 | 57 | 37 | 40 | 46 |
| Connally | A lot | 35 | 25 | — | — | — |
| | Some | 36 | 30 | — | — | — |
| | Not much | 36 | 31 | — | — | — |
| Anderson | A lot | 46 | 40 | 57 | 42 | 40 |
| | Some | 34 | 26 | 52 | 48 | 50 |
| | Not much | 22 | 28 | 41 | 34 | 40 |
| Kennedy | A lot | 36 | 25 | 25 | 30 | 32 |
| | Some | 42 | 26 | 27 | 25 | 32 |
| | Not much | 48 | 37 | 33 | 38 | 36 |
| Ford | A lot | — | — | 64 | — | — |
| | Some | — | — | 71 | — | — |
| | Not much | — | — | 67 | — | — |

*Note:* Entries are percent favorable, based on those respondents willing to judge.

*Source:* CBS News/*New York Times* monthly surveys.

their attention to the campaign are presumably better able to make judgments on other grounds are just as influenced by candidates' campaign successes and failures as the rest of the public. This fact suggests that the information on which to base other kinds of judgment is in short supply. There is no surprise in the fact that those who pay attention to the contest are more likely to respond to journalists' interpretations. As analyses by Patterson in 1976 and Robinson in 1980 showed, those interpretations focus heavily on winning and losing, rather than on the candidates' qualities and policies.[14]

Interestingly, attentive citizens began the campaign in January 1980 with more favorable impressions of those new candidates destined to do well (Bush and Anderson) than did less attentive citizens; further, they had less favorable views of those destined to be losers (Dole, Crane, Connally, Brown; Baker is the exception) than did the less attentive. The better-known candidates (Carter, Kennedy, and Reagan) were less well liked by the attentive than the nonattentive, and this difference persisted throughout the campaign. This phenomenon could be described as prescience by the attentive public, but it might also result from the fact that the attentive public was more likely to participate in the nomination process and thus to affect the outcome in ways consistent with their opinions.

A final observation concerning the public's use of a candidate's success as a criterion for judging him comes from the popularity of vanquished candidates after their defeat. After the primaries concluded, most of the defeated candidates for whom we have data made "comebacks" in popularity, lending metaphorical support to Thomas B. Reed's observation that "a statesman is a dead politician."[15] Bush and Kennedy were resurrected in June 1980. In 1976, Jackson was more popular in June than he was just before he quit the race in April. Udall was more popular in May, after journalistic coroners had tagged the toe of his campaign, than he was in April as an active contestant. Church's popularity in June was far higher than in May, a function perhaps both of his late successes and the conclusion of the contest. Three other Democrats (Glenn, Mondale, and Stevenson) included in the CBS News/*New York Times* June survey as potential vice-presidential candidates were rated more highly by respondents than any presidential contender. Of course, we cannot know how they might have been rated in January or February had they been active candidates, but the high ratings (which cut across party lines) lend further support to the notion that the public applies different standards after the active contest for the nomination than during it.

## THE INFLUENCE OF PARTISANSHIP AND IDEOLOGY
## ON PUBLIC OPINION OF CANDIDATES

While we have seen the impact of a candidate's success and failure on his popularity, it is clear that candidates are not liked or disliked solely on the basis of their effectiveness in playing the nominating game. Two traditional bases of opinion are partisanship and ideological orientation. These allow citizens to make rational choices aimed at selecting leaders consistent with their political beliefs, while at the same time minimizing the investment of time spent gathering information about the various candidates' values and issue positions.

Partisanship and ideology are not, however, easily employed by citizens during the nominations. Since most states do not permit crossover voting in primaries, partisanship is not particularly relevant to a specific nomination decision. Furthermore, a candidate's ideological leaning is often ambiguous. Many citizens are uncomfortable with liberal-conservative terminology and are unwilling to locate themselves ideologically or do so in ways quite inconsistent with the conventionally accepted meaning of the terms. As we saw in Chapter 5, a majority of the public was unable to describe any candidate except Carter in ideological terms. Nevertheless, journalists frequently describe candidates as liberal or conservative and some citizens attempt to make use of this information in orienting themselves toward the candidates.

To what extent do partisanship and ideology affect the popularity of candidates in the nomination period? How does this influence vary with the nomination cycle? To answer these questions, we examined the popularity of the candidates through the nomination period with our samples divided according to party identification and ideological self-placement. In addition, we performed a multiple regression of candidate popularity on partisanship and ideology (not shown here) so as to estimate the independent effects of each on opinions about the candidates.

Patterson found in 1976 that the effects of partisanship were weaker during the primaries than during the general election: "Apparently, partisanship is not as strong a psychological defense in the primaries—election day is still months away, and the voters' partisan biases are not fully mobilized."[16] Patterson attributes this phenomenon to a variety of factors including competition within the party during the primaries, the delay in making voting decisions characteristic of recent elections, and the politically neutral character of news during the primaries.

Candidates vary considerably in how similarly they are viewed across parties. In general, better-known candidates are viewed less similarly by Democrats and Republicans. Tables 7.2 and 7.3, which show opinions of the candidates divided by party of respondent, reveal relatively wide gaps between partisans for Carter, Reagan, Kennedy, and Connally in 1980. The newcomers, particularly Dole, Baker, Crane, and Anderson, were rated more similarly across parties. Our confidence in this generalization is lessened somewhat by the more distinct partisan reaction to newcomers Udall, Shriver, and Bayh in 1976, and to a lesser extent to Carter and Church. The gap between partisans was small for Brown in 1976, and it narrowed over time for Church.

The argument that partisanship has less impact on public opinion during nominations is more clearly supported when we consider the *response* of partisans to the events of the campaign. Citizens of different parties tend to react similarly to important campaign events during the nomination period, but not during the general election. Figures 7.1 through 7.4, impressions of candidates in New Jersey during the primaries, show that the opinions of Democrats and Republicans were roughly parallel, changing direction together in response to the vagaries of the campaign. After the primaries concluded, the partisan lines for Carter and Reagan (not shown here) tended to diverge.[17]

According to our regression analysis, ideological self-identification has a weaker impact on opinions than does party identification for most of the candidates in 1976 and 1980. The exceptions, however, point to the power of ideology under certain conditions. Table 7.5 shows opinions about the candidates divided according to respondent's ideology. Some candidates were labeled as ideologues. For example, Reagan was better liked by conservatives than by liberals, and the difference was between 20 and 30 percent throughout the campaigns in 1976 and 1980. But the independent impact of ideology, determined through multiple regression, was greater in 1976 when Reagan was perceived as outside the mainstream of the Republican Party, than in 1980 when he was viewed as in the mainstream. Kennedy, as we might expect, was much better liked by liberals than conservatives. In June 1980, the gap in favorable impressions between the two groups was 24 percent. Yet only in January 1980 was Kennedy liked by a majority of liberals, and amazingly, as many liberals in June liked Reagan as Kennedy.

Anderson is the other candidate in 1980 for whom ideology played an important role. We noted earlier that after the Iowa

## TABLE 7.5

**Opinion of Selected Candidates in 1976 and 1980, by Respondent's Ideology**

| Candidate | Respondent's Ideology | 1976 | | | | |
|---|---|---|---|---|---|---|
| | | February | March | April | May | June |
| Reagan | Liberal | 44% | 33% | 38% | 42% | 44% |
| | Moderate | 59 | 56 | 55 | 60 | 58 |
| | Conservative | 72 | 67 | 68 | 66 | 68 |
| Udall | Liberal | 71 | 70 | 67 | 54 | — |
| | Moderate | 66 | 46 | 30 | 44 | — |
| | Conservative | 44 | 27 | 19 | 44 | — |

| Candidate | Respondent's Ideology | 1980 | | | | |
|---|---|---|---|---|---|---|
| | | January | February | March | April | June |
| Reagan | Liberal | 47 | 35 | 31 | 38 | 48 |
| | Moderate | 46 | 43 | 44 | 54 | 55 |
| | Conservative | 61 | 53 | 65 | 69 | 72 |
| Kennedy | Liberal | 57 | 42 | 37 | 41 | 47 |
| | Moderate | 42 | 27 | 31 | 30 | 30 |
| | Conservative | 37 | 25 | 21 | 23 | 23 |
| Anderson | Liberal | 21 | 41 | 56 | 58 | 59 |
| | Moderate | 41 | 23 | 54 | 42 | 47 |
| | Conservative | 27 | 31 | 41 | 36 | 31 |

*Note:* Entries are percent favorable, based on those willing to judge.
*Source:* CBS News/*New York Times* monthly surveys.

caucuses Anderson's popularity increased among our New Jersey samples but not in the CBS News/*New York Times* polls. However, the CBS News/*New York Times* data, when divided by ideology, reveal a different picture. Table 7.5 shows that among liberals, favorable impressions of Anderson increased from 21 percent to 41 percent between January and February, while among moderates they declined a lot. Due to the small number of cases, inferences must be drawn cautiously, but it is noteworthy that opinions of Anderson among liberals continued to become more favorable, while among conservatives they ultimately declined to a level near that of January. Anderson started out the campaign more popular among conservatives, but by June was more popular among liberals by nearly 30 percent.

Udall was frequently referred to as the candidate of the liberal wing of the Democratic Party in 1976. Among the small segment of the population with an opinion of him, he was very much judged on ideology. Over the three months of his active candidacy, Udall declined only 4 percent in popularity among liberals, but among moderates and conservatives his fall was precipitous. In April, nearly 50 percentage points separated the liberal and conservative impressions of him. Somewhat anomalously, this gap closed considerably in May when twice as many respondents had an opinion of him as in April.

Perceptions of a candidate's ideology are likely to vary considerably from person to person, given the multidimensionality of the concept and the relatively loose usage of it in the press. Consequently we might expect to see some perceptual distortion of a candidate's ideology according to whether the citizen likes him or not. Some of this distortion can be labeled rationalization, a process by which an individual first decides whether or not to like a candidate, and then begins to perceive the candidate as ideologically compatible or incompatible, depending upon what the judgment was. The CBS News/ *New York Times* studies asked respondents where the candidates stood ideologically. In Table 7.6 we show the correlation between the respondents' ideological self-placement and where the candidate was placed, separating those respondents with favorable impressions of the candidate from those with unfavorable impressions. The data presented here are for March of 1976 and 1980. Data for other months are similar to these.

For all candidates in both years, we observe a fairly strong tendency for those respondents who like a candidate to see him as close to them ideologically, and we see the opposite effect for those who don't like the candidate. While we might expect the effect to be strongest for the candidates who are least well known, such a tendency is not evident. Tau-B is a fairly conservative measure of correlation; the actual percentages give a better notion of the extent to which citizens' perception of candidate ideology is related to their own ideology. Among those with a favorable impression of Bush in March 1980, 46 percent of conservatives thought Bush was conservative, while only 17 percent of liberals thought so. Among those with an unfavorable impression of Bush, half of the liberals thought he was conservative, while only one fourth of conservatives thought so. The strongest effect in 1980 is seen among those with an unfavorable

## TABLE 7.6

### Relationship Between Respondent's Ideological Self-Placement and Perception of Candidate's Ideology
### (Tau–B Correlations)

| Candidate | Whole sample | Has favorable opinion of candidate | Has unfavorable opinion of candidate |
|---|---|---|---|
| March 1976 | | | |
| Reagan | .05 | .28 | -.16 |
| Udall | -.06 | .17 | -.20 |
| Jackson | .01 | .24 | -.21 |
| Carter | .11 | .22 | -.18 |
| Ford | -.05 | .08 | -.25 |
| Wallace | -.05 | .13 | -.15 |
| Humphrey | -.00 | .21 | -.17 |
| March 1980 | | | |
| Reagan | .08 | .24 | -.12 |
| Carter | .03 | .15 | -.12 |
| Kennedy | -.03 | .24 | -.10 |
| Bush | -.00 | .24 | -.18 |
| Anderson | -.07 | .16 | -.33 |
| Ford | .11 | .23 | -.04 |

*Note:* Entries are Tau–B's for the correspondence between respondent's ideological self-placement and his placement of the candidate's ideology.
*Source:* CBS News/*New York Times* monthly surveys.

impression of Anderson. Two thirds of conservatives who didn't like Anderson felt he was liberal, while only 12 percent of liberals thought so; 42 percent of liberals said he was conservative, but only 12 percent of conservatives thought so.

Jimmy Carter is thought to have profited in 1976 from a strategy of "calculated ambiguity." By being "fuzzy on the issues," it was said that he made it easier for citizens who liked him to perceive him as closer to their point of view. If Carter was in fact more successful at this than the other candidates, it should be reflected in a high correlation between respondents' own ideology and their perception of Carter's ideology. Table 7.6 shows, however, that the correlation for those who liked Carter was no higher than for those who liked Reagan, Jackson, or Humphrey.

## EFFECTS OF DIRECT EXPOSURE TO A CAMPAIGN: NEW JERSEY REACTION TO THE PENNSYLVANIA PRIMARY

Our New Jersey data provide us with a measure of citizens' "disinterested reaction" to the nomination process since New Jersey's own primary came in June, on the last day of primaries. While we presume that politically interested citizens make mental links between the campaign news they hear and the eventuality that they may need to make a vote choice, for most of the late winter and spring no immediate decision is required. More important, no campaign is directed at them. The overall flow of information is lower than during a campaign; such information as there is comes chiefly through national news media. In a campaign, mailings and phone calls reach many citizens who would otherwise avoid the campaign, and perhaps most significantly, television advertising brings information to those citizens who don't watch the news.

Learning, opinion information, and attitude change are presumably facilitated by a campaign. Yet the New Jersey primary was essentially irrelevant to the outcome in 1980, and the candidates made little effort there. Thus our data are not particularly useful in allowing us to ascertain the public opinion effects of a campaign directed at the state's residents. However, New Jersey's unusual media environment and its proximity to Pennsylvania provide us with a unique opportunity to assess the effects of information flow.

New Jersey has no VHF commercial television stations of its own. Residents in the northern part of the state are served by stations in New York City while residents in the southern part of the state are served by stations in Philadelphia. For the most part, New Jersey residents read in-state, regionally-oriented newspapers. Information about the Pennsylvania primary on Philadelphia television would be seen by residents of southern, but not northern New Jersey. Northern and southern residents are fairly similar demographically and politically, and they shared an important characteristic for this analysis: they were all "onlookers" at the Pennsylvania primary. Thus by dividing our sample according to region of residence, and comparing change in the regional subgroups from before the primary to after it, we have natural treatment and control groups for ascertaining the effects of televised communication about the campaign in Pennsylvania.

The Pennsylvania primary was held on April 22, 1980, and while both parties' races were nearly settled, Bush and Kennedy viewed this primary as their last best hope to demonstrate their popularity and the weaknesses of their opponents. Both invested heavily of their remaining campaign resources, and both did well in the voting: Kennedy finished slightly ahead of Carter, 45.7 percent to 45.4 percent; among Republican voters Bush had 50.2 percent to 42.5 percent for Reagan. The data presented here include 611 interviews conducted during the two weeks before the primary, and 636 interviews conducted between April 23 and May 1. It should be noted that some subgroups in the analysis had relatively few cases.*

The campaign had a clear impact on awareness of the candidates (defined as being able to name them spontaneously) for those New Jersey residents living in the southern part of the state (see Table 7.7). The effects are clearest for Republicans; all four candidates made larger gains in awareness among southern than northern Republicans. Democrats displayed a tendency to forget candidates. In the north each candidate was named by 9 percent fewer Democrats after the primary than before it. In the south, the Democrats at least held

---

*Neither segment of interviews constituted an independent sample. Yet each day's interviewing was effectively, though not perfectly, random. The two segments were quite similar demographically, providing some reassurance that observed changes from the first to the second were real and not artifacts of the way in which the data were manipulated. The major exception to this—and to the overall equivalence of the northern and southern subgroups—is on the size of place variable. The southern post-primary group was 12 percentage points more "rural" than the southern pre-primary group; in general, the northern subgroup was considerably more "urban" than the southern subgroup. Here are selected demographics by region and segment:

| | % Male | | % Urban | | % Suburban | | % Rural | | % Democratic | | % Republican | |
|---|---|---|---|---|---|---|---|---|---|---|---|---|
| | North | South | North | South | North | South | North | South | North | South | North | South |
| Mar 31–Apr 21 | 51 | 51 | 24 | 14 | 64 | 67 | 9 | 17 | 60 | 62 | 40 | 38 |
| Apr 23–May 1 | 52 | 53 | 26 | 9 | 60 | 61 | 11 | 29 | 58 | 62 | 42 | 38 |

*Note:* Numbers of cases for tables discussed in the text can be found in Appendix C.

**TABLE 7.7**

**Percent with Awareness of Candidates Before and After 1980 Pennsylvania Primary, by Party and Region of Residence in New Jersey**

|  | Democrats | | | Republicans | | |
|---|---|---|---|---|---|---|
|  | Before | After | Percent change | Before | After | Percent change |
| Kennedy |  |  |  |  |  |  |
| North | 83 | 74 | −9 | 85 | 87 | +2 |
| South | 87 | 86 | −1 | 75 | 93 | +18 |
| Carter |  |  |  |  |  |  |
| North | 87 | 76 | −9 | 86 | 89 | +3 |
| South | 87 | 86 | −1 | 83 | 90 | +7 |
| Bush |  |  |  |  |  |  |
| North | 60 | 51 | −9 | 64 | 69 | +5 |
| South | 61 | 74 | +13 | 60 | 76 | +16 |
| Reagan |  |  |  |  |  |  |
| North | 82 | 73 | −9 | 86 | 90 | +4 |
| South | 86 | 86 | 0 | 74 | 90 | +16 |

*Note:* Entries are percentage of respondents able to name the candidate when asked to name the candidates for nomination. Party groups include "leaners." *Source:* Eagleton Poll of Rutgers University.

steady in their ability to name Reagan, Carter, and Kennedy, and 13 percent more could name Bush after the primary than could do so before it.

Meanwhile, change in opinion holding was less dramatic and appeared to depend on factors other than the salience of the candidates (see Table 7.8). Among the better-known candidates, only for Reagan was there an increase in opinion-holding among residents of either region (7 percent among Republicans in southern New Jersey). Opinion-holding about Kennedy declined 10 percent among Democrats in the south, a point to which we will return in a moment. As discussed in Chapter 6, after the first round of primaries, opinion-holding about Bush had stabilized at just below 50 percent for the whole sample, substantially below the level for Reagan, Carter, and Kennedy. Thus he had not reached the ceiling imposed by the chronically disengaged segment of the public which we have labeled as the "apathetics." The campaign in Pennsylvania raised southern New Jersey residents' level of opinionation about Bush to within 10 percent of that seen for Reagan.

Related to opinionation is willingness to state a preference among the candidates. Table 7.9 shows the percentages of undecided respondents and respondents supporting candidates other than the four actively contesting the primary. Despite the fact that New Jersey residents were not faced with a choice themselves, the campaign had the effect of substantially reducing the level of indecision among those living in southern New Jersey, but had no such effect on those in the north.

The primary also produced significant changes in the direction of opinions about the candidates, and most of this change occurred among residents of southern New Jersey. Table 7.10 shows these

**TABLE 7.8**

**Percent with Opinion of Candidates Before and After 1980 Pennsylvania Primary, by Party and Region of Residence in New Jersey**

|  | Democrats | | | Republicans | | |
|---|---|---|---|---|---|---|
|  | Before | After | Percent change | Before | After | Percent change |
| Kennedy |  |  |  |  |  |  |
| North | 81 | 78 | -3 | 84 | 83 | -1 |
| South | 87 | 77 | -10 | 86 | 88 | +2 |
| Carter |  |  |  |  |  |  |
| North | 80 | 77 | -3 | 84 | 81 | -3 |
| South | 84 | 80 | -4 | 89 | 85 | -4 |
| Bush |  |  |  |  |  |  |
| North | 46 | 51 | +6 | 60 | 61 | +1 |
| South | 47 | 58 | +11 | 70 | 80 | +10 |
| Reagan |  |  |  |  |  |  |
| North | 74 | 69 | -5 | 80 | 78 | -2 |
| South | 71 | 67 | -4 | 81 | 88 | +7 |

*Note:* Entries are percentage of respondents with a favorable or unfavorable impression of the candidate.

*Source:* Eagleton Poll of Rutgers University.

**TABLE 7.9**

**Percent Undecided or Preferring Other Candidates
Before and After the 1980 Pennsylvania Primary,
by Party and Region of Residence in New Jersey**

|  | Before the primary | After the primary |
|---|---|---|
| Republicans |  |  |
| Undecided: North | 24 | 24 |
| Undecided: South | 25 | 10 |
| Other Candidate: North | 22 | 23 |
| Other Candidate: South | 28 | 15 |
| Democrats |  |  |
| Undecided: North | 28 | 37 |
| Undecided: South | 27 | 19 |
| Other Candidate: North | 3 | 3 |
| Other Candidate: South | 1 | 0 |

*Note:* Entries are percentages of respondents.
*Source:* Eagleton Poll of Rutgers University.

data. All candidates except Carter enjoyed large increases in popularity among their own partisans in the south. At the same time, all candidates except Bush suffered large declines in popularity among opposite party identifiers in the south. Except for Bush, who gained as much in the north as the south, and Carter, who gained 6 percent in the north among Republicans, there was almost no change in popularity among residents of northern New Jersey. In these data, we are presented with evidence that partisanship begins to operate as a perceptual filter when information flow increases and becomes more overtly persuasive, as it did for the southern New Jersey residents exposed to the campaign via television. Carter and Kennedy became less well liked by Republicans in the south, while Reagan had a similar decline among Democrats in the south. Bush, as the lesser-known candidate, made gains among all the subgroups, although the mechanism of change in the south was different from that in the north. Awareness of and opinionation about Bush increased substantially in the south, but not in the north; consequently we may infer that at least part of his increased popularity resulted from "new

**TABLE 7.10**

Popularity of Candidates Before and After 1980 Pennsylvania Primary, by Party and Region of Residence in New Jersey

|  | Democrats | | | Republicans | | |
|  | Before | After | Percent change | Before | After | Percent change |
|---|---|---|---|---|---|---|
| Kennedy | | | | | | |
| North | 43 | 45 | +2 | 12 | 12 | 0 |
| South | 40 | 59 | +19 | 20 | 11 | -9 |
| Carter | | | | | | |
| North | 59 | 57 | -2 | 28 | 34 | +6 |
| South | 53 | 53 | 0 | 33 | 20 | -13 |
| Bush | | | | | | |
| North | 43 | 59 | +16 | 58 | 71 | +13 |
| South | 61 | 76 | +15 | 62 | 75 | +13 |
| Reagan | | | | | | |
| North | 32 | 34 | +2 | 72 | 72 | 0 |
| South | 45 | 30 | -15 | 67 | 81 | +14 |

*Note:* Entries are percent favorable, based on those willing to judge.
*Source:* Eagleton Poll of Rutgers University.

opinion" about him in the south, while his gains in the north were more likely to have come from "changed opinion." Without panel data, this must remain an inference.

Returning to an earlier observation, we noted that 10 percent fewer Democrats in the south had an opinion of Kennedy after the primary than before. Yet favorable impressions of Kennedy among Democrats in the south increased 20 points, from 40 percent favorable to 60 percent favorable. Why? Kennedy's campaign and his success was obviously effective in rallying Democrats to him, but starting from a position of relative unpopularity among Democrats, one reasonably could expect some Democrats who were impressed with Kennedy's performance to be reluctant to change their opinion dramatically in a short time span. Instead, some of those who had an initially negative view of Kennedy may have "become undecided" as a halfway house to liking Kennedy.

Changes in preferences among the candidates underscore the differences between first-hand and second-hand exposure to the campaign. As noted above, a chief effect of the campaign was to reduce the proportion of undecided respondents in southern New Jersey. Among Republicans in the south, Reagan benefited from this as much as Bush did, despite finishing second in the voting. But his support among northern New Jersey residents fell 10 percent, while Bush's increased by a similar amount. Among Democrats in the south, Kennedy gained nearly 10 percent while Carter held steady. In the north, Kennedy held steady and Carter declined 8 percent.

Thus in both parties, *the losing candidates did worse among those partisans who only heard about the loss than among those who were exposed to more extensive information in the campaign.* The residents of northern New Jersey behaved much like they had during the earlier events of the nomination, while those in the south, directly exposed to a campaign, behaved very differently.

This phenomenon should raise doubts about a system in which so much depends on the second-hand reaction of citizens to the wins and losses in faraway places. If Udall is correct, a candidate's case in one state is prejudiced by his performance in another, perhaps very different state. Winnowing occurs partly because of these second-hand reactions. Losing in Pennsylvania did not hurt the images of Reagan and Carter among those partisans in New Jersey who saw the campaign; perhaps the same thing would have been true in other primaries for candidates such as Udall, Baker, or Brown. While only a case study, our data from the Pennsylvania primary lend further support to the contention that many important decisions in the new nominating system are based upon incomplete and perhaps inappropriate kinds of information.

## INTRAPARTY POLARIZATION

The public intraparty battling inherent in a nomination system based on a series of highly visible primaries logically leads to some deleterious, if ephemeral, effects on intraparty support of candidates. Despite the Republicans' "11th Commandment" forbidding denigration of other Republicans, candidates of both parties found it necessary to attack their fellow partisans in the heat of battle. Does the nomination campaign lead to intraparty polarization among the public, and if so, how serious is this? The answer to this question bears upon the role of the nominating system in strengthening the

## TABLE 7.11

### Opinion About Candidate Pairs, by Party, 1980

| | January | | February | | March | | April | | June | |
|---|---|---|---|---|---|---|---|---|---|---|
| | Repub-licans | Demo-crats | Repub-licans | Demo-crats | Repub-licans | Demo-crats | Repub-licans | Demo-crats | Repub-licans | Demo-crats |
| Carter and Kennedy | | | | | | | | | | |
| Favorable both | 10 | 31 | 9 | 29 | 5 | 23 | 5 | 17 | 7 | 19 |
| Favorable Carter | 26 | 39 | 36 | 50 | 32 | 45 | 26 | 39 | 15 | 27 |
| Favorable Kennedy | 14 | 22 | 7 | 11 | 7 | 17 | 10 | 23 | 9 | 29 |
| Unfavorable both | 50 | 8 | 49 | 10 | 57 | 15 | 59 | 21 | 69 | 25 |
| Number of cases | (236) | (414) | (278) | (476) | (302) | (459) | (326) | (573) | (293) | (524) |
| Reagan and Bush | | | | | | | | | | |
| Favorable both | 42 | 10 | 37 | 20 | 37 | 12 | 33 | 14 | 54 | 19 |
| Favorable Bush | 16 | 17 | 33 | 32 | 20 | 25 | 18 | 22 | 8 | 25 |
| Favorable Reagan | 28 | 19 | 22 | 10 | 32 | 18 | 38 | 25 | 33 | 18 |
| Unfavorable both | 14 | 55 | 8 | 38 | 12 | 44 | 11 | 39 | 6 | 38 |
| Number of cases | (106) | (158) | (184) 84 | (289) | (168) | (221) | (191) | (273) | (176) | (239) |

*Note:* Entries are percentage of respondents, by party, based on respondents with opinions of both candidates. Columns sum to 100 percent.

*Source:* CBS News/*New York Times* monthly surveys.

parties. If the open nominating system encourages dissension within the parties, greater democracy in the selection of the nominee will have been achieved at a very high cost.

The case of 1980 in the Democratic Party is particularly interesting given the strange and sudden opinion shifts that occurred in late 1979 following the seizure of American diplomatic personnel by Iranian militants. Prior to that incident, Carter's popularity among Democrats was quite low, while Kennedy's was correspondingly high. By January 1980, a complete reversal had occurred. Other factors were involved, but it appeared that many Democrats could not simultaneously hold favorable impressions of the two men. Of course, as rivals for the nomination and spokesmen for separate segments of the Democratic Party, both contributed to this with their rhetoric; Carter promised to "whip his ass" if Kennedy ran; Kennedy ran and attacked the President as vigorously as the Republicans did.

On the Republican side, Reagan and his strongest rival, Bush, jousted vigorously but without the rancor which characterized the Democratic contest. Bush labeled Reagan's taxing and spending proposals "Voodoo Economics" while Reagan sandbagged Bush with his amiability by agreeing to an exclusive debate with Bush in New Hampshire, and then inviting the excluded candidates onto the stage as his surprised opponent sulked.

Within each party, citizens responded to the campaign by becoming more polarized. Table 7.11 shows for each party the percentage of respondents with similar and dissimilar opinions about the two candidates for their party's nomination (based on those respondents with opinions of both candidates). In January over 40 percent of Republicans had favorable impressions of both Reagan and Bush. As the campaign progressed, this figure declined; in April, only one third of Republicans liked both Reagan and Bush. A reconciliation occurred after the primaries concluded, as over half of the Republicans said they liked both men.

The bitterness of the Democratic race, and the persistence of Kennedy despite defeat, is evident in the data for the Democrats. Less than one third of the Democrats began the campaign with favorable impressions of both men, and by June, this figure had dropped below 20 percent. An omen for November, one fourth of Democrats said they didn't like either Kennedy or Carter.

The open nominating system probably contributed to Carter's defeat in November. By providing Kennedy with a convenient platform from which to attack the president, the system exacerbated Carter's inability to hold traditional Democratic voters. And while early closure of the nominations is one of the new system's most important flaws, intraparty polarization might be expected to be worse when early closure does not occur.

## THE IMPACT OF THE CONVENTIONS

An important consequence of the early closure characteristic of the new nominating system has been to eliminate the heretofore chief function of the parties' national conventions. But conventions are now important as a means of promoting party unity after divisive intraparty battling in the primaries. Much has been made of the irrelevance of recent conventions. Having only a "bit part" to play in the drama of the nomination, the conventions in 1980 attracted less attention than usual. The three major television networks still sent nearly 2,000 employees, but gave the proceedings less live coverage than in the past. Even the nation's best newspapers sent fewer reporters than in 1976. *Boston Globe* foreign-domestic editor David Greenway expressed the sentiments of many people when he said, "I think it will be a big yawn. A lot of it is traditional, a huge, four-year feast for political junkies."[18]

Yet despite the lack of hard news generated by the conventions, data from our New Jersey samples indicate that the conventions had an impact on public opinion. Carter had suffered a steep decline in popularity among both Democrats and Republicans. The Democratic convention, which featured strident denunciations of the Republicans and reaffirmation of some of the party's basic principles, provided Carter with a big boost among his own partisans. His popularity among Democrats rose 17 percentage points from interviews conducted before the convention to those conducted during and after the convention. At the same time, the popularity of Anderson among Democrats fell 10 percent and Reagan's declined 6 percent.

The effects on the respondents' expressed preference among the three candidates is even more dramatic. Figure 7.5 shows these data. In the interviews conducted before the Democratic convention, Reagan led Carter 38 percent to 18 percent. After the convention, Carter led Reagan narrowly, 29 percent to 27 percent. Though we must be cautious in inferring individual-level change from cross-sectional data, all of the change does not appear to have been a result of Reagan supporters switching to Carter. Instead, Anderson's support is involved as well. Among Republicans, Reagan declined 7 percent, Carter was unchanged, and Anderson gained 7 percent.

**FIGURE 7.5**

**Effect of Party Conventions on New Jersey Voter Preference, 1980**

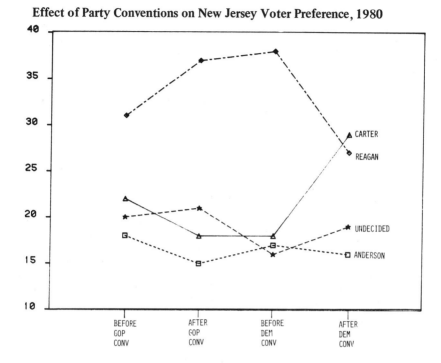

Among Democrats, Carter gained 15 percent, while Anderson declined 9 percent and Reagan declined 5 percent.

These data suggest that the main effect of the convention was to activate "latent partisans" who, until then, had been responding to the campaign on bases other than partisanship. Carter had been judged by Democrats more on his perceived failings as president (a theme repeated by Kennedy) than as a candidate for reelection against Republican opponents. Throughout the primaries, Anderson had been more popular with Democrats than with Republicans (and considerably more popular than Carter with Democrats). As a forceful speaker and a moderate, he was a romantic figure for Democrats who yearned for something Carter was not providing. Yet he was a Republican, and as speculation persisted that his presence as an independent candidate would hurt Carter more than Reagan, he was vulnerable to a reactivation of partisanship among Democrats.

Thus conventions in the new system may not be deliberative bodies with a meaningful role to play in determining the nominee, but they remain consequential for their role in promoting public fidelity to the parties. Where most aspects of the new system work to tear the party asunder, the convention is one of the few elements that serves to bring it together.

## TAKING STOCK: THE FORMATION AND CHANGE OF PUBLIC OPINION DURING PRESIDENTIAL NOMINATIONS

At this point it may be useful to offer an overview of the analysis of the past five chapters. In examining data from the most recent nominating contests we see important regularities in how the public comes to know and judge aspirants to the presidency. We believe these regularities contribute to our understanding of the origin and development of public opinion toward politicians and bear upon the quality of decisions made in nominations.

First, most of the observable movement of public opinion occurs during a fairly brief period, early in the nomination campaigns. While this may result in part from early closure of the nomination, public opinion appears to be relatively fixed even before journalists begin saying that the outcomes are determined. And despite the fact that candidates destined to lose continue to campaign in most cases, the public learns little after the first few events of the campaign season. At the beginning of a nomination contest, citizens vary considerably in what they know about the active candidates; similarly, the candidates vary in their overall visibility to the public. Most of the citizens appear to learn something new about most of the candidates during the early stages of the campaign. Some merely become aware of heretofore unknown candidates; others learn candidates' issue positions or characteristic traits. Some candidates remain invisible to portions of the public. But for almost all of the public, measureable movement ceased soon after the start of the primaries. Learning does not occur gradually, building with exposure to the campaign over time; rather it is associated with prominent early events of the campaign.

Second, on an absolute level, the general public learns relatively little about the candidates. This results both from the low level of public attention to nominations and the scarcity of useful information about the candidates. Individual citizens vary in how much they know about candidates, and this variation is related to their interest in and attentiveness to the race. Yet both attentive and inattentive citizens learn at about the same rate, suggesting that the information environment has not been rich enough to allow highly-motivated citizens to increase the "knowledge gap" between themselves and less-motivated citizens.

Third, the public judges candidates by criteria specific to presidential nominations and related to the kind of information available. The most important factor in public judgment appears to be competence in the electoral arena. The public reacted to nothing so much as a candidate's success in playing the nominating game. Candidate popularity clearly changed in response to the early contests; yet the public knew so little about the candidates at this point that most of the change must have been a result of the fortunes of the candidates, rather than any new information about their character, intelligence, or ideological perspectives. Patterson's 1976 content analysis showed that campaign news stresses the competitive positions of the candidates, and his surveys found that citizens remembered where the candidates stood in the "horserace."[19] Research on primary voting by Williams and his colleagues showed that voters may use a single salient characteristic in judging a candidate.[20] Our data strongly suggest that in the absence of better information, many citizens do indeed form impressions—and make decisions—based simply on candidate success.

Our case study of public response to the Pennsylvania primary demonstrates that other factors may enter the citizen's calculus when more information is available. Furthermore, the increased flow of information leads many undecided citizens to choose among the candidates, and many others to change their preference. From this, we may infer that decisions made by primary voters are based on more than just how well the candidates have done up to the time of their primary. Yet because of the winnowing that occurs early in the process—and the early closure of the race that often follows—and because the electorate in early states is not a microcosm of the public, early public judgments based on scant information exert a significant and distorting influence upon the outcome.

Fourth, while our data show that citizens learn more about the personal qualities of candidates than about issue positions or ideological stances, ideology in particular is important to some citizens in judging candidates. Downs has argued that ideological voting is easier than issue voting because it saves the citizen the information costs associated with becoming informed about numerous candidate issue positions. We find a relatively strong tendency for citizens to believe that candidates they like are close to them ideologically, and for some candidates (in particular, those referred to by the press in ideological terms—Edward Kennedy, Ronald Reagan, and Morris Udall) citizen ideology is related to candidate popularity. Still, despite relatively consistent labeling of the candidates by journalists, citizens varied considerably in where they located particular candidates on the ideological spectrum, suggesting that some of the congruence between candidate popularity and ideological proximity results from rationalization by the citizen. Further, data from the Center for Political Studies help to put into perspective the overall importance of ideological labeling: less than two thirds of the public could label Jimmy Carter; just over one half could label Reagan or Kennedy; and less than one third could label John Anderson or George Bush.

These generalizations paint a picture of a system in which chance and circumstance play an important role in determining which candidates succeed and which ones fail. The system is not well structured to reward the "best" candidates, regardless of whether "best" is defined as the most skillful, the smartest, the most honest, or the ones most attuned to the wishes of their party's members. Because most of the "action" occurs during the early stages of the campaign, early events and contests have disproportionate weight in the outcome; while this is a "regularity" it has the effect of magnifying the importance of atypical and unrepresentative constituencies and settings for campaigns, and increases the chances that otherwise insignificant events will influence the outcome. Because journalists are somewhat unpredictable in what they will find noteworthy, we cannot even conclude that winning early contests always pays dividends: George Bush won a primary in the second round of elections, but was ignored by a press infatuated with John Anderson. The attention paid to Anderson, who was almost certainly doomed to failure from the beginning, may have deprived the other moderate Republicans—Bush and Howard Baker—of needed attention at a time when public opinion was still malleable. Who knows how Baker might have done a month later in a different part of the country? While the system makes it possible for an occasional candidate to "strike it rich," most of the rest of the candidates—regardless of their merits—will not receive serious consideration from those doing the choosing.

## NOTES

1. Quoted in Jules Witcover, *Marathon: The Pursuit of the Presidency 1972–1976* (New York: The Viking Press, 1977), pp. 692–93.

2. See, for example: American Political Science Association Committee on Political Parties, "Toward a More Responsible Two-Party System," *American*

*Political Science Review* 44 (Supplement 1950); David S. Broder, *The Party's Over* (New York: Harper and Row, 1971); Ruth K. Scott and Ronald J. Hrebenar, *Parties in Crisis: Party Politics in America* (New York: John Wiley and Sons, 1979), pp. 300–301.

3. John A. Crittenden, *Parties and Elections in the United States* (Englewood Cliffs, N.J.: Prentice-Hall, 1982), p. 258.

4. For a concise summary of the decline in public trust of government, see David B. Hill and Norman R. Luttbeg, *Trends in American Electoral Behavior* (Itasca, Illinois: F. E. Peacock, 1980), Chapter 4.

5. Eagleton Poll Press Release: 43-3, "New Jerseyans Unimpressed by Politicians: But New Jersey Politicians Better Than Most" (Eagleton Institute of Politics, Rutgers University, New Brunswick, N.J., February 17, 1981).

6. David O. Sears and Richard E. Whitney, *Political Persuasion* (Morristown, N.J.: General Learning Press, 1973), pp. 11–14.

7. Richard Fenno, "If, As Ralph Nader Says, Congress is 'the Broken Branch,' How Come We Love Our Congressmen So Much?" in *Congress in Change*, ed. Norman J. Ornstein (New York: Praeger, 1975), pp. 277–88.

8. Herbert A. Simon, "Bandwagon and Underdog Effects and the Possibility of Election Predictions," *Public Opinion Quarterly* 18 (1954), pp. 245–53; George Gallup, "Polls and the Political Process: Past, Present and Future," *Public Opinion Quarterly* 29 (1965), p. 546; Charles K. Atkin, "The Impact of Political Poll Reports on Candidate and Issue Preferences," *Journalism Quarterly* 46 (1969), p. 519.

9. Thomas E. Patterson, *The Mass Media Election* (New York: Praeger, 1980), pp. 125–32; in addition to Patterson's research, James B. Lemert's 1976 panel study in Oregon found that citizens' perceptions of the candidates were affected by their fortunes in the early primaries: James B. Lemert, *Does Mass Communication Change Public Opinion After All?: A New Approach to Effects Analysis* (Chicago: Nelson-Hall, 1981), pp. 63–80.

10. Bernard C. Cohen, *The Press and Foreign Policy* (Princeton, N.J.: Princeton University Press, 1963), p. 13.

11. Michael J. Robinson, "The Media in 1980: Was the Message the Message?" in *The American Elections of 1980*, ed. Austin Ranney (Washington, D.C.: American Enterprise Institute for Public Policy Research, 1981), pp. 206–10.

12. Robinson makes this argument in his essay, "A Statesman is a Dead Politician: Candidate Images on Network News," *What's News: The Media in American Society*, ed. Elie Abel (San Francisco: Institute for Contemporary Studies, 1981), pp. 159–86.

13. Thomas Patterson, *The Mass Media Election* (New York: Praeger, 1980), pp. 129–30.

14. Ibid., p. 147.

15. Reed actually said, "A statesman is a successful politician who is dead."

16. Thomas Patterson, *The Mass Media Election* (New York: Praeger, 1980), p. 147.

17. See Scott Keeter and Cliff Zukin, "The 1980 Presidential Election: Tracking Citizens' Opinions and Preference," paper presented at the 1981 Annual Meeting of the Midwest Political Science Association, Cincinnati, Ohio, April 15–18, 1981.

18. Quoted by Dom Bonafede, "The Press Makes News in Covering the 1980 Primary Election Campaign," *National Journal* 12 (July 12, 1980), p. 1134.

19. Thomas E. Patterson, *The Mass Media Election* (New York: Praeger, 1980), Chapters 3, 11.

20. Daniel C. Williams et al., "Voter Decision Making in a Primary Election: An Evaluation of Three Models of Choice," *American Journal of Political Science* 20 (February 1976), p. 47. See also Mark J. Wattier, "Voting in the 1980 Democratic Presidential Primaries," paper presented at the Annual Meeting of the Southern Political Science Association, October 1982, Atlanta, Georgia.

# 8

# JUDGING THE SYSTEM

The tide of reform is now going out. Surprised by unintended consequences of the post-1968 changes in the nominating process, the Democratic Party has taken steps to strengthen the role played by its leaders in the nominating process. Such a move could be viewed as anti-democratic, but democracy comes in many different forms. While presidential nominations in the United States presently embody a kind of democracy in which the voter directly controls the outcome, a system of representative decision making can also be called democratic. Given our analysis of public opinion and participation in presidential nominations, the task before us now is to consider how the particular version of democracy embodied in our nominating system comports with a variety of standards by which a political process may be judged. We will begin this chapter with an overview of the findings of our study, and discuss the pertinence of these findings to an evaluation of the system. Next, we will describe the gap between what the reformers intended when they changed the system and the consequences of those changes. We then turn to more general standards by which to judge the system. Finally, we discuss the possible impact of "counterrevolution" within the Democratic Party, and speculate about alternative procedures for nominating presidential candidates.

## THE FINDINGS

Our examination of public attitudes in the 1976 and 1980 nominations turned up a number of new observations about political behavior. Yet more striking than what was new was the essential continuity of our findings with widely-accepted theories of the formation and change of public opinion and the behavior of voters. While the overall portrait of the public may not be surprising to students of mass political behavior, the findings bear directly upon the assessment of a system now based mostly upon mass participation.

The public was not much interested or engaged in nomination politics. Some citizens became more interested over the course of the campaign, but many others lost interest. Concomitantly, we found that most citizens learned little about the candidates despite the length of the campaign and its prominence in the news. Some citizens learned almost nothing, including the names of the contestants. Yet we are not impelled by these findings to a conclusion that the public is indifferent about the nominations, or does not want to have a role in them, or is incapable of meaningful participation. A number of factors account for the low level of citizen engagement we observed.

First, in three of the four races in 1976 and 1980, the outcome was decided relatively early in the process. Despite the fact that the campaigns ran from January to June, for almost three months of that time there was no suspense about the outcome and no compelling reason (except perhaps for ritualistic satisfaction) for the citizen to observe or to participate. We should, therefore, be less surprised to find relatively little growth in interest. The absolute level of interest we observed leads to a second consideration: what is an appropriate standard for judging the public's interest? While only a minority of the public (about one third) claimed to be very much interested in February of 1980, this is at least as high as the level of interest observed in the midst of the general election. Thus while nominations are more confusing than general elections, and maybe of less intrinsic interest to the one third of the public who are Independents, and while voting in a primary may be a more difficult act than voting in a general election, public interest in nominations is about as high as in the general election. Of course, since the task at hand—choosing a nominee—is a more difficult one than voting in a general election, it may require a higher level of interest (both individually and collectively) for a well-informed public decision.

Third, our analysis is based for the most part on national data, or on data which examine the "disinterested" response of citizens in places where the campaign was not focused. For those citizens at whom a campaign is aimed, public opinion may be substantially different. Our data allow us only a few glimpses of such effects. New Hampshire primary voters reported paying much more attention to the nomination than did a national sample of citizens interviewed at the same time. Citizens in New Jersey who were exposed to the television version of the primary campaign in Pennsylvania learned more about the candidates and were more likely to express a candidate preference than were comparable New Jersey residents not exposed to the campaign. But of course national public opinion affects the outcome by giving cues to the media and to potential supporters of different candidates, even if those with a direct voice in the process—*the primary electorates*—are more interested in the campaign and better informed about the candidates than the public at large.

Despite relatively low levels of interest and information, most of the public form impressions and make judgments about the candidates, judgments that indirectly (through polls) and directly (through support and votes) determine the outcome of the nomination. The bases on which citizens make these judgments are not entirely clear, but our analysis indicates the most important factor is the competitive standing of the candidates. Candidates who do well, especially early in the process, become more popular while those who don't do well become less popular. This phenomenon may have a rational component for some; party members might reasonably be impressed by evidence of a candidate's electability as demonstrated in a primary (even if in a state very different from the rest of the nation). But this interpretation probably applies to a relatively small part of the public. Moreover, we observed that citizens of *both* parties tended to react similarly to candidate successes and failures during the nomination campaign. The public learns what the media stress, and the media stress the competitive standing of the candidates.[1]

Because public opinion is influenced by the outcome of campaign tests and the way those tests are interpreted by journalists, the seriality of the nomination contests becomes an independent influence upon the outcome. Early contests affect later ones by sensitizing and predisposing the electorates in later states to the candidates. This is in part what is meant by "momentum," which while not ensuring the nomination of a candidate who temporarily finds himself in possession of it, makes short work of those candidates who don't have any of it. Citizens who live in states with early contests invariably have both more power and a different kind of power than those in the later states. The system may not always lead to closure as early as seen in 1976 and 1980, but as long as the campaign moves from state to state over a period of months, power among the states will be unbalanced. To the extent that early closure *is* characteristic of future nominations, we will continue to see a large part of the public chronically disengaged and disenfranchised from the nomination process and perhaps increasingly cynical about the disjuncture between the democratic goals of the system and its "snap judgment" reality.

## IMPLEMENTING THE REFORM GOALS: INTENTIONS AND OUTCOMES

The nominating process was changed in response to demands for greater openness in the selection of the nominee and a greater sensitivity to political change. In short, the objective of reform was a democratization of the process. The most noteworthy means by which this democratization was effected—a proliferation of primaries—was not intended by the reformers. Before inveighing against the new system, an examination of the ways in which it has not conformed to the intentions of the reformers may be instructive.

Although many people had a hand in shaping the recent evolution of the nominating system, the Democratic Party's McGovern-Fraser Commission was, by most accounts, the impetus for contemporary changes. The 1968 Democratic National Convention selected Hubert Humphrey as the nominee over candidates with greater popular support, and the McGovern-Fraser Commission subsequently recommended changes in party procedures which would serve to increase the representativeness of convention delegates. But as Austin Ranney, a member of the McGovern-Fraser Commission, has noted, primaries were not favored as the best method for attaining greater representativeness. Ranney has written:

> Indeed, we hoped to prevent any such development by reforming the delegate-selection rules so that the party's nonprimary process would be open and fair, participation in them would greatly increase, and consequently the demand for more primaries would fade away.... But we got a rude shock.... We accomplished the opposite of what we intended.[2]

For several reasons, states chose to adopt primaries instead of changing rules for caucuses and conventions. Some states viewed primaries as the easiest and safest way to conform to the new rules so as to avoid a possible convention challenge to the legitimacy of their delegation. Others genuinely believed that primaries best satisfied the goals of an open system. The growth of primaries was also facilitated by allies of particular candidates who believed that primaries were their best hope for success.

Two other important sets of actors viewed primaries as the preferred method of nominations. One was the news media, whose notion of democracy might best be described as "rule by unfiltered public opinion." Although journalists may strive to report the news in an unbiased fashion, their preference for unmediated citizen control of nominations has been noted by many observers. Richard Rubin, drawing on a content analysis of CBS News coverage of nominations from 1968 to 1976, describes the nature and form of this bias:

> The basic political posture of television journalism toward alternative nomination processes was to favor primaries versus state caucus/convention methods, both in amount of coverage and in the positive nature of story treatment. The positive treatment of the primaries *as a process* was in part due to the fact that television, compared to print journalism, had (and still has) far more difficulty in covering stories of complex elite negotiations (such as occur in caucuses and state conventions) than election campaigns and action-oriented events.[3]

Journalists may favor a process based on primaries because they have greater power to influence the outcome under such a system. But perhaps a more important basis for the attitude of the press is its belief in the divinity of direct democracy: a genuine ideological predisposition toward the making of political choices in the "marketplace of ideas." Pluralistic politics, while not entirely opaque to television, is always suspect in the mind of the journalist precisely because it attempts to bring order to politics. As Weaver argues, this may explain part of the journalistic fascination with the New Hampshire primary, where "retail" politics of face-to-face campaigning occurs, as opposed to a state like New York, which features "wholesale" politics with interest group activity (such as by labor unions) exerting an important influence on the voting.[4]

The other important set of actors that supported the spread of primaries was an amalgam of conservatives and nonideological party activists who feared that open caucuses would be captured by ideological zealots to the detriment of the party's chances in the general election. McCorkle and Fleishman, writing about the "intellectual ironies" of party reform, note that direct democracy has traditionally been opposed by many conservatives.[5] Yet within the Democratic Party, fears arose after McGovern's nomination in 1972 that open caucuses were too easily commandeered by liberal, programmatic activists. The caucuses were open enough to invite take-overs by small cadres of highly committed supporters of ideological candidates, but still too obscure for wide participation by mainstream Democrats (who tended to be less knowledgeable about participation). At the same time, the voice of the voter was becoming increasingly conservative, as evidenced by the results of various referenda and George Wallace's success in primaries. Thus , contend McCorkle and Fleishman, an important historical foe of primaries did not step forward to oppose their growth.

More generally, the timing and direction of the reforms can be linked with important social and political changes of the period.[6] Technological change facilitated the independence of candidates from party organizations that previously had been the only realistic base for extensive campaigning. With such innovations as the jet airplane, television and its vast audience, polling, and computer targeting and mailing, candidates were much less dependent on the party and could even run against it. Both the party leaders who once arbitrated the nomination and those who supported control of nominations by the party organization, found themselves opposed by a new generation of candidates prepared to "go it alone." Further, the parties were experiencing internal divisions over the shape and direction of policy. The displacement of these painful, internal conflicts onto an electoral arena may have been the only way to resolve them.

Finally we should note that the public favored giving itself direct control of nominations. Gallup polls over the last thirty years have offered respondents the choice between a national primary and the convention system, and the public has consistently favored a national primary. Even after the number of state primaries had increased so that the public directly selected a majority of delegates, the polls still indicated a preference for a national primary.[7] Somewhat different evidence is found in a *Los Angeles Times* poll taken in December 1979 among a national sample. Over three fourths of those interviewed said that they were satisfied with the present, primary-based system. Respondents were also asked who they thought should have influence over the nomination. Forty percent more respondents said that the influence of party leaders and officeholders should be reduced than said it should be increased. The difference was even greater among those who felt that the nominating system was currently not sound. In a mirror image of these opinions, the poll found considerable sentiment for strengthening the role of the primary voter, particularly among those respondents with a negative view of the present nominating process.[8]

One wonders if the public knows that the horse it is beating is dead. Perhaps the poll's respondents favored further changes because the present system often renders participation irrelevant, a problem correctable by a national primary. Yet other findings of the poll suggest otherwise. Nearly half of the respondents didn't know what kind of selection process—a primary or a caucus/convention—was used in their state. This suggests that the sentiment expressed in the poll is more of an anti-party bias familiar to students of public opinion than a considered opinion about the merits of different systems for selecting nominees. The poll also found the public dissatisfied with the information environment of the primaries. As a reporter for the *Los Angeles Times* wrote: "They admit to learning little during the primaries about a candidate's leadership qualities, administrative abilities, solutions to problems, and trustworthiness."[9]

## WERE THE REFORM GOALS ACHIEVED?

Thus, while the party reformers sought to open the party to participation by its members, they did not necessarily seek to establish a nominating system based mostly on primaries. Instead, they were swept along by a confluence of forces that characterized the reform period. The new system was viewed as desirable by the press and the public: anti-organizational sentiment was tapped and put to work by opportunistic candidates. Still, even if the structure of the new system is not what the reformers intended, it is possible that their goals were realized and achieved. Are nomination decisions in the postreform period likely to be made in a manner that more faithfully represents the wishes of the party rank-and-file?

While elections would appear to be the simplest and most direct means by which an authoritative accounting of citizen preference can be made, three general problems impinge upon the ability of primary elections to do this. First, elections vary in form, and the form of the election affects how well the outcome reflects public opinion. Most primaries potentially distort the expression of the public's will. Second, while elections are perhaps the easiest mode of participation, turnout is far from universal, and thus biases of representation may occur if the citizen's propensity to vote is related to his or her preference among the candidates. Third, the primaries themselves play a role in the creation of public sentiment. Thus a more theoretical question asks whether it is meaningful to conceive of public opinion apart from the structure in which it is expressed; that is, it may not make sense to presuppose the existence of preferences and judge the nominating system by how well it mirrors those preferences. We will examine each of these problems in turn.

As the review of primary elections in Chapters 1 and 2 demonstrates, primaries are quite complicated, both in the rules governing their operation and in the choices they present to the voter. The late E. E. Schattschneider believed in elections as a tool for effecting democracy (though he was no fan of intraparty democracy), but he warned that they needed to be simple to work efficiently. Where the voter was presented a choice between two candidates, the electorate can be said to have unambiguous control of the direction that government would take, within the limits of that choice.[10] But primary elections are not simple, and place substantial informational burdens upon the citizen. In order to make an intelligent choice, the voter must often know about more than two candidates, and as we have seen, the information environment is not conducive to such learning. In addition to knowledge of the candidates, the citizen must know something about the structure of the election and how the vote is translated into delegate support. A citizen who wanted to assure that his primary vote mattered might cast a very different vote under winner-take-all rules than under proportional rules. The prospective fortunes of the candidates—which ones are likely to survive and which ones are not—may also affect the voter's calculus. In short, presidential primaries ask a lot of the voter; there is often no optimal solution to the voter's dilemma, even when he or she is very well informed. As Chapter 2 shows, the meaning of contests held under such conditions is usually ambiguous, and this ambiguity confers great power upon those who structure the information and are in a position to offer prompt and authoritative interpretation of the results: the media. The party rank-and-file are thus sovereign, but because they are not omniscient, they must share their power in ways not anticipated by the reformers.

The second problem concerns the representativeness of the participants. Compared with other forms of participation, primaries would appear to be the "least expensive" to the citizen. Although information costs can be very high, the citizen is not required to pay them. (Of course, in terms of the quality of participation, you get what you pay for.) Voting is a brief act, accomplished at a place likely to be familiar to the voter. For this reason, primaries would seem to be less likely than other participatory forms—such as caucuses—to discourage potential participants. Given the relationship between socioeconomic status and participation, the less costly the form, the more representative the profile of the participants. As our data have shown, primary voters look very much like voters in the general election. Primary voters are better educated than the general electorate, but in terms of political attitudes they are very much like general election voters. Scholars disagree about the significance of the differences between participants and nonparticipants. James Lengle makes a persuasive case that primaries distorted the expression of Democrats' will in 1972 and perhaps in 1976.[11] This distortion is potentially compounded by the seriality of the system which gives early electorates—which by Lengle's standards are even more unrepresentative of the bulk of party followers—special influence in the process.

Much of the analysis of representation to this point, and most of the criticism of the system reveiwed here, assumes that party identifiers have preferences among the candidates that preexist the actual delegate selection process in their state. This assumption raises a third problem concerning the evaluation of primaries as reflecting public sentiment. While much of the evidence presented in this book shows that citizen opinions in presidential nominations are ephemeral and dynamic, analyses of representation tend to adopt a static model of opinion. But in fact opinions interact with participation. The intention to participate almost certainly motivates information gathering, reflection, and choice. Opinions in turn affect the likelihood of participation. Intense opinions may be more likely to be acted upon. While we accept that democracy implies political equality, democracy may also legitimately take account of intensity of preference. The decision not to vote may be a passive one resulting from burdens imposed by the act, but it may also be a political statement itself. Polls, which are used to establish the standard by which the representativeness of outcomes is judged, are ill-equipped to take account of these contingencies. They are inherently conservative because they cannot reveal what sort of opinion might have been produced had deliberation and participation occurred. Thus it may be misleading to compare the results of primaries with the sentiments of citizens in places where no campaign has been waged or among those who were not stirred to become engaged in the process. All opinions are not equal, and an analysis that forces them to be equal inevitably introduces its own set of distortions into the conclusions.

A postscript to this discussion concerns another goal of the reformers. Participation was viewed as valuable for the benefits it confers upon the participant, not just for the efficacy with which the public's views are made known to or accounted for by the system. One strand of democratic theory has long held that participation in politics promotes the growth of the individual. By engaging in the process of mutual accommodation with others, citizens are educated about their own values and wishes and learn to mesh these more harmoniously with others. Elections may provide some of these benefits, though voting, as a highly individualistic act, does not require discussion, deliberation, or accommodation. Many of the reformers felt that open caucuses were the ideal forum for democratic participation. Owing to the increased attention paid to them, some caucuses were well-attended in 1980. Advocates of caucuses believe they can ultimately be more representative than primaries precisely because decision making in them is not atomistic or individual; the caucus participants may be forced at least to consider the broader interests of the party before making a decision, and in this sense the needs and desires of nonparticipants may get more consideration.

The system of primary elections thus institutionalizes a particular kind of representation. The system is undoubtedly more open to public participation than it was before the reforms and it is more responsive to political change than it was. It is more representative in a demographic sense and in its capacity to reflect and respond to pressures from those who do not control the party machinery. At the same time, the system better represents wishes and interests of other actors than just the party rank-and-file. Because public opinion is more important, so too are those who influence the character of information in the system. The media may act in formulaic and politically neutral ways in choosing which events and facts of the nomination to report or to ignore, but even if we accept that the biases of the media are structural rather than willful, journalists are now a stronger force in determining the outcome than they have ever been.

Ultimately, a definitive answer to the question of representativeness is not possible. The structure of the system renders it transparent to some constituencies and interests and opaque to others. This statement is true regardless of the particular structure chosen.[12] The present system places more power in the hands of citizens, but because of its particular configuration (i.e., the serial primaries, the panoply of rules and procedures, the habits of candidates and journalists) the hands of the citizens are not directed solely by their owners. As we have suggested, it is misleading to conceive of representation as merely a set of forms by which preexisting public opinion is reflected. Public opinion arises within those forms, and might be very different were different forms employed.

## BEYOND REPRESENTATION

Representativeness is such a fundamental concern that it is easy to lose sight of the fact that the ultimate purpose of the nominating system is to select leadership. There are a number of other standards by which the nominating *process* may be judged that relate more directly to the *outcome* of the process: What is the quality of decision making within the system? How sensitive is the system to forces for change? Does the system promote nominees that offer the general electorate meaningful choice? Does the system recruit able candidates and test skills necessary for effective leadership and governance?

The following discussion of these standards is necessarily speculative in some cases; deciphering who has been a "good" leader is a job best left to historians. And any nominating system may produce both statesmen and buffoons. In measuring the new system by the standards suggested above two points should be kept in mind. First, when discussing the nominating system we must be careful not to take the term "system" for granted. In this case the system refers to a structure (laws and rules) within which three principal actors interact—candidates, the press, and the public. A change in the role or behavior of any one element causes changes in the behavior of the others.

Second, implicit in evaluating any nominating system is the notion of tradeoffs. Any system will promote certain values at the expense of others. These values cannot be examined in isolation for they are strongly interrelated, and are in some cases competing. For example, our current system prizes openness. A system that maximizes openness, however, is also one that minimizes experience and party ties. Thus the benefit of a system that makes it easier for outsiders to run and win, thus giving the (early-voting) electorate a wider field of potential presidents from which to choose, may have the cost of electing presidents who lack the experience and the organizational contacts to govern effectively.

## THE QUALITY OF DECISION MAKING

The primary consideration in the quality of public decision making is whether citizens have sufficient information for the task at hand. On this point our data are clear. As has been apparent throughout, we find nomination politics to have been relatively peripheral to the concerns of much of the public. Citizens did not learn much about the candidates, and while those who participated may have known more than the average member of the public, the rest of the public's lack of knowledge may be an important factor in its low rate of participation. The limited public learning is likely a function of the general parameters of citizen interest coupled with the way in which the nomination is portrayed by journalists and the early closure of three of the four contests examined here. Whatever the reason, public opinion about the candidates did not rest upon a rich base of information. The criteria applied to judgments about candidates appeared to be severely constricted if not inappropriate.

While public interest is modest, interest is not a precondition to learning. Even those with little interest in the primary elections learned the names of central candidates and knew of their prominent successes. But even the most interested learned little beyond this. Largely, people learned what was in the information environment. The media—specifically television news—could do a far better job of educating the public if they took responsibility for this role. Granted, this is not a role the electronic media have asked for. Yet with 65 percent of the public receiving most of their election information from television it is a role they indeed play. The responsibility to educate the public must come with this role, particularly since it is the public's air-waves that commercial stations are using to make profits.

We are pessimistic about the possibilities of noncosmetic change in media behavior. Three of the obstacles to reform are deeply ingrained in the structure of television news. First, we must recognize that "reporting the news" and "educating the public" are not synonymous, and in some ways success at the former guarantees failure at the latter. The definition of "news" used by most working journalists is simply dysfunctional for citizen learning. Journalists often have difficulty defining news in conceptual terms. It is a sense, or as former Supreme Court Justice Potter Stewart commented on trying to define pornography, "I know it when I see it." But most, if not all journalists would agree that news is a "happening" or "what we now know that we didn't know before." Thus journalists focus on what changes in an election campaign—gaffes, primary results, campaign strategy. A candidate who changes positions makes the news for this, and is pictured as disingenuous or making a strategic appeal to a particular group; a candidate who restates a consistent position is instead shown more colorfully at a campaign rally.[13] If news abhors a vacuum, it also chokes on repetition. Human beings, however, learn by repetition. Thus in some ways the problem of citizen learning is endemic to the commonly accepted definition of news.

The second reason centers around the structural constraints on the electronic media. Television news is particularly important here, given its prominence in the campaign. Unlike the newspaper which can simply run more pages if there is a great deal of news, network television evening news has only 22½ minutes to summarize the day's news. The nightly news shows produced by the networks are largely headline services. Stories about the campaign are short and must be kept simple. There is not enough time to explore candidates' histories and issue stances in a responsibly detailed fashion. Moreover, because television is a visual medium, "pictures" command a high news value. Action footage is preferred to "talking heads." Thus the focus is more often on where the candidate was and the size of the crowd than on what the candidate said. It is not difficult to reconcile instant analysts' proclamations after presidential debates that there was "nothing new—their standard raps," with studies showing the public does in fact learn from debates.[14] People had simply never heard the full standard raps before. The story is how the candidate is trying to get elected, not what he will do if elected.

Third, given the fact that over 60 percent of the public relies primarily on television for its political information, we must not lose sight of the fact that television news is a business: the ultimate goal is not to inform the public but to maintain and attract an audience to increase revenues. Certainly most television newspeople think of themselves as journalists, and prize the values of promoting the public interest. But the style and format of TV news are shaped by commercial considerations and the competitive tension among the networks. The consequence is that the public receives information of dubious value. The internetwork competition has elevated the news value of "being first" to preposterous proportions. It makes little difference to people whether they learn who is elected at 8:02 or 8:04, or 10:30 for that matter. This is not news people *need* to know immediately in order to live their lives. If the networks invested all the energy, creativity, and resources that now goes into "projecting winners" into informing the public—before the election—we would doubtlessly have a more knowledgeable electorate and more evidence of "informed choice." However, for the reasons mentioned we do not expect much improvement—television is personality over policy, style over substance, form over content; and television news is, after all, television.

Coupled with the shortage of useful information is the inflexibility of decision making in the new system. As Wilson Carey McWilliams has argued, a good decision-making process values the properties of deliberation and reconsideration. But primary votes are irrevocable, with no possibility of reconsideration. As a consequence of the serial arrangement of primaries, "early support matters more than considered support."[15] The heightened importance of the early contests means that otherwise irrelevant or trivial events during this period also get magnified. The public knows so little about the candidates in the first weeks of the nominating contests—while its judgments are so final—that almost anything that happens in the campaigns takes on an artificial significance. In this way, chance and luck also have a very big hand, and the quality of the decision-making process is further diminished.

## SENSITIVITY TO POLITICAL CHANGE

A second standard for judging the nominating system is its sensitivity to social movements and new issues. This question is, in many ways, similar to that of representation, but here the focus is not on the adequacy of the system to represent the wishes of individuals, but rather its ability to respond to broader forces in the party and society. The new nominating system is much more open, allowing the nominations to be won by candidates who stand for what is "new." Our last two presidents have come to the White House running as "outsiders"—particularly Jimmy Carter, who met many party leaders only *after* he had secured the Democratic nomination in 1976. In the wake of the political scandal known as Watergate, which included the obstruction of justice and abuse of power at the highest level of government, Jimmy Carter offered himself as a decent, religious country man who said simply "Trust me, I'll never lie to you." Given the nation's recent history and mood this was enough in 1976. And we might well look at this as a virtue of the "new system." After all, does not the individual who best puts his finger on the public pulse have the most rightful claim to leadership?

However, the events of 1980 counsel caution before accepting this assertion. Poll reading is always something of a mysterious activity, but by 1980 the dominant public impression of Carter seemed to be "he's a nice guy who is in over his head."[16] Decency was sufficient for candidate Carter in 1976, but was not enough for President Carter in 1980. The electorate valued strong leadership more in 1979 than in 1976,[17] and perhaps seeking to correct for its earlier myopia, perceived in Ronald Reagan the strength of leadership that Jimmy Carter lacked. But with Reagan also came vast policy changes, as the new president reacted to a self-perceived and self-proclaimed mandate. In terms of basic values and principles it is difficult to argue the country was any more conservative in 1980 than 1976.[18] If New Jersey is representative of the nation (and we believe it to be on this question[19]), support for the kind of sweeping changes instigated by President Reagan dissipates upon casual examination. Half of the public did not vote in 1980, of those voting half did not support Reagan, and of those supporting Reagan, half said they were voting more *against* Carter than *for* Reagan.* Mandates should be made of more than 13 percent.

Viewed from the perspective of the Republican Party, the nomination of Reagan in 1980 can be seen as a legitimate expression of the dominant forces within the party (although as Barbara Farah pointed out, the GOP convention delegates favoring Reagan were much more conservative than the average Republican[20]). But the successive cases of Carter and Reagan suggest that the sensitivity of a nominating system to ephemeral forces affects the capacity of the system to yield meaningful choices in the general election. Because the selection of the nominees is based on more idiosyncratic predilections than in the past, voters in general elections may increasingly wonder what the implications of their votes will be. Ideally, a political structure should provide enough stability and continuity that the society can make predictions about the future course of public policy and can adjust its behavior accordingly. Such continuity lends itself to democratic control, for predictability allows meaningful retrospective voting.[21] If the public knows what to expect from Democrats and Republicans, an intelligent choice can be made between them, and voters can exercise real political control. To the extent that the same party stands for very different policies each time an election occurs, the public's control is loosened. While this may not be a necessary logical consequence—after all, the party may stand for something different from the other party, even if it also stands for something different from itself in the last election— imperfect information in elections means that not all citizens will be

---

*Data on turnout and vote division are from the New Jersey Department of State. Data on support for/against candidates are from an Eagleton Poll conducted in late October, 1980.

informed of the "new" stand, and the very fact of change raises the prospect that the voter may find that once unwrapped at home, the merchandise is not what was expected.

Thus paradoxically, a nominating system that maximizes a party's sensitivity to ephemeral opinions and currents for change may ultimately produce an electoral system that weakens popular control of public policy. This outcome is particularly plausible if the openness of the nomination promotes personalistic rather than ideological candidacies. Despite fears that the reforms would encourage ideologues or demagogues and lead to greater polarization of the parties, the concern now is that, as McCorkle and Fleishman put it, ". . . the marketplace politics of the nominating process reduces potential presidents into smaller-than-life characters in the political equivalent of an often unfunny situation comedy or, even worse, mere consumer products."[22] As the personal qualities of candidates become more important as criteria in presidential selection, the public's control of public policy through elections is severely attenuated.

Yet even when candidate appeals are substantive rather than personal, the net effect of a system open to any candidate able to strike a responsive chord is public confusion over the goals and ideals of the party. As James Ceaser has put it:

> At a minimum, the primary path to the nomination has provided greater access to candidates who seek to redefine what the parties stand for, and in recent nomination contests, many aspirants have run on programs that allegedly have been designed to build fundamentally new coalitions. . . . This incentive to attempt to form new coalitions can, of course, be destabilizing, eroding the very stability of a party that enables it to sustain change over the course of several elections. The result could be a greater appearance of change with less capacity in the political system to effectuate it.[23]

Theories of democracy that posit elections as the means of popular control assume that the public's verdicts in general elections provide much of the impetus for change in what the parties stand for. Public opinion is not thought to be an appropriate vehicle for *defining* the alternatives because more information and deliberation are needed than ordinarily are found in elections. Our data lend support to such an argument.

Change in the political system does not necessarily have to come from the two parties, of course. Third-party challenges may periodically allow for the adequate expression of sentiments not reflected in the cleavage between the two parties. While such challenges are viewed by many observers as likely to be weak and inconsequential, Ceaser argues that they have become much more credible since 1968.[24] He also suggests that the absence of strong third-party efforts may be indicative of the flexibility and responsiveness of the two major parties, and not just evidence of the inefficacy of such movements. Given this responsiveness, there would seem to be less need for the parties to open themselves to rapid change.

Thus by the standards of the quality of decision making and its contribution to an appropriate balance between change and stability, the new nominating system has important flaws. These flaws are a function of the greater power possessed by citizens in the process. The flaws stem not from the inadequacies of the public, but from the way in which the public's power is exercised. The system of serial primary elections cedes power to the public but without the institutional arrangements to ensure that public opinion develops in an appropriate fashion and is expressed without the intrusion of chance and happenstance. The sensitivity of the outcome to ephemeral opinion and random events renders general elections less meaningful as institutions of popular control. In all phases of presidential selection, the citizen has more formal power and less real control. The people do not rule; *no one rules.*

## ELECTABILITY VERSUS THE ABILITY TO GOVERN

The new system encourages certain kinds of candidates to run for president. Ambition is more important in the new system, and due to the long, labor-intensive campaign, the lack of an important or time-consuming job may be a prerequisite for a successful candidate. Campaigning ability per se, while always important, was in the past neither sufficient nor always necessary for a politician to receive serious consideration for the presidency; now it is both.

Electioneering skills would be important under any nominating system. Even under a system closed to popular participation, party leaders would be loath to select a candidate who was terribly deficient in such skills to carry the party's standard into the general election. But the more the system is based on primary elections, the more important electioneering skills will be. The current nominating system tests such skills to a far greater degree than its predecessor. The critical question is whether the skills necessary to *win elections* are also the ones necessary to *govern effectively.*

To be sure, it is difficult to say what skills are important for governance, or to rate presidents as to how well they have governed. Each president has brought his own peculiar mix of skills to office, and the historical conditions and crises each faced have been similarly unique. Yet all presidents must deal with Congress to establish an agenda, set priorities, and move bills into laws. While Congress takes an active role in determining domestic policy, the president must be the "chief manager" of government. Useful skills for these tasks include: knowledge of the institutional workings of Congress, experience in Washington, the ability to command party loyalty for programmatic support, political savvy in coalition building, managerial skills including the ability to attract and coordinate a talented White House staff and cabinet, and the ability to persuade both public officials and the public at large. Moreover, the president is singularly responsible for the conduct of foreign policy, making experience in this realm a useful commodity.

Very few of these talents are tested under our present nominating system. While Ronald Reagan has a number of talents, perhaps the only skill out of the forementioned group that he has in great abundance is the ability to persuade the public, and through them, elected leaders. Reagan, after all, was a professional actor, with consummate communication skills. His policy victories in 1981 and 1982 are due more to this strength than to genuine coalition building. Time and again Reagan appealed directly "to the people" for support. But one can go to the well only so often; the 98th Congress appears to be far less supportive (and cowed) than its predecessor. We do not mean to disparage the skill of persuading the public; real leadership cannot be exercised without it. But beyond being transitory we note that there is no guarantee that the nominating system will produce presidents with this quality; one need look no further than Jimmy Carter for a prime example of a president who was unable to motivate the public or harness public opinion.

It is no easy task to define the characteristics of a system that in succession produced Carter and Reagan. They are as night and day in many fundamental ways: Carter was knowledgeable about the details of policies and problems, worked long hours, was an unemotional and uninspiring speaker, was sensitive to the inequitable distribution of wealth and the plight of the poor but appeared "cold." The reverse is true of Reagan. Yet there are some commonalities that bear on the general question of the ability to govern. First, both men were "outsiders." They had little experience in dealing with the Washington establishment (which can be a virtue, although we believe it to generally be a liability) and less in the conduct of foreign affairs. Moreover, since both men won election to office largely independent of the party organization or officeholders, both had to build coalitions from scratch. Reagan was more successful than Carter, as he was more talented at manipulating public opinion.* But this is not a reliable base to rest on; the popularity of all presidents spirals downward with the passage of time.[25]

It is admittedly difficult to deduce what type of candidates are advantaged under the new system by discussing Carter and Reagan. However, it may be possible to shed a bit more light on the topic by looking at the inverse question: What types of potential candidates would be disadvantaged? The system appears to be structured against candidates without a burning desire for power, those who cannot campaign on a fulltime basis in the year before the first delegate selection events of the election, and candidates with "baggage." Walter Mondale declined to make the race in 1976, saying he was not "hungry enough" to spend the time campaigning and fundraising. It took a stint in the vice-presidency to whet his appetite sufficiently for his candidacy in 1984. Jules Witcover found the word "marathon" best summed up Jimmy Carter's successful quest for the nomination in 1976.[26] As Hubert Humphrey found out in 1972 and in 1976, the new system demands an early and total commitment of energy and resources from the men who seek the presidency. California Senator Alan Cranston, seeking the 1984 Democratic nomination, had been to New Hampshire half a dozen times before the end of 1982. Party statesmen such as Hubert Humphrey or Adlai Stevenson will be turned to less often than they were under the old system.

Those with fulltime jobs requiring their presence are also discriminated against by the new system. The case of Howard Baker provides an interesting example. Baker's campaign managers and professional observers see his inability to leave his duties in Washington as a serious deficiency of his aborted 1980 campaign.[27] His competition had no such problems (nor did Jimmy Carter in 1976); Reagan, Bush, and Connally had no public responsibilities calling them; Anderson had renounced his house seat. Perhaps seeing how the game must be played, Baker said he will not seek reelection to the Senate—giving

---

*Reagan's communication skills in defining and claiming a "mandate" doubtlessly served him well in this stead during the first part of his presidency. But part of the credit must also be given to the highly effective work of Senate Majority Leader Howard Baker, Robert Dole, and others in leadership positions.

up the position of Majority Leader—but has not ruled out a future run for the presidency. We have also noted the public enjoys its "new romance" with previously unknown candidates who are successful in early campaign tests. This may not augur well for persons with long records of public service. The more "hard choices" (such as SALT ratification or abortion decisions) officials have had to make in their careers, the greater the likelihood of offending various groups.[28] This results in "political baggage" old warhorses must carry against wartless newcomers. It is considerably easier to *create* a favorable impression than to *change* a mixed or unfavorable one. For these reasons the new system says to potential candidates, "If you have the time and energy, and if you run from outside government, you have a better chance to win."

The absence of party ties also has consequences for staffing the government. Candidates who must set up their own staffs to contest the nomination carry that campaign team into the general election, and if victorious, into the White House.[29] Many in the Nixon White House came from the J. Walter Thompson advertising agency, Carter brought his "Georgia Mafia" with him to government, Reagan is surrounded by long-time California advisors, with a sprinkling of outsiders. Part of this is natural: presidents need men they can trust, and trust comes with experience over time. However, by running outside the party, and from being involved in politics outside the purview of the national party, presidents in the reform era are more likely to be unaware of "potential talent" that could be tapped for their administrations.

Our current nominating system may well produce presidents with the appropriate qualities for governing. But if it does, it is largely accidental. To be sure there is some overlap in the skills necessary to win elections and to govern effectively but the disjuncture is greater than the intersection. We counsel against overly deterministic conclusions—a system that better tested coalition building, experience, and managerial skills would not necessarily produce more talented governors. But, as the purpose of the nominating system is to select an effective leader for the country, less thought should be given to reforms designed to make the process more representative and more thought given to reforms designed to test skills more useful in governing.

## TURNING BACK THE CLOCK

Sentiment for returning discretion in presidential nominations to the party leadership is strong, though some believe that the cure for the ills of the primary-based system is to be found in regional or national primaries. The Democratic Party has already adopted several changes in delegate selection rules for its 1984 convention, though at this writing the effect of these changes on the timing and the number of state primaries to be held in 1984 is not yet known. Despite our criticism of the nominating system we believe that many of the flaws in the system are relatively easy to correct, and some of the changes made by the Democrats are significant steps in the right direction.

Four major modifications were recommended by the Democratic Party's Commission on Presidential Nomination chaired by James B. Hunt, Governor of North Carolina, and adopted by the Democratic National Committee in March 1982.[30] First was the addition of 550 unpledged delegate positions—so-called "superdelegates"—to be filled by party leaders and elected officials, constituting almost 15 percent of the delegates to the convention. According to the Hunt Commission, the presence of superdelegates addresses much of the criticism of the system reviewed earlier in this chapter: it would "increase the *representativeness* of mainstream Democratic constituencies . . . restore *peer* review to the process, subjecting candidates to review by those who know them best. It would put a premium on *coalition building* . . . that would help us campaign and govern effectively. It would *strengthen party ties* among officials . . . and . . . would help return *decision-making discretion and flexibility* to the convention."[31] These delegates would be formally independent of the primaries and public opinion, but in fact the primaries would likely serve to instruct their behavior.

The second modification is a shortening of the "nominating season" by limiting delegate selection activities to the period between the second Tuesday of March and the second Tuesday of June. Iowa received an exemption to hold its local caucuses fifteen days in advance, and New Hampshire will be permitted to hold its primary seven days earlier. Still, the period of delegate selection in 1984 will be about five weeks shorter than in 1980. The evidence presented in the preceding chapters suggests that this change is a good one, but should be taken further. The length of the campaigns in 1976 and 1980 did not contribute to citizen learning; most of the learning and opinion formation we observed occurred very early in the period, and appeared to cease even before the contests were effectively closed. Some observers fear that putting the Iowa caucuses one week before the New Hampshire primary will merely serve to accentuate the effects of the outcome in Iowa. Had this rule applied in 1980, the argument goes, Reagan might not have had time to recover, and been dealt a fatal blow in New Hampshire.

A third change is the loosening of the rules binding delegates to a vote. While candidates have a right to expect that delegates pledged to support them are in fact bona fide supporters, the meaning of representation is distorted if delegates are owned by the candidates rather than the voters. As Terry Sanford put it, "Parties should ponder whether they need a convention at all if a delegate represents a candidate rather than the voting constituency."[32]

A fourth change was motivated by concern about "front loading"— the trend among states to move their primaries closer to the beginning of the process so as to avoid being rendered irrelevant by early closure. The Hunt Commission recommended reinstituting the "loophole primary," in which states may select delegates on a winner-take-all basis at the level of the Congressional district. States would have the option of continuing with a system of proportional representation, but the logic of the change was that larger states could increase their clout by using the district-level winner-take-all rule to increase the potential payoff to a candidate who did well. Proportional representation was supposed to avoid early closure by fragmenting delegations and denying any candidate a "knockout punch" early. However, the fact that the large field of candidates could not afford to maintain their campaigns through several states meant that one emerged as a leader early. Proportionality then guaranteed that he would continue to protect his lead by adding delegates even in states where he did not finish first. Thus the loophole primary promises a candidate who falls behind in the smaller, early states the opportunity to make a dramatic comeback in a large, later loophole state. Knowing this, the argument goes, larger states (such as California, New York, or Pennsylvania) will have less incentive to try to rush to the front in order to have an impact on the outcome.

But unintended and negative consequences may flow from this change. First, if the "clout" argument is correct, states that presently use caucuses or conventions to select delegates may decide to switch to primaries, an outcome decidedly not favored by the Hunt Commission. Second, a large state might maximize its impact by having a loophole primary *and* having it early.* Third, our data suggest that

---

*If, as seems likely, the AFL-CIO endorses a Democratic candidate before

proportional representation is preferable because it simplifies the voter's calculus. If the voter believed that his voice would be heard— even if among a minority—because his candidate would get some representation at the convention, then he would vote for his preferred candidate. In a near winner-take-all system, the choice is more complicated. A vote for a likely loser is a wasted vote, and the voter may have to consider whether or not to cast a negative vote in order to defeat a disliked candidate. Of course, a primary voter may be unaware of the rules under which the election is conducted; if so, the simplest choice—to vote for the candidate who is best liked— may be an irrational one.

The range of plans for changing the system is almost limitless.[33] If the experience of Democratic Party reformers of the past fourteen years is any guide, the only certainty is that structural changes invariably have unanticipated political consequences. Still, if one is willing to specify the values a nominating system should serve and the role the political party *as an institution* should play in it, educated guesses about the effects of certain alternative systems are possible. We agree with the arguments advanced by such observers as Schattschneider and McWilliams that primary elections do not work well as mechanisms for determining what a party will stand for. The information burden of multi-candidate, decentralized elections is too great. The task of informing the citizen—the chief outside determinant of the outcome—falls to the candidate organizations and the mass media. Successful candidates then tend to be of one type, those highly ambitious individuals skilled in electioneering; successful candidates may have other important political skills for governing, but if they do it is only by coincidence since the public is not well suited to judge those skills, nor as Thomas Patterson has argued, are the media well-suited to the task of organizing choices in elections.[34]

These flaws of elections would inhere whether the system has a series of state primaries, regional primaries, or a national primary. Each form would have certain advantages and disadvantages, depending on one's values. All involve important tradeoffs. The national primary would reduce the impact of media interpretations of contests in small states, though journalists might retain much of this power through their capacity to interpret polls and other evidence

---

the primaries, the effect of this endorsement would be greatly magnified by the loophole system since the AFL-CIO's strength is greatest in those large states likely to adopt loophole primaries.

of candidate support before the primary. If the national primary directly selected the nominee, some form of runoff would be essential, assuming no candidate received a majority of votes. The runoff would reintroduce media interpretation as a factor, and the historically low turnout in runoffs might exacerbate the problem of demographic unrepresentativeness.

Regional primaries, particularly if held over a shorter period (say, one per week for five weeks) might allow more candidates to stay in the race for the duration, thus increasing the chances of a deliberative convention. But even if the order of the regional contests were determined by lottery, the sequence effects and their attendant biases would still occur. Should the first primary be held in the midwest a favorite son, such as John Glenn, for example, would be expected to do much better than had a western primary led the parade. Given the dynamics we have observed we would then expect the media to devote disproportionate attention to Glenn, propelling his candidacy into the public consciousness and stimulating fund raising, recruitment of workers, campaign morale, and endorsements. Had the midwestern primary been held last, Glenn might have been winnowed from the field or his reputation damaged by the time midwesterners were called upon to state their preferences.

Both the national and regional primary plans would eliminate a prominent feature of the existing system: the early contests in small states that allow less well known politicians to be serious candidates for the presidency. A national primary would have eliminated Jimmy Carter from the pool of potential presidents in 1976. Such a system may be considered either good or bad, depending on which values one prefers to see maximized in nomination politics. On the one hand the system would be biased in favor of "insiders"—people with experience—an important component of governing ability. On the other hand, such a system is more closed to fresh leadership and those persons who may be more prescient in reading the mood of the public.

Despite the unrepresentativeness of the early states, we believe there is merit in retail politics as a *part* of the input that determines a nomination. The problem in recent nominations has been the *finality* with which judgments rendered in Iowa, New Hampshire, Vermont, and a few other states have been felt on the field of aspirants. If steps were taken—and the Hunt Commission changes include some such steps—to ensure that party conventions could not be automatically "locked up" by the primaries, the media might treat the early contests in more appropriate fashion. However, as we have argued, we do not expect media behavior to change unless other aspects of the system also change. One way to preserve the quality of retail politics while minimizing the dysfunctional impact of the first test would be to ensure that more than one state is in the lead-off position. If voters in Iowa, New Hampshire, and Oregon, for example, held delegate-selection activities at the same time the regional and cultural differences would probably yield a mixed verdict. A divided outcome would temper the media's tendency to "rush to judgment" but still give clues (and more accurate ones) to candidates' strengths.[35] Should one candidate do well in all three states, that candidate would better deserve the avalanche of media coverage sure to follow.

It is more difficult, of course, to run simultaneously in three states. Yet if small states were selected, thus avoiding expensive media markets, the system bias against unknowns would not be overly severe. Moreover, having to raise slightly more seed money (even with federal matching funds) may in fact be a desirable screen to eliminate those who cannot command sufficient support to make the race. Such reforms are relatively minor but could make the system work better. Primaries can still ensure that the base of participants in the nomination decision is expanded, and primary voters have a right to expect that their voices will be heard at the conventions. The way to guarantee this is to prevent artificial factors from denying any primary voters a chance to judge those who seek the nomination or rendering their votes meaningless.

The failings of the nominating system do not constitute a failure of democracy. The kind of democracy envisioned by the party reformers never materialized. Instead, primaries proliferated. The public's will must develop within this awkward system, accentuating the weaknesses of public opinion rather than its strengths. The expression of the public will is then distorted by rules and circumstances that combine to deny each participant a fair share of influence. Undue power flows to other actors, particularly those who report and interpret the events of the nominating process, since what *seems to be* is often more consequential than what *is*. Citizens in the United States today have more power over presidential nominations than they have ever had, but must exercise that power within a structure that hinders its wise use.

## NOTES

1. See Thomas E. Patterson, *The Mass Media Election* (New York: Praeger, 1980), Chapter 11; Michael Robinson and Margaret Sheehan, *Over the Wire and on TV: CBS and UPI in Campaign '80* (New York: Basic Books, 1983).

2. Ranney is quoted by James Ceaser, *Presidential Selection: Theory and Development* (Princeton, N.J.: Princeton University Press, 1979), p. 263. Ceaser provides good reasons for the increased use of primaries and much of this discussion is drawn from his analysis.

3. Richard L. Rubin, *Press, Party, and Presidency* (New York: W. W. Norton, 1981), p. 192. The content analysis was performed by Charles Skop, a student at Columbia University, 1979. Similar observations were made by Paul Weaver after he examined CBS coverage of the 1976 nomination campaign. See Paul Weaver, "Captives of Melodrama," *New York Times Magazine* (August 29, 1976). pp. 6, 48–57.

4. Paul Weaver, "Captives of Melodrama," *New York Times Magazine* (August 29, 1976), pp. 6, 48–57.

5. Pope McCorkle and Joel L. Fleishman, "Political Parties and Presidential Nominations: The Intellectual Ironies of Reform and Change in the Mass Media Age," in *The Future of American Political Parties: The Challenge of Governance*, ed. Joel L. Fleishman (Englewood Cliffs, N.J.: Prentice-Hall, 1982), pp. 147–60.

6. See Richard L. Rubin, *Press, Party and Presidency* (New York: W. W. Norton, 1981), pp. 185–86.

7. James W. Ceaser, *Reforming the Reforms* (Cambridge, Mass.: Ballinger, 1982), pp. 87–88.

8. The data and analysis of this poll can be found in essays by George Skelton and by William Schneider and I. A. Lewis in *Nominating a President: The Process and the Press* (New York: Praeger, 1980), pp. 139–147.

9. George Skelton in *Nominating a President: The Process and the Press* (New York: Praeger, 1980), pp. 139–141.

10. E. E. Schattschneider, *Two Hundred Million Americans in Search of a Government* (New York: Holt, Rinehart and Winston, 1969).

11. James I. Lengle, *Representation and Presidential Primaries: The Democratic Party in the Post-Reform Era* (Westport, Conn.: Greenwood Press, 1981), Chapter 7.

12. Two expositions of the rule are: Gerald M. Pomper, "New Rules and New Games in Presidential Nominations," *Journal of Politics* 41 (August 1979), pp. 784–805; and James I. Lengle and Byron Shafer, "Primary Rules, Political Power, and Social Change," *American Political Science Review* 70 (March 1976), pp. 25–40.

13. Donald Matthews, "Winnowing," in *Race for the Presidency*, ed. James David Barber (Englewood Cliffs, N.J.: Prentice-Hall, 1978), pp. 55–78; Thomas E. Patterson, *The Mass Media Election* (New York: Praeger, 1980), p. 29.

14. There are a number of studies. See particularly: Arthur Miller and Michael MacKuen, "Learning About the Candidates: The 1976 Presidential Debates," *Public Opinion Quarterly* 43 (Fall 1979), pp. 326–46; Steven Chaffee and Sun Yuel Choe, "Time of Decision and Media Use during the Ford-Carter Campaign," *Public Opinion Quarterly* 44 (Spring 1980), pp. 53–69; Lee Becker, Idowu Sobowale, Robin Cobbey, and Chaim Eyal, "Debates' Effects on Voters' Understanding of Candidates and Issues," *The Presidential Debates*, eds. George Bishop,

Robert Meadow, and Marilyn Jackson-Beeck (New York: Praeger, 1978), pp. 126-39. For a general review see Sidney Kraus and Dennis Davis, "Political Debates," *Handbook of Political Communication*, eds. Dan Nimmo and Keith Sanders (Beverly Hills, Calif.: Sage, 1981), pp. 273-96.

15. Wilson Carey McWilliams, "The Meaning of the Election," *The Election of 1980*, ed. Gerald M. Pomper (Chatham, N.J.: Chatham House, 1981), pp. 171-73.

16. Cliff Zukin and J. Robert Carter, Jr., "The Measurement of Presidential Popularity: Old Wisdoms and New Concerns," in *The President and the Public*, ed. Doris Graber (Philadelphia: Institute for the Study of Human Issues (ISHI), 1982), pp. 207-41.

17. Stephen J. Wayne, "Expectations of the President," *The President and the Public*, ed. Doris Graber (Philadelphia: ISHI, 1982), pp. 17-38.

18. Robert Entman and David Paletz, "Media and the Conservative Myth," *Journal of Communication* 30 (1980), pp. 154-65.

19. Cliff Zukin and J. Robert Carter, Jr., "The Measurement of Presidential Popularity: Old Wisdoms and New Concerns," *The President and the Public*, ed. Doris Graber (Philadelphia: ISHI, 1982), pp. 216-17.

20. Barbara G. Farah, "The Representativeness of Direct Primaries: Linkage Between Partisan Voters and Convention Delegates 1972, 1976, and 1980," unpublished manuscript, Center for Political Studies, University of Michigan, 1982, p. 20.

21. Morris Fiorina, *Retrospective Voting in American National Elections* (New Haven: Yale University Press, 1981).

22. Pope McCorkle and Joel L. Fleishman, "Political Parties and Presidential Nominations: The Intellectual Ironies of Reform and Change in the Mass Media Age," in *The Future of American Political Parties: The Challenge of Governance*, ed. Joel L. Fleishman (Englewood Cliffs, N.J.: Prentice-Hall, 1982), p. 165.

23. James W. Ceaser, *Reforming the Reforms* (Cambridge, Mass.: Ballinger, 1982), pp. 104-5.

24. Ibid., pp. 99-106.

25. Lee Sigelman, "The Dynamics of Presidential Support," *Presidential Studies Quarterly* 9 (Spring 1979), pp. 206-16; James Stimson, "Public Support for American Presidents: A Cyclical Model," *Public Opinion Quarterly* 40 (Spring 1976), pp. 1-21.

26. Jules Witcover, *Marathon* (New York: The Viking Press, 1977).

27. Jonathan Moore, ed., *The Campaign for President: 1980 in Retrospect* (Cambridge, Mass.: Ballinger, 1981), Chapters 1, 3.

28. This is the logic in John Mueller's "Coalition of Minorities" variable used to explain falling presidential popularity. In the course of making decisions (on the SALT treaty, for/against the budget, etc.) a president will over time alienate an increasing number of the groups initially supporting him. See "Presidential Popularity from Truman to Johnson," *American Political Science Review* 64 (March 1970), pp. 18-34.

29. Sidney Blumenthal, *The Permanent Campaign* (Boston: Beacon Press, 1980).

30. For a complete description of the changes and the rationale behind them, see "The Report of the Commission on Presidential Nomination" (Washington, D.C.: Democratic National Committee, 1982).

31. "The Report of the Commission on Presidential Nomination" (Washington, D.C.: Democratic National Committee, 1982), p. 16. Emphasis in original.

32. Terry Sanford, *A Danger of Democracy: The Presidential Nominating Process* (Boulder, Colo.: Westview Press, 1981), p. 70.

33. Ceaser offers a detailed overview of several plans and an assessment of the likely consequences of them. See *Reforming the Reforms* (Cambridge, Mass.: Ballinger, 1982), Chapter 5.

34. Thomas Patterson, *The Mass Media Election* (New York: Praeger, 1980), pp. 173–76.

35. Christopher Arterton, "Campaign Organizations Confront the Media-Political Environment," *Race for the Presidency*, ed. James David Barber, (Englewood Cliffs, N.J.: Prentice-Hall, 1978), pp. 3–24.

# APPENDIX A
# METHODS AND DATA

This appendix presents a general overview of the three sources of data used in the book. Table A.1 shows the survey timing, sample sizes, and relationship of interviewing dates to the significant formal events of the campaign. Each of the three sources is described, with a brief discussion of each one's strengths and weaknesses.

## EAGLETON POLL–NEW JERSEY DATA

The New Jersey data were collected on a series of 17 telephone interviews conducted with cross sections of voting-age residents of the state. Approximately 15,000 people were interviewed between October 1979 and October 1980. The data were collected by the Eagleton Poll, a research center of the Eagleton Institute of Politics, Rutgers University. Each survey was an independent probability sample of the New Jersey population. Sampling procedures for each survey were identical.

As there was no sponsor for the election surveys many of the questions were "piggybacked" on other ongoing research projects. Thus we had only minimal control over the timing of some of the surveys. We occasionally found ourselves in the awkward position of being in the field on both sides of a significant primary or in the middle of a convention. This led to an analytic quandary. Preserving each survey as an independent statewide sample gives confidence that observed changes from one survey to the next are real, and error calculable. However, in cases where a significant campaign event bisected field interviewing the benefit of preserving the purity of the

**TABLE A.1**

**Campaign Events, Survey Dates, and Sample Sizes, 1980**

| Selected Campaign Events and Dates | Survey Dates | | |
| --- | --- | --- | --- |
| | Eagleton New Jersey | CBS/*New York Times* National | CPS/NES† National |
| Iowa Caucus—Jan 26 | Oct 19–28 (1,134) | Jan 9–13 (1,468) | Jan 22 to Feb 25 (1,008) |
| New Hampshire—Feb 26 | Feb 14–26 (1,701) | Feb 13–17 (1,536) | |
| Mass., Vermont—Mar 4 | Feb 27–Mar 2* (764) | | |
| New York, Conn.—Mar 25 Wisconsin—Apr 1 | Mar 13–25* (323) | Mar 12–15 (1,468) | |
| Pennsylvania—Apr 22 | Apr 6–21* (611) | Apr 10–14 (1,605) | April 2 to May 2 (965) |
| | Apr 22–May 1 (636) | | |
| Texas, Ind., Tenn., North Carolina—May 6 | May 1–15 (942) | | |
| Michigan, Oregon—May 20 | May 16–22 (817) | | |
| Calif., N.J., Ohio—June 3 | June 23–July 1 (840) | June 18–22 (1,517) | June 4 to July 13 (843) |

Republican Convention–July 14–17

July 15–28 (818)
July 31–Aug 10 (456)*

Democratic Convention–Aug 11–14

Aug 12–20 (360)*

General Election Surveys

Reagan-Anderson Debate, Sept 21

Sept 11–18 (562)

Sept 22–27 (564)
Sept 27–Oct 1 (809)
Oct 1–5 (828)
Oct 16–20 (821)
Oct 20–23 (939)

Reagan-Carter Debate, Oct 28

Oct 29–30 (1,134)

Sept 2 to Oct 1 (769)
Sept 2 to Nov 3 (1,614)

POST ELECTION SURVEYS

Nov 5 to Nov 25 (764)
Nov 5 to Nov 26 (818)
Nov 5 to Dec 17 (1,408)

*Not an independent sample.
†The National Election Study was designed to interview three separate panels.
Panel 1 Waves: Jan 22 to Feb 25; Jan 4 to July 13; Sept 2 to Oct 1; Nov 5 to Nov 25
Panel 2 Waves: Apr 2 to May 2; Nov 5 to Nov 26
Panel 3 Waves: Sept 2 to Nov 3; Nov 5 to Dec 17.

sample had to be weighed against the cost of not being able to observe the event's impact on the public.

An alternative approach is to consider the studies as one large sample of continuous interviewing. We may select for analysis interviews completed during any given segment of days—those leading up to one of the parties' conventions, for example. Citizens' knowledge or attitudes during this period can be then compared with knowledge or attitudes from interviews done during the several days following the convention. The cost of this strategy of analysis is that sampling error may be greater. Ultimately, 13 of the 17 samples retained full integrity, while the remaining four were "cut" around significant events of the campaign. These are noted by the asterisks in Table A.1.

While we were able to conduct a large number of surveys, and to interview a large number of respondents, resource constraints limited the amount of time available, or the number of questions that could be asked on any one survey. The limited amount of time defines the scope of the study to a considerable extent. In most of the analysis of the New Jersey data our primary independent variable is "time." By cutting the interviewing points around significant campaign events our design allows us to observe changes, and to make inferences about events of the election that might be responsible for those changes. Hence we are better able to trace the dynamics of public opinion than to explain those dynamics with this data source. The principal advantage of the Eagleton data is in the number of observations made and the concomitant ability to closely tie those observations to the formal events of the primary campaign.

There are three attributes of the Eagleton data that may be considered disadvantages. First, as has been mentioned, the data are not deep; there is a general lack of explanatory variables other than "time." Second, the data are from cross-sectional surveys, making statements about individual-level change inferential. Finally, the data came from a single state and may be suspect on grounds of external validity, although we do not find this to be particularly troubling. At relevant places in the book we have presented evidence to demonstrate that the dynamics of public opinion in New Jersey are not dissimilar from the nation as a whole in the cases of presidential popularity or nomination politics. Of somewhat greater concern is the fact that New Jersey holds its primary at the end of the nominating season in June. Under this condition citizens may be less likely to "tune in." However, we also consider this factor to be a virtue of sorts. Because of this timing we are able to observe the effects of the national media and national campaign "uncontaminated," for the most part, by a direct campaign aimed at voters. However, because New Jersey is served by New York and Philadelphia media we were able to observe the impact of candidates' targeted campaigns and make inferences about the effects of direct campaigning (see Chapter 7).

## CENTER FOR POLITICAL STUDIES, NATIONAL ELECTION STUDY– NATIONAL DATA

The design of the 1980 National Election Study represents a radical departure from earlier studies. Until 1980 the CPS surveys had focused only on the general election period; preelection interviews were conducted in September/October while follow-up interviews were conducted after the November election. The first wave of data collection in 1980 began in February after the Iowa caucus and before the New Hampshire primary. The second wave was conducted in April, after the early primaries had concluded, with an independent cross-sectional sample of the continental United States. The first panel re-interviews were conducted at the end of the primary season in June, when approximately 85 percent of the respondents first contacted in February were successfully re-interviewed. Overall, the 1980 design included three separate panel studies, as described at the bottom of Table A.1.

The strengths and weaknesses of the CPS data are the exact opposite of the Eagleton data. Among its strengths are its national scope, the panel design that allows us to trace individual change from the beginning to the end of the campaign, and its depth. There are over 2,000 variables that may be used for analytic purposes.

There are three primary disadvantages of the CPS/NES study given our purposes. First, the long time interval between interview waves— both cross-sectional and panel—renders the data set virtually useless for tracing the dynamics of public opinion during the nomination period. So much happens so fast, and opinion is so reactive to specific campaign events, that each wave of interviewing at best provides only a summary of the movement that has taken place. From analyzing the other data sources available to us we know that the CPS data set does not in some cases catch countervailing movements of the electorate within a given period of time. This data set is far better suited to *explaining*, rather than *describing* knowledge growth, opinion formation, and image changes. If a goal of the National Election Study is to illuminate the dynamics of public opinion in nomination politics, the design will have to be refined in subsequent studies to interview in early-primary and caucus states and tie early national samplings more closely to the initial events of the campaign.

A second weakness of the CPS/NES study is that there are serious deficiencies in the information collected about the two men who emerged as prominent newcomers in 1980–John Anderson and George Bush. Questions about Anderson were not asked until the second survey in April, well after he became widely known. In addition to lacking baseline data on Anderson his omission from the first interview schedule means that individual-level panel data (from the second wave conducted in June) is also missing. The problem with regard to Bush is that the first wave of interviewing began in late January, after substantial changes in the public's view of Bush occurred due to his "victory" in the Iowa caucus, and after lesser but still significant changes had occurred in the public image of other candidates according to the Eagleton and CBS/*New York Times* data.

A further limitation of the CPS/NES data set (for our purposes) comes from the structure of the interviewer schedule and use of filter questions. Only those saying they "knew something about" the candidates, for example, were asked for their opinion about the contestants. Those who "had heard of" candidates were not asked follow-up questions. The problem here, as the Eagleton data show, is that many of those who only recognized candidates' names, knowing little else about them, did indeed have opinions about them. There are other problems of "excessive screening" with regard to knowledge of the candidates' ideologies, issue positions, and character traits. These are discussed more fully in the appropriate sections of Chapter 5.

## CBS NEWS/*NEW YORK TIMES*–NATIONAL DATA

We have used data collected by CBS News and the *New York Times* in both 1980 and 1976. In both election years five national cross-sectional studies of the U.S. public were conducted. The timing and sample sizes of the 1980 surveys are shown in Table A.1; the 1976 surveys in Table A.2, below.

In terms of relative advantages and disadvantages the CBS/*New York Times* data fall somewhere between the Eagleton and CPS/NES data. This series of cross-sectional surveys are better than the CPS but not as good as the Eagleton data for measuring the public before and after most of the significant events of the campaign. They are

## TABLE A.2

### Campaign Events, Survey Dates, and Sample Sizes
### CBS News/*New York Times*, 1976

| Campaign Event | Survey Date | Sample Size |
|---|---|---|
| Iowa Caucus—Jan 19 | | |
| | Feb 2-8 | 1,459 |
| New Hampshire—Feb 24 | | |
| Massachusetts—March 2 | | |
| Florida—March 9 | | |
| Illinois—March 16 | | |
| | March 18-24 | 1,524 |
| Wisconsin—April 6 | | |
| | April 10-15 | 1,464 |
| Pennsylvania—April 27 | | |
| Indiana—May 4 | | |
| Nebraska—May 11 | | |
| Michigan, Maryland—May 18 | | |
| | May 19-23 | 1,501 |
| Tennessee, Kentucky, Oregon, Idaho—May 25 | | |
| Rhode Island, Montana—June 1 | | |
| California, New Jersey, Ohio—June 8 | | |
| | June 15-20 | 1,454 |

national samples, while the Eagleton data are from one state. However, questions about Baker, Connally, Crane, and Dole were not asked after February and questions about Jerry Brown were not asked after March of 1980. Collected for journalistic rather than academic purposes, the lack of continuity in issues and candidates asked about from one month to the next places some limits on the usefulness of this data set.

# APPENDIX B
# PUBLIC OPINION STRATA

The 1980 National Election Study conducted by the Center for Political Studies (CPS) afforded us an opportunity to operationalize and test hypotheses about the behavior of different strata. We have serious reservations about using the CPS data to trace citizen learning through the primaries. The interview waves are spaced too far apart to faithfully describe how people reacted to the events of the campaign. However, the February-to-June panel study lets us observe *individual* change from shortly after the election's first significant event, the Iowa caucuses, to the end of the primaries in June. Moreover, the CPS data are national in scope, with greater external validity than Patterson's data from Erie, Pennsylvania and Los Angeles and our data from New Jersey.

Sacrifices inevitably must be made when moving from the conceptual to the operational world. Our conceptual formulation of the opinion-strata was based on a number of attributes including: interest in the election and general public affairs, type of motivation for monitoring political communications, media exposure and dependency, and interpersonal discussion among others.[1] For practical reasons, including the limitations inherent in secondary analysis, we have used a more parsimonious strategy in operationally defining the strata, as described in the text.

The size of the various groups remained fairly constant through the course of the primaries, although there appears to have been some activation of the inadvertent public between April and June. The latent public increased by about 15 percentage points while the inadvertent public declined by about 10 points. However, the individual strata changes, presented in the table below, show a good deal

**Individual-Level Change in Opinion Strata, February to June**
**(in percent)**

|  | June | | | | Total | (n) |
|---|---|---|---|---|---|---|
|  | Attentives | Latents | Inadvertents | Apathetics | | |
| February | | | | | | |
| Attentives | 69 | 23 | 6 | 2 | 100 | (209) |
| Latents | 13 | 64 | 18 | 5 | 100 | (277) |
| Inadvertents | 5 | 48 | 36 | 12 | 101 | (257) |
| Apathetics | 6 | 30 | 15 | 49 | 100 | (80) |

*Note:* Entries show the distribution of respondents among the four strata in June, based upon their classification in the February interviews.
*Source:* CPS National Election Study, 1980.

of movement from February to June. While there is change in both directions, the small activation effect of the campaign is most clearly seen in the lower strata. Almost half of the inadvertent public became more attentive to the media as the primary season progressed. Only half of the apathetic public in February remained totally uninterested in June. Among the half that became activated most fell into the latent category. This particular movement is contrary to our expectations, although with a group sample size of 89, only 27 persons are in this cell. Not all of the movement away from the apathetic group is attributable to the election, however. Among the half who were no longer in the apathetic group in June, 21 percent were found to have exhibited greater interest in the election while 13 percent became more interested in general public affairs. Sixteen percent exhibited more interest in both during their June interview.

The interstratum movement from February to June is not surprising, given that we observed a good deal of individual-level change in interest (as noted in Chapter 3), a principal operational component of the strata. Moreover, we would expect some movement from the inadvertent to latent strata as a function of some individuals paying more attention to the campaign as the nomination cycle moved to a close. However, the amount of movement is certainly troubling to the notion of relatively static groups in the electorate. While we believe that these groups may be more dynamic than we originally envisioned we are also certain that the measurement strategy could be significantly improved in future studies. We are more certain of the existence of some form of layering than that we have measured it accurately.

## NOTE

1. For a more extended discussion and rationale, see Cliff Zukin, "Mass Communication and Public Opinion," *Handbook of Political Communication* (Beverly Hills, California: Sage, 1981), pp. 359-90. See also, Scott Keeter and Cliff Zukin, "Citizen Learning in the 1980 Election: Public Opinion Strata in Nomination Politics," presented at the 1982 Midwest Political Science Association Meeting, April 28-May 1, Milwaukee, Wisconsin.

# STATISTICAL BACKGROUND

This appendix presents the number of cases for figures, and for tables when there would have been too much clutter to place them with other statistical information in the main body. Sample sizes, standard deviations, and relevant statistical notes are grouped under the appropriate numbers and titles.

**Figure 4.1: Percentage Able to Volunteer Candidates' Names, New Jersey, 1980.**

**Figure 4.2: Percentage Feeling They "Knew Something About" Candidates, 1980.**

Numbers of cases are as shown in Table A.1, Appendix A.

**Figure 4.3: Percentage Feeling They "Knew Something About" Candidates by Party, 1980.**

|              | February | April | June | September |
|--------------|----------|-------|------|-----------|
| Democrats    | 402      | 409   | 341  | 658       |
| Independents | 354      | 293   | 258  | 557       |
| Republicans  | 238      | 244   | 224  | 362       |

**Figure 4.4: Percentage Feeling They "Knew Something About" Candidates, by Opinion-Strata, 1980.**

|              | February | April | June |
|--------------|----------|-------|------|
| Attentives   | 240      | 250   | 200  |
| Latents      | 330      | 288   | 374  |
| Inadvertents | 330      | 298   | 166  |
| Apathetics   | 100      | 115   | 92   |

Figure 5.1: Average Number of Issue Positions Ascribed to Candidates, 1980.

Standard Deviations and Sample Size

|  | February | April | June | September |
|---|---|---|---|---|
| Carter | 1.24 | 1.29 | 1.26 | 1.27 |
| Reagan | 1.65 | 1.59 | 1.54 | 1.35 |
| Kennedy | 1.52 | 1.55 | 1.53 | 1.47 |
| Bush | 1.53 | 1.71 | 1.71 | — |
| Anderson | — | 1.60 | 1.68 | 1.50 |
| Brown | 1.67 | 1.68 | — | — |
| Connally | 1.69 | — | — | — |
| Baker | 1.60 | — | — | — |
| Numbers of cases | (999) | (946) | (832) | (1,577) |

Figure 5.2: Comparison of Issue and Trait Awareness, 1980

Standard Deviations and Sample Size

|  | February | April | June | September |
|---|---|---|---|---|
| Reagan–Trait | 1.58 | 1.38 | 1.27 | 1.01 |
| Reagan–Issue | 2.10 | 2.41 | 2.42 | 2.49 |
| Anderson–Trait | — | 1.85 | 1.92 | 1.82 |
| Anderson–Issue | — | 1.60 | 1.68 | 1.50 |
| Bush–Trait | 1.80 | 1.94 | 1.96 | — |
| Bush–Issue | 1.53 | 1.71 | 1.71 | — |
| Numbers of cases | (999) | (946) | (832) | (1,577) |

Figure 5.4: Comparison of Average Issue Scores by Opinion-Strata.

Sample Sizes

|  | Attentives | Latents | Inadvertents | Apathetics |
|---|---|---|---|---|
| February | 241 | 329 | 325 | 104 |
| April | 254 | 289 | 299 | 119 |
| June | 209 | 277 | 257 | 83 |
| September | 201 | 250 | 243 | 62 |

**Figure 6.1: Percentage Not Expressing Opinions About Candidates, New Jersey, 1980.**

**Sample Sizes**

| | Oct 1979 Pre-Iowa | Feb 14–26 Post-Iowa Pre-N.H. | Feb 27–Mar 2 Post-N.H. Pre-Mass. | Mar 13–25 Post-Mass. Pre-N.Y. | Apr 6–21 Post-N.Y. Pre-Penn. | Apr 22–May 1 Post-Penn. | May 1–16 Scattered Primaries | May 16–22 Pre-N.J., Cal., Ohio | June 23–July 11 Post-primary |
|---|---|---|---|---|---|---|---|---|---|
| Reagan | 1,123 | 1,684 | 756 | 320 | 605 | 630 | 809 | 933 | 839 |
| Bush | 601 | 1,463 | 680 | 291 | 574 | 598 | 776 | 885 | 805 |
| Brown | 987 | 1,563 | 699 | 290 | 558 | 574 | | | |
| Anderson | 306 | 816 | 413 | 275 | 532 | 560 | 727 | 791 | |
| Baker | 816 | 1,394 | 680 | 265 | | | | | |
| Connally | 998 | 1,548 | 695 | 294 | | | | | |

**Figure 6.2: Percentage of Republicans Not Expressing Opinions About Republican Candidates, New Jersey, 1980.**

**Sample Sizes**

| | Oct 1979 Pre-Iowa | Feb 14–26 Post-Iowa Pre-N.H. | Feb 27–Mar 2 Post-N.H. Pre-Mass. | Mar 13–25 Post-Mass. Pre-N.Y. | Apr 6–21 Post-N.Y. Pre-Penn. | Apr 22–May 1 Post-Penn. | May 1–16 Scattered Primaries | May 16–22 Pre-N.J., Cal., Ohio | June 23–July 11 Post-primary |
|---|---|---|---|---|---|---|---|---|---|
| Reagan | 353 | 571 | 212 | 95 | 186 | 198 | 345 | 244 | |
| Bush | 211 | 524 | 199 | 88 | 178 | 196 | 336 | 237 | |
| Anderson | 103 | 299 | 134 | 86 | 171 | | | | |
| Baker | 280 | 501 | 192 | 86 | | | | | |
| Connally | 325 | 438 | 198 | 91 | | | | | |

**Figure 6.3: Percentage Not Expressing Opinions About Candidates, 1976**

Sample Sizes

| February | March | April | May | June |
|---|---|---|---|---|
| 1,459 | 1,524 | 1,464 | 1,501 | 1,454 |

## Chapter 6: Points of Information

The following table displays the percentage of Democrats and the total sample not expressing opinions about candidates in 1976.

| | January | February | March | April | June |
|---|---|---|---|---|---|
| Carter–total | 78 | 46 | 39 | 29 | 39 |
| Carter–Democrats | 75 | 43 | 36 | 26 | 32 |
| Udall–total | 92 | 89 | 72 | 45 | — |
| Udall–Democrats | 92 | 89 | 72 | 46 | — |
| Church–total | 81 | 80 | 66 | 41 | — |
| Church–Democrats | 82 | 82 | 68 | 41 | — |
| Brown–total | — | — | 76 | 54 | — |
| Brown–Democrats | — | — | 78 | 54 | — |
| Reagan–total | 47 | 36 | 30 | 22 | 23 |
| Ford–total | 20 | 10 | 15 | 13 | 14 |
| Number of cases–total | (1,459) | (1,524) | (1,464) | (1,501) | (1,454) |
| –Democrats | (589) | (609) | (560) | (617) | (638) |

The following table displays the percentage of Republicans and the total sample not expressing opinions about candidates in 1980.

| | January | February | March | April | June |
|---|---|---|---|---|---|
| Anderson–total | 83 | 79 | 55 | 50 | 53 |
| Anderson–Republicans | 82 | 78 | 54 | 43 | 47 |
| Bush–total | 70 | 50 | 47 | 51 | 52 |
| Bush–Republicans | 69 | 43 | 43 | 46 | 46 |
| Reagan–total | 20 | 16 | 31 | 26 | 29 |
| Reagan–Republicans | 16 | 14 | 27 | 19 | 18 |
| Number of cases–total | (1,468) | (1,536) | (1,468) | (1,605) | (1,517) |
| –Republicans | (488) | (490) | (502) | (554) | (341) |

**Table 7.1: Opinion of Republican Candidates Before and After the 1980 Iowa Precinct Caucuses**

**Sample Sizes**

|  | October 1979 | February 1980 |
|---|---|---|
| **Bush** | | |
| Republicans | 94 | 304 |
| Democrats | 126 | 359 |
| **Anderson** | | |
| Republicans | 30 | 137 |
| Democrats | 51 | 170 |
| **Baker** | | |
| Republicans | 153 | 277 |
| Democrats | 240 | 312 |
| **Connally** | | |
| Republicans | 220 | 370 |
| Democrats | 361 | 495 |
| **Reagan** | | |
| Republicans | 291 | 447 |
| Democrats | 455 | 607 |

## Table 7.2: Opinion of Candidates, January–June 1980, by Party

**Sample Sizes**

|            | January | February | March | April | June |
|------------|--------:|---------:|------:|------:|-----:|
| Carter     |         |          |       |       |      |
| Republicans | 381    | 438      | 456   | 525   | 316  |
| Democrats   | 625    | 760      | 675   | 798   | 599  |
| Kennedy    |         |          |       |       |      |
| Republicans | 426    | 422      | 453   | 503   | 305  |
| Democrats   | 700    | 652      | 645   | 757   | 560  |
| Brown      |         |          |       |       |      |
| Republicans | 334    | 356      | 327   | —     | —    |
| Democrats   | 493    | 556      | 380   | —     | —    |
| Reagan     |         |          |       |       |      |
| Republicans | 408    | 422      | 368   | 446   | 279  |
| Democrats   | 621    | 690      | 489   | 610   | 437  |
| Bush       |         |          |       |       |      |
| Republicans | 150    | 281      | 285   | 298   | 186  |
| Democrats   | 233    | 402      | 367   | 417   | 300  |
| Anderson   |         |          |       |       |      |
| Republicans | 86     | 106      | 229   | 314   | 182  |
| Democrats   | 142    | 177      | 320   | 412   | 285  |
| Dole       |         |          |       |       |      |
| Republicans | 130    | 169      | —     | —     | —    |
| Democrats   | 184    | 222      | —     | —     | —    |
| Baker      |         |          |       |       |      |
| Republicans | 194    | 230      | —     | —     | —    |
| Democrats   | 306    | 336      | —     | —     | —    |
| Crane      |         |          |       |       |      |
| Republicans | 69     | 96       | —     | —     | —    |
| Democrats   | 81     | 122      | —     | —     | —    |
| Connally   |         |          |       |       |      |
| Republicans | 326    | 320      | —     | —     | —    |
| Democrats   | 518    | 534      | —     | —     | —    |

**Table 7.3: Opinion of Candidates, February–June 1976, by Party**

**Sample Sizes**

|  | February | March | April | May | June |
|---|---|---|---|---|---|
| **Carter** | | | | | |
| Republicans | 52 | 160 | 176 | 200 | 149 |
| Democrats | 145 | 349 | 362 | 454 | 433 |
| **Ford** | | | | | |
| Republicans | 230 | 300 | 266 | 262 | 250 |
| Democrats | 460 | 528 | 488 | 527 | 524 |
| **Wallace** | | | | | |
| Republicans | 224 | 256 | 236 | 241 | – |
| Democrats | 480 | 512 | 474 | 532 | – |
| **Humphrey** | | | | | |
| Republicans | 231 | 259 | 235 | 244 | – |
| Democrats | 504 | 518 | 492 | 527 | – |
| **Church** | | | | | |
| Republicans | – | 80 | 73 | 117 | 167 |
| Democrats | – | 107 | 103 | 195 | 362 |
| **Brown** | | | | | |
| Republicans | – | – | 91 | 139 | – |
| Democrats | – | – | 124 | 287 | – |
| **Reagan** | | | | | |
| Republicans | 165 | 232 | 224 | 221 | 236 |
| Democrats | 294 | 379 | 411 | 484 | 465 |
| **Udall** | | | | | |
| Republicans | 25 | 69 | 94 | 152 | – |
| Democrats | 44 | 130 | 160 | 333 | – |
| **Shriver** | | | | | |
| Republicans | 95 | – | – | – | – |
| Democrats | 191 | – | – | – | – |
| **Bayh** | | | | | |
| Republicans | 50 | – | – | – | – |
| Democrats | 83 | – | – | – | – |
| **Jackson** | | | | | |
| Republicans | 67 | 143 | 136 | – | 156 |
| Democrats | 152 | 279 | 263 | – | 323 |
| **Harris** | | | | | |
| Republicans | 17 | 62 | 65 | – | – |
| Democrats | 47 | 89 | 118 | – | – |

## Table 7.4: Opinions of Candidates 1980 by Attention to the Campaign

### Sample Sizes

| Candidate | Amount of Attention | January | February | March | April | June |
|-----------|---------------------|---------|----------|-------|-------|------|
| Carter | A lot | 199 | 210 | 273 | 383 | 339 |
| | Some | 488 | 586 | 558 | 651 | 694 |
| | Not much | 447 | 583 | 493 | 459 | 341 |
| Dole | A lot | 100 | 114 | — | — | — |
| | Some | 151 | 211 | — | — | — |
| | Not much | 97 | 122 | — | — | — |
| Baker | A lot | 135 | 138 | — | — | — |
| | Some | 247 | 291 | — | — | — |
| | Not much | 174 | 216 | — | — | — |
| Crane | A lot | 50 | 68 | — | — | — |
| | Some | 73 | 113 | — | — | — |
| | Not much | 36 | 70 | — | — | — |
| Reagan | A lot | 200 | 196 | 247 | 347 | 298 |
| | Some | 497 | 568 | 450 | 525 | 547 |
| | Not much | 463 | 523 | 307 | 300 | 235 |
| Brown | A lot | 167 | 191 | 213 | — | — |
| | Some | 427 | 476 | 377 | — | — |
| | Not much | 349 | 383 | 238 | — | — |
| Bush | A lot | 106 | 157 | 203 | 273 | 240 |
| | Some | 190 | 356 | 348 | 351 | 365 |
| | Not much | 138 | 258 | 219 | 163 | 121 |
| Connally | A lot | 182 | 184 | — | — | — |
| | Some | 411 | 456 | — | — | — |
| | Not much | 354 | 336 | — | — | — |
| Anderson | A lot | 62 | 85 | 189 | 272 | 250 |
| | Some | 102 | 125 | 291 | 351 | 350 |
| | Not much | 89 | 113 | 180 | 179 | 125 |
| Kennedy | A lot | 203 | 199 | 269 | 382 | 327 |
| | Some | 516 | 535 | 557 | 611 | 676 |
| | Not much | 558 | 501 | 463 | 425 | 318 |
| Ford | A lot | — | — | 261 | — | — |
| | Some | — | — | 511 | — | — |
| | Not much | — | — | 415 | — | — |

## Table 7.5: Opinion of Selected Candidates in 1976 and 1980, by Respondent's Ideology

**Sample Sizes**

| Candidate | Respondent's Ideology | 1976 | | | | |
|---|---|---|---|---|---|---|
| | | February | March | April | May | June |
| Reagan | Liberal | 195 | 220 | 262 | 298 | 321 |
| | Moderate | 307 | 345 | 344 | 387 | 379 |
| | Conservative | 213 | 340 | 370 | 404 | 352 |
| Udall | Liberal | 32 | 71 | 113 | 221 | — |
| | Moderate | 47 | 116 | 112 | 261 | — |
| | Conservative | 24 | 101 | 158 | 292 | — |

| | | 1980 | | | | |
|---|---|---|---|---|---|---|
| | | January | February | March | April | June |
| Reagan | Liberal | 232 | 261 | 189 | 229 | 236 |
| | Moderate | 491 | 574 | 437 | 504 | 517 |
| | Conservative | 390 | 397 | 338 | 391 | 276 |
| Kennedy | Liberal | 249 | 245 | 243 | 258 | 296 |
| | Moderate | 525 | 553 | 540 | 619 | 604 |
| | Conservative | 442 | 388 | 443 | 477 | 341 |
| Anderson | Liberal | 47 | 76 | 144 | 154 | 162 |
| | Moderate | 93 | 127 | 290 | 345 | 338 |
| | Conservative | 101 | 110 | 201 | 280 | 193 |

## Table 7.6: Relationship Between Respondent's Ideological Self-Placement and Perception of Candidate's Ideology

### Sample Sizes

| Candidate | Whole sample | Has favorable opinion of candidate | Has unfavorable opinion of candidate |
|---|---|---|---|
| March 1976 | | | |
| Reagan | 806 | 446 | 360 |
| Udall | 238 | 121 | 118 |
| Jackson | 482 | 270 | 212 |
| Carter | 646 | 493 | 154 |
| Ford | 1,079 | 681 | 398 |
| Wallace | 963 | 381 | 598 |
| Humphrey | 953 | 477 | 477 |
| March 1980 | | | |
| Reagan | 1,102 | 413 | 420 |
| Carter | 1,160 | 584 | 497 |
| Kennedy | 1,081 | 299 | 688 |
| Bush | 640 | 262 | 209 |
| Anderson | 620 | 260 | 164 |
| Ford | 1,118 | 697 | 266 |

**Table 7.7: Awareness of Candidates Before and After 1980
Pennsylvania Primary, by Party and Region of Residence
in New Jersey**

**Sample Sizes**

|  | Democrats | | Republicans | |
|---|---|---|---|---|
|  | Before | After | Before | After |
| **Kennedy** | | | | |
| North | 332 | 219 | 219 | 157 |
| South | 92 | 66 | 57 | 41 |
| **Carter** | | | | |
| North | 332 | 220 | 219 | 157 |
| South | 92 | 66 | 57 | 41 |
| **Bush** | | | | |
| North | 331 | 220 | 219 | 158 |
| South | 92 | 65 | 57 | 41 |
| **Reagan** | | | | |
| North | 332 | 219 | 219 | 156 |
| South | 92 | 66 | 57 | 41 |

**Table 7.8: Percent with Opinion of Candidates Before and After
the 1980 Pennsylvania Primary, by Party and Region of
Residence in New Jersey**

**Sample Sizes**

|  | Democrats | | Republicans | |
|---|---|---|---|---|
|  | Before | After | Before | After |
| **Kennedy** | | | | |
| North | 332 | 221 | 219 | 158 |
| South | 92 | 66 | 57 | 41 |
| **Carter** | | | | |
| North | 333 | 221 | 219 | 158 |
| South | 92 | 66 | 57 | 41 |
| **Bush** | | | | |
| North | 320 | 202 | 208 | 156 |
| South | 88 | 65 | 53 | 40 |
| **Reagan** | | | | |
| North | 330 | 219 | 217 | 158 |
| South | 92 | 66 | 57 | 41 |

## Table 7.9: Percent Undecided or Preferring Other Candidates Before and After the 1980 Pennsylvania Primary, by Party and Region of Residence in New Jersey

### Sample Sizes

|  | Before | After |
| --- | --- | --- |
| **Republicans** |  |  |
| North | 217 | 154 |
| South | 57 | 39 |
| **Democrats** |  |  |
| North | 333 | 218 |
| South | 92 | 65 |

## Table 7.10: Popularity of Candidates Before and After the 1980 Pennsylvania Primary, by Party and Region of Residence in New Jersey

### Sample Sizes

|  | Democrats | | Republicans | |
| --- | --- | --- | --- | --- |
|  | Before | After | Before | After |
| **Kennedy** |  |  |  |  |
| North | 268 | 172 | 183 | 131 |
| South | 80 | 51 | 49 | 36 |
| **Carter** |  |  |  |  |
| North | 267 | 170 | 185 | 128 |
| South | 77 | 53 | 51 | 35 |
| **Bush** |  |  |  |  |
| North | 148 | 104 | 125 | 95 |
| South | 41 | 38 | 37 | 32 |
| **Reagan** |  |  |  |  |
| North | 243 | 152 | 174 | 123 |
| South | 65 | 44 | 46 | 36 |

Figure 7.1: **Opinion of Reagan and Connally, 1980, by Party (New Jersey data).**

Sample Sizes

| | Oct 1979 Pre-Iowa | Feb 14–26 Post-Iowa Pre-N.H. | Feb 27–Mar 2 Post-N.H. Pre-Mass. | Mar 13–25 Post-Mass. Pre-N.Y. | Apr 6–21 Post-N.Y. Pre-Penn. | Apr 22–May 1 Post-Penn. | May 1–16 Scattered Primaries | May 16–22 Pre-N.J., Cal., Ohio |
|---|---|---|---|---|---|---|---|---|
| Reagan | | | | | | | | |
| Democrats | 455 | 607 | 249 | 114 | 198 | 192 | 269 | 236 |
| Republicans | 291 | 447 | 164 | 71 | 150 | 158 | 281 | 193 |
| Connally | | | | | | | | |
| Democrats | 361 | 495 | 210 | 96 | — | — | — | — |
| Republicans | 220 | 370 | 124 | 56 | — | — | — | — |

Figure 7.2: **Opinion of Carter and Anderson, 1980, by Party (New Jersey data).**

Sample Sizes

| | Oct 1979 Pre-Iowa | Feb 14–26 Post-Iowa Pre-N.H. | Feb 27–Mar 2 Post-N.H. Pre-Mass. | Mar 13–25 Post-Mass. Pre-N.Y. | Apr 6–21 Post-N.Y. Pre-Penn. | Apr 22–May 1 Post-Penn. | May 1–16 Scattered Primaries | May 16–22 Pre-N.J., Cal., Ohio |
|---|---|---|---|---|---|---|---|---|
| Carter | | | | | | | | |
| Democrats | 495 | 653 | 302 | 141 | 223 | 221 | 330 | 308 |
| Republicans | 313 | 484 | 171 | 81 | 158 | 162 | 294 | 214 |
| Anderson | | | | | | | | |
| Democrats | 51 | 170 | 76 | 76 | 120 | 115 | 183 | 197 |
| Republicans | 30 | 137 | 61 | 44 | 85 | 114 | 176 | 133 |

**Figure 7.3: Opinion of Kennedy and Baker, 1980, by Party (New Jersey data).**

**Sample Sizes**

|  | Oct 1979 Pre-Iowa | Feb 14–26 Post-Iowa Pre-N.H. | Feb 27–Mar 2 Post-N.H. Pre-Mass. | Mar 13–25 Post-Mass. Pre-N.Y. | Apr 6–21 Post-N.Y. Pre-Penn. | Apr 22–May 1 Post-Penn. | May 1–16 Scattered Primaries | May 16–22 Pre-N.J., Cal., Ohio |
|---|---|---|---|---|---|---|---|---|
| **Kennedy** |  |  |  |  |  |  |  |  |
| Democrats | 484 | 634 | 289 | 122 | 230 | 220 | 319 |  |
| Republicans | 287 | 501 | 180 | 86 | 155 | 166 | 297 |  |
| **Baker** |  |  |  |  |  |  |  |  |
| Democrats | 240 | 312 | 131 | 66 | – | – | – |  |
| Republicans | 153 | 277 | 88 | 41 | – | – | – |  |

**Figure 7.4: Opinion of Bush and Brown, 1980, by Party (New Jersey data).**

**Sample Sizes**

|  | Oct 1979 Pre-Iowa | Feb 14–26 Post-Iowa Pre-N.H. | Feb 27–Mar 2 Post-N.H. Pre-Mass. | Mar 13–25 Post-Mass. Pre-N.Y. | Apr 6–21 Post-N.Y. Pre-Penn. | Apr 22–May 1 Post-Penn. | May 1–16 Scattered Primaries | May 16–22 Pre-N.J., Cal., Ohio |
|---|---|---|---|---|---|---|---|---|
| **Bush** |  |  |  |  |  |  |  |  |
| Democrats | 126 | 359 | 132 | 63 | 113 | 139 | 194 |  |
| Republicans | 94 | 304 | 113 | 52 | 109 | 127 | 203 |  |
| **Brown** |  |  |  |  |  |  |  |  |
| Democrats | 370 | 474 | 199 | 90 | 156 | 158 | – |  |
| Republicans | 224 | 385 | 132 | 62 | 121 | 126 |  |  |

**Figure 7.5: Effect of Party Conventions on New Jersey Voter Preference, 1980.**

**Sample Sizes**

| Before Republican Convention | After Republican Convention | Before Democratic Convention | After Democratic Convention |
|---|---|---|---|
| 840 | 818 | 456 | 360 |

# BIBLIOGRAPHY

Aldrich, John. *Before the Convention: Strategies and Choices in Presidential Nomination.* Chicago: University of Chicago Press, 1981.

Alexander, Herbert. *Financing Politics.* Washington, D.C.: Congressional Quarterly, 1976.

American Enterprise Institute Forum. *Regulation of Political Campaigns—How Successful?* Washington, D.C.: American Enterprise Institute, 1977.

American Political Science Association Committee on Political Parties. "Toward a More Responsible Two-Party System." *American Political Science Review* 44 (1950): Supplement.

Arrow, Kenneth. *Social Choice and Individual Values.* New York: John Wiley and Sons, 1963.

Arterton, Christopher. "Campaign Organizations Confront the Media-Political Environment." In *Race for the Presidency,* edited by James D. Barber, pp. 3-24. Englewood Cliffs, N.J.: Prentice-Hall, 1978.

——"The Media Politics of Presidential Campaigns." In *The Race for the Presidency,* edited by James D. Barber, pp. 25-54. Englewood Cliffs, N.J.: Prentice-Hall, 1978.

——"Political Money and Party Strength." In *The Future of American Political Parties: The Challenge of Governance,* edited by Joel L. Fleishman, pp. 101-139. Englewood Cliffs, N.J.: Prentice-Hall, 1982.

Asher, Herbert. *Presidential Elections and American Politics,* 2nd ed. Homewood, Ill.: Dorsey Press, 1980.

Atkin, Charles K. "The Impact of Political Poll Reports on Candidate and Issue Preferences." *Journalism Quarterly* 46 (1969): 515-521.

Becker, Lee, Idowu Sobowale, Robin Cobbey, and Chaim Eyal. "Debates' Effects on Voters' Understanding of Candidates and Issues." In *The Presidential Debates,* edited by George Bishop, Robert Meadow, and Marilyn Jackson-Beeck. New York: Praeger, 1978.

Bennett, Stephen. "Consistency Among the Public's Social Welfare Policy Attitudes in the 1960s." *American Journal of Political Science* 17 (1973): 544-570.

Berelson, Bernard, Paul Lazarsfeld, and William McPhee. *Voting.* Chicago: University of Chicago Press, 1954.

Blumenthal, Sidney. *The Permanent Campaign.* Boston: Beacon Press, 1980.

Blumer, Jay, and Denis McQuail. *Television in Politics.* Chicago: University of Chicago Press, 1969.

Bonafede, Dom. "The Press Makes News in Covering the 1980 Primary Election Campaign." *National Journal* 12 (1980): 1132-1135.

Broder, David S. *The Party's Over.* New York: Harper and Row, 1971.

Campbell, Angus. "Has Television Reshaped Politics?" *Columbia Journalism Review* 6 (1962): 10-13.

Ceaser, James W. *Presidential Selection: Theory and Development.* Princeton, N.J.: Princeton University Press, 1979.

——*Reforming the Reforms: A Critical Analysis of the Presidential Selection Process.* Cambridge, Mass.: Ballinger, 1982.

Chaffee, Steven, and Sun Yuel Choe. "Time of Decision and Media Use During the Ford-Carter Campaign." *Public Opinion Quarterly* 44 (1980): 53-69.

Clarke, Peter, and Eric Fredin. "Newspapers, Television and Political Reasoning." *Public Opinion Quarterly* 42 (1978): 143-160.

Cohen, Bernard C. *The Press and Foreign Policy.* Princeton, N.J.: Princeton University Press, 1963.

Commission on Party Structure and Delegate Selection. George S. McGovern, Chair. *Mandate for Reform.* Washington, D.C.: Democratic National Committee, 1970.

Commission on Presidential Nominations: James B. Hunt, Jr., Chair. *Report of the Commission on Presidential Nominations.* Washington, D.C.: Democratic National Committee, 1982.

Converse, Phillip. "Information Flow and the Stability of Partisan Attitudes." In *Elections and the Political Order,* edited by Angus Campbell, Phillip Converse, Warren Miller, and Donald Stokes, pp. 136-157. New York: John Wiley and Sons, 1966.

——"The Natures of Belief Systems in Mass Publics." In *Ideology and Discontent*, edited by David Apter, pp. 206-261. New York: The Free Press, 1964.

Crittenden, John A. *Parties and Elections in the United States.* Englewood Cliffs, N.J.: Prentice-Hall, 1982.

Crotty, William. *Political Reform and the American Experiment.* New York: Harper and Row, 1977.

Davis, James W. *Presidential Primaries: Road to the White House.* Westport, Conn.: Greenwood Press, 1980.

Eagleton Poll. "New Jerseyans Unimpressed by Politicians: But New Jersey Politicians Better than Most." New Brunswick, N.J.: Eagleton Institute of Politics. Release 43-3, February 27, 1981.

Entman, Robert, and David Paletz. "Media and the Conservative Myth." *Journal of Communication* 30 (1980): 154-165.

Farah, Barbara G. "The Representativeness of Direct Primaries: Linkage Between Partisan Voters and Convention Delegates 1972, 1976, and 1980." Ann Arbor: University of Michigan, Center for Political Studies, 1982.

Fenno, Richard F., Jr. "If, as Ralph Nader Says, Congress is 'The Broken Branch,' How Come We Love our Congressmen so Much?" In *Congress in Change*, edited by Norman J. Ornstein, pp. 277-288. New York: Praeger, 1975.

Fiorina, Morris. *Retrospective Voting in American National Elections.* New Haven: Yale University Press, 1981.

Fitzsimmon, Steven, and Hobart Osburn. "The Impact of Social Issues and Public Affairs Television Documentaries." *Public Opinion Quarterly* 32 (1969): 379-397.

Gallup, George. "Polls and the Political Process: Past, Present and Future." *Public Opinion Quarterly* 29 (1965): 544-549.

Germond, Jack W., and Jules Witcover. *Blue Smoke and Mirrors.* New York: The Viking Press, 1981.

Hammond, Thomas H. "Another Look at the Role of 'The Rules' in the 1972 Democratic Presidential Primaries." *Western Political Quarterly* 33 (1980): 50-72.

Hill, David B., and Norman R. Luttbeg. *Trends in American Electoral Behavior.* Itasca, Ill.: F. E. Peacock, 1980.

Hofstetter, C. R. *Bias in the News*. Columbus: Ohio State University Press, 1976.

——"Perceptions of News Bias in the 1972 Presidential Campaign." *Journalism Quarterly* 56 (1979): 370-374.

Katz, Elihu, and Paul Lazarsfeld. *Personal Influence*. New York: The Free Press, 1955.

Keech, William R., and Donald R. Matthews. *The Party's Choice*. Washington, D.C.: The Brookings Institution, 1977.

Keeter, Scott, and Cliff Zukin. "Citizen Learning in the 1980 Election: Public Opinion Strata in Nomination Politics." Paper presented at the 1982 Midwest Political Science Association Meeting, April 28-May 1, 1982, Milwaukee, Wisconsin.

——"The 1980 Presidential Election: Tracking Citizens' Opinions and Preferences." Paper presented at the 1981 Annual Meeting of the Midwest Political Science Association, Cincinnati, Ohio, April 15-18, 1981.

Key, V. O., Jr. *Public Opinion and American Democracy*. New York: Alfred A. Knopf, 1961.

Kirkpatrick, Jeane J. "Representation in American National Conventions: The Case of 1972." *British Journal of Political Science* 5 (1975): 265-322.

Kraus, Sidney, and Dennis Davis. "Political Debates." In *Handbook of Political Communication*, edited by Dan Nimmo and Keith Sanders, pp. 273-296. Beverly Hills, Calif.: Sage, 1981.

Lazarsfeld, Paul, Bernard Berelson, and Hazel Gaudet. *The People's Choice*. New York: Columbia University Press, 1944.

Lemert, James B. *Does Mass Communication Change Public Opinion After All? A New Approach to Effects Analysis*. Chicago: Nelson-Hall, 1981.

Lengle, James I. "Primary Rules, Political Power and Social Change." *American Political Science Review* 70 (1976): 25-40.

——*Representation and Presidential Primaries: The Democratic Party in the Post-Reform Era*. Westport, Conn.: Greenwood Press, 1981.

Lengle, James I., and Byron Shafer. *Presidential Politics: Readings on Nominations and Elections*. New York: St. Martin's Press, 1980.

Lippman, Walter. *Public Opinion*. New York: The Free Press, 1922.

Madison, James. "Federalist 10." In *The Federalist Papers*, Alexander Hamilton, John Jay, and James Madison, pp. 77-84. New York: Mentor, 1961.

Marshall, Thomas R. *Presidential Nominations in a Reform Age.* New York: Praeger, 1981.

Matthews, Donald R. "Presidential Nominations: Processes and Outcomes." In *Choosing the President*, edited by James D. Barber, pp. 35-70. Englewood Cliffs, N.J.: Prentice-Hall, 1974.

——"Winnowing." In *Race for the Presidency*, edited by James D. Barber, pp. 55-78. Englewood Cliffs, N.J.: Prentice-Hall, 1978.

May, Ernest, and Janet Fraser. *Campaign '72: The Managers Speak.* Cambridge, Mass.: Harvard University Press, 1973.

McCorkle, Pope, and Joel L. Fleishman. "Political Parties and Presidential Nominations: The Intellectual Ironies of Reform and Change in the Mass Media Age." In *The Future of American Political Parties: The Challenge of Governance*, edited by Joel L. Fleishman, pp. 147-160. Englewood Cliffs, N.J.: Prentice-Hall, 1982.

McLeod, Jack, Carl Bybee, and Jean Duvall. "Equivalence of Informed Participation: The 1976 Presidential Debates as a Source of Influence." *Communication Research* 6 (1979): 463-487.

McLeod, Jack, and Lee Becker. "The Uses of the Gratifications Approach." In *Handbook of Political Communications*, edited by Dan Nimmo and Keith Sanders, pp. 67-100. Beverly Hills, Calif.: Sage, 1981.

McWilliams, Wilson Carey. "The Meaning of the Election." In *The Election of 1980*, edited by Gerald Pomper, pp. 170-188. Chatham, N.J.: Chatham House, 1981.

Mendelsohn, H., and Garrett O'Keefe. *The People Choose a President.* New York: Praeger, 1976.

Mikulski, Barbara. *A Report of the Commission on Delegate Selection and Party Structure.* Washington, D.C.: Democratic National Committee, 1973.

Miller, Arthur, and Michael MacKuen. "Learning About the Candidates: The 1976 Presidential Debates." *Public Opinion Quarterly* 43 (1979): 326-346.

Moore, Jonathan, ed. *The Campaign for President: 1980 in Retrospect.* Cambridge, Mass.: Ballinger, 1981.

Moore, Jonathan, and Janet Fraser, eds. *Campaign for President: The Managers Look at '76*. Cambridge, Mass.: Ballinger, 1977.

Mueller, John. "Presidential Popularity from Truman to Johnson." *American Political Science Review* 64 (1970): 18-34.

Nie, Norman, and Kristi Anderson. "Mass Belief Systems Revisited: Political Change and Attitude Structure." *Journal of Politics* 36 (1974): 540-587.

O'Keefe, G., and L. Atwood. "Communication and Election Campaigns." In *Handbook of Political Communication*, edited by Dan Nimmo and Keith Sanders, pp. 329-347. Beverly Hills, Calif.: Sage, 1981.

Orren, Gary. "The Changing Style of American Party Politics." In *The Future of American Political Parties: The Challenge of Governance*, edited by Joel L. Fleishman, pp. 4-41. Englewood Cliffs, N.J.: Prentice-Hall, 1982.

Paletz, David, and Robert Entman. *Media Power Politics*. New York: The Free Press, 1981.

Paris, David C., and Richard D. Shingles. "Preference Representation and the Limits of Reform: The 1976 Democratic Convention." *Journal of Politics* 44 (1982): 201-211.

Patterson, Thomas. *The Mass Media Election*. New York: Praeger, 1980.

Patterson, Thomas, and Robert McClure. *The Unseeing Eye*. New York: G. P. Putnam and Sons, 1976.

Pierce, John. "1970 Party Identification and the Changing Role of Ideology in American Politics." *Midwest Journal of Political Science* 14 (1970): 25-42.

Pitkin, Hannah F. *The Concept of Representation*. Berkeley: University of California Press, 1967.

Polsby, Nelson W. *Consequences of Party Reform*. New York: Oxford University Press, 1983.

Pomper, Gerald M. "New Rules and New Games in Presidential Nominations." *Journal of Politics* 41 (1979): 784-805.

——"The Nominating Contest." In *The Election of 1980*, edited by Gerald M. Pomper, pp. 1-37. Chatham, N.J.: Chatham House, 1981.

——"The Nomination Contests and Conventions." In *The Election of 1976: Reports and Interpretations*, edited by Marlene Pomper, pp. 1-34. New York: David McKay, 1977.

Quarles, Rebecca. "Mass Media and Voting Behavior: The Accuracy of Political Perceptions Among First-Time and Experienced Voters." *Communication Research* 6 (1979): 407–436.

Ranney, Austin. *Curing the Mischiefs of Faction*. Berkeley: University of California Press, 1975.

——"Turnout and Representation in Primary Elections." *American Political Science Review* 66 (1972): 21–37.

Repass, David. "Issue Salience and Party Choice." *American Political Science Review* 65 (1971): 389–400.

Roberts, C. "Media Use and Difficulty of Decision in the 1976 Presidential Campaigns." *Journalism Quarterly* 56 (1979): 794–802.

Robinson, Michael. "A Statesman is a Dead Politician: The Media in American Society." In *What's News: The Media in American Society*, edited by Elie Abel, pp. 159–186. San Francisco: Institute for Contemporary Studies, 1981.

——"The Impact of the Televised Watergate Hearings." *Journal of Communications* 24 (1974): 17–30.

——"Media Coverage in the Primary Campaign of 1976." In *The Party Symbol*, edited by W. Crotty, pp. 178–191. New York: Freeman, 1980.

——"The Media in 1980: Was the Message the Message?" In *The American Elections of 1980*, edited by Austin Ranney, pp. 177–211. Washington, D.C.: American Enterprise Institute for Public Policy Research, 1981.

Robinson, Michael, and Margaret Sheehan. *Over the Wire and on TV: CBS and UPI in Campaign '80*. New York: Basic Books, 1983.

Rubin, Richard L. *Press, Party and Presidency*. New York: W. W. Norton, 1981.

Sabato, Larry. *The Rise of Political Consultants*. New York: Basic Books, 1981.

Sanford, Terry. *A Danger of Democracy: The Presidential Nomination Process*. Boulder, Colo.: Westview Press, 1981.

Schattschneider, E. E. *Two Hundred Million Americans in Search of a Government*. New York: Holt, Rinehart and Winston, 1969.

Schneider, William, and I. A. Lewis. "Public Opinion and the Nominating Process." In *Nominating a President: The Process and the Press*, edited by

John A. Foley, Dennis A. Britton, and Eugene B. Everett, Jr., pp. 141-147. New York: Praeger, 1980.

Schumpeter, Joseph. *Capitalism, Socialism and Democracy*, 3rd ed. New York: Harper, 1950.

Scott, Ruth K., and Ronald J. Hrebenar. *Parties in Crisis: Party Politics in America.* New York: John Wiley and Sons, 1979.

Sears, David O., and Richard W. Whitney. *Political Persuasion*. Morristown, N.J.: General Learning Press, 1973.

Sigelman, Lee. "Dynamics of Presidential Support." *Presidential Studies Quarterly* 9 (1979): 206-216.

Simon, Herbert A. "Bandwagon and Underdog Effects and the Possibility of Election Predictions." *Public Opinion Quarterly* 18 (1954): 245-253.

Skelton, George. "Los Angeles Times Poll." In *Nominating a President: The Process and the Press*, edited by John A. Foley, Dennis A. Britton, and Eugene B. Everett, Jr., pp. 139-141. New York: Praeger, 1980.

Stimson, J. "Public Support for American Presidents: A Cyclical Model." *Public Opinion Quarterly* 40 (1976): 1-21.

Vance, Cyrus. "Reforming the Electoral Reforms." *New York Times Magazine*, February 22, 1981, pp. 16ff.

Wamsley, Gary, and Richard Pride. "Television Network News: Rethinking the Iceberg Problem." *Western Political Quarterly* 25 (1972): 434-450.

Wattier, Mark J. "Voting in the 1980 Democratic Presidential Primaries." Paper presented at the annual meeting of the Southern Political Science Association, October 1982 in Atlanta, Georgia.

Wayne, Stephen. "Expectations of the President." In *The President and the Public*, edited by Doris Graber, pp. 17-38. Philadelphia: Institute for the Study of Human Issues, 1982.

Weaver, Paul. "Captives of Melodrama." *New York Times Magazine*, August 29, 1976, pp. 6ff.

Williams, Daniel C., Stephen J. Weber, Gordon A. Haaland, Ronald H. Mueller, and Robert E. Graig. "Voter Decision Making in a Primary Election: An Evaluation of Three Models of Choice." *American Journal of Political Science* 20 (1976): 37-49.

Witcover, Jules. *Marathon: The Pursuit of the Presidency 1972-1976*. New York: The Viking Press, 1977.

Wray, J. Harry. "Comment on Interpretations of Early Research into Belief Systems." *Journal of Politics* 41 (1979): 1173-1181.

Zukin, Cliff. "Mass Communication and Public Opinion." In *Handbook of Political Communication*, edited by Dan Nimmo and Keith Sanders, pp. 359-390. Beverly Hills, Calif.: Sage, 1981.

Zukin, Cliff, and J. Robert Carter, Jr. "The Measurement of Presidential Popularity: Old Wisdoms and New Concerns." In *The President and the Public*, edited by Doris Graber, pp. 207-241. Philadelphia: Institute for the Study of Human Issues, 1982.

# INDEX

Connally, John, 12, 21, 22, 68, 69, 70, 75, 80, 81, 85, 86, 90, 99, 120, 133, 147, 155, 157, 195
Connecticut, 1980 primary, 20, 22
constraints on media and election, 189
Crane, Philip, 21, 22, 75, 80, 81, 86, 90, 135, 147, 153, 155, 157
Cranston, Alan, 195
crossover voting, 31

Daley, Richard, 9
data sources and limitation, 6ff, 178
Democratic National Convention, 1968, 9, 27, 180; 1972, 10, 28; 1980, 28
Democratic Party, 197
Democratic primary, 1976, 16ff; 1980, 18ff
Democratic primary rule changes for 1984, 30, 197
democratic theory, 5
distortion of representation, 29ff
District of Columbia, 13
Dole, Robert, 19, 21, 68, 75, 81, 86, 90, 135, 147, 155, 157
Downs, Anthony, 173
dynamics of learning, 65ff

Eagleton Poll, 6, 66, 74, 99, 118, 141, 144, 170
effects of early primaries, 179
effects of losing primaries, 146ff
effects of winning primaries, 151ff
electability versus ability to govern, 193
Erie, Pennsylvania, 54

Farah, Barbara, 32, 33, 191
felt issue-knowledge, 97
Fenno, Richard, 142
Florida, 1972 primary, 34; 1976 primary, 15, 17; 1980 primary, 149
Ford, Gerald, 2, 14, 15, 18, 22, 32, 35, 38, 65

formation and change of public opinion during presidential nominations, 172ff

Gallup Poll, 16, 182
Georgia, 1976 primary, 15
Glenn, John, 155, 200
Greenway, David, 170

Harris, Fred, 17, 64, 124
Humphrey, Hubert, 3, 9, 16, 27, 34, 65, 149, 161, 180, 195
Hunt Commission, 197, 200; recommendations, 197ff
Hunt, James B., 197

Idaho, 1976 primary, 15, 18, 151
ideology and public opinion, 157
ideology of electorate, 49
Illinois, 1976 primary, 15, 17; 1980 primary, 13, 22
Illinois primary electorate, 43
impact of conventions, 170ff
impact of nomination reforms, 3
inadvertent public, 81ff
Indiana, 1976 primary, 15
information and nominations, 187
information environment, 101ff
information sources, 58
interest in elections, 53
interest in nomination politics, 178ff
interest in primaries, 60
intraparty polarization, 167
Iowa, 1976 caucus, 16, 17, 125, 149; 1980 caucus, 21, 128, 129, 130, 142, 147, 152; general, 31, 35, 54, 66, 74, 99, 119, 120, 145, 153, 157, 197-98, 200, 201
Iowa debates, 1980, 19
Iranian hostage crisis, 19, 57, 169
issue awareness and primaries, 101ff
issue positions of electorate, 45, 49

Jackson, Henry, 17, 18, 64, 125, 149, 155, 161
Johnson, Lyndon, 9, 34

Jordan, Hamilton, 16
journalistic interpretation and public opinion, 153
journalists, 181ff

Kennedy, Edward, 16, 18, 19, 20, 28, 39, 40, 43, 54, 71, 75, 80, 93, 94, 99, 101, 106, 118, 120, 133, 149, 155, 157, 162, 163, 166, 167, 169, 171, 174
Kennedy, John, 29
Kennedy, Robert, 9, 34
Kentucky, 1976 primary, 15
Key, V. O., Jr., 71
Kirkpatrick, Jeane, 27, 32
knowledge about candidates, 75, 89, 184
knowledge and learning of candidate character traits, 107ff
knowledge and learning of ideology, 93ff
knowledge and learning of issue positions, 95ff
knowledge and the voting public, 110ff
knowledge change during primaries, 75ff
knowledge gap, 172
knowledge of politics, 45

latent public, 81ff
Lazarsfeld, Paul, 55
League of Women Voters, 79
learning about candidates, 77, 172, 184
learning during 1976 campaign, 64ff
learning in 1980 elections, 63
learning in nomination politics, 178ff
Lengle, James, 35, 45, 50, 185
Lippman, Walter, 53
Loeb, William, 21
loophole primary, 198
Los Angeles, 54
*Los Angeles Times* Poll, 182

Madison, James, 26
Marshall, Thomas, 65, 117
Maryland, 1976 primary, 18, 126, 151
Massachusetts, 1976 primary, 15, 17, 147; 1980 primary, 20, 22, 68, 69, 128, 129, 130, 147; general, 31
Massachusetts primary electorates, 43
McCorkle and Fleishman, 181, 182, 192
McGovern, George, 10, 34, 140, 181
McGovern-Fraser Commission, 3, 9, 25, 27, 180
McWilliams, Wilson Carey, 190, 199
media and communication between candidates and voters, 106ff
media coverage of Iowa caucus, 53-54
media exposure and attention, 58
media exposure and learning, 179
media stimulation of interest, 59
Michigan, 1972 primary, 34; 1976 primary, 15, 126; 1980 primary, 22, 69, 99
Mikulski, Barbara, 10
Mikulski Commission, 10
Mondale, Walter, 155, 195
Montana, 1976 primary, 15, 18, 151
motivation and learning, 105
motivation and opinion formation, 127ff
Mudd, Roger, 19
Muskie, George, 10

Nashua debate, 21, 42
National Election Study, 6, 44, 59
National Rifle Association, 106
nationalization of politics, 8
Nebraska, 1976 primary, 15, 151
Nevada, 1976 primary, 15, 18, 151
New Hampshire, 1968 primary, 34; 1976 primary, 15, 17, 149; 1980 primary, 20, 21, 120, 152;

Reagan, Ronald, 2, 14, 15, 20, 21,
22, 32, 35, 38, 43, 54, 68, 69,
71, 75, 77, 78, 80, 85, 90, 93,
94, 97, 99, 105, 106, 107, 108,
109, 110, 112, 118, 120, 124,
127, 130, 133, 136, 142, 144,
146, 152, 155, 157, 161, 162,
163, 167, 169, 170, 171, 174,
191, 194, 195, 196
recognition of candidates, 66, 86,
121
Reed, Thomas, 155
reforms, 2, 3, 9ff, 180, 183ff
regional primaries, 199ff
Republican primary, 1976, 15;
1980, 20ff
representation, 26ff
representation in presidential nominations, 25
representativeness of early primaries, 35
representativeness of primary electorates, 184, 185
Rhode Island, 1976 primary, 15
Robinson, Michael, 152, 155
Rubin, Richard, 181

Schapp, Milton, 17
Schnattschneider, E. E., 184, 199
Schumpeter, Joseph, 26
Sears, David, and Richard Whitney,
142
sensitivity to political change, 190
Shah of Iran, 19
Shriver, Sargent, 17, 157
Smith, Al, 3
South Carolina, 1980 primary, 22
South Dakota, 1976 primary, 15

Soviet Union, 19
states in the nomination process, 29
Stevenson, Adlai, III, 155, 195
Stewart, Potter, 188
subjective knowledge, 74
Survey Research Center (SRC), 117

Tennessee, 1976 primary, 15
Texas, 1976 primary, 15; 1980
primary, 22
third parties, 192

Udall, Morris, 17, 39, 64, 124, 126,
139, 149, 152, 155, 157, 159,
167, 174

Vermont, 1976 primary, 17; 1980
primary, 20, 22, 68, 69, 127, 129,
130, 147; general, 200, 201
Vietnam war, 9, 34
voters and nonvoters, 112

Wallace, George, 9, 16, 17, 65, 182
Watergate, 11, 190
Weaver, Paul, 181
West Virginia, 1960 primary, 29;
1976 primary, 15; 1980 primary,
13
winnowing primary field, 173
Williams, Daniel, 173
winner-take-all versus proportional
primaries, 184
Wisconsin, 1968 primary, 34; 1972
primary, 34; 1976 primary, 126,
149; 1980 primary, 20, 22, 149;
general, 17ff, 139
Wisconsin primary electorates, 43
Witcover, Jules, 195

# ABOUT THE AUTHORS

**SCOTT KEETER** is Assistant Professor of Political Science at Rutgers University in New Brunswick, New Jersey. His teaching and research interests are in the areas of public opinion and research methodology. He has worked for NBC News as an analyst of election day voter surveys.

**CLIFF ZUKIN** is Associate Professor of Political Science at the Eagleton Institute of Politics, Rutgers University. He is director of the Eagleton Poll, a quarterly survey of the New Jersey public, and Chairman of the Executive Council of the Network of State Polls. His principal research interests are in the areas of mass media and public opinion, and have been published in the *Handbook of Political Communication, Public Opinion Quarterly, Journalism Quarterly,* and the *Journal of Communication.*

DATE DUE